THE

MAKING

OF

MARTIN

LUTHER

The Making of Martin Luther

RICHARD REX

PRINCETON UNIVERSITY PRESS
PRINCETON AND OXFORD

Published by Princeton University Press,
41 William Street, Princeton, New Jersey 08540

In the United Kingdom: Princeton University Press,
6 Oxford Street, Woodstock, Oxfordshire OX20 1TR
press.princeton.edu

Jacket design by Amanda Weiss

Library of Congress Cataloging-in-Publication Data

Names: Rex, Richard, author.
Title: The making of Martin Luther / Richard Rex.
Description: Princeton, NJ : Princeton University Press, 2017. |
Includes an index.
Identifiers: LCCN 2017009884 | ISBN 9780691155159
(hardcover : alk. paper)
Subjects: LCSH: Luther, Martin, 1483–1546. | Reformation.
Classification: LCC BR325 .R524 2017 | DDC 284.1092 [B]—dc23
LC record available at https://lccn.loc.gov/2017009884

British Library Cataloging-in-Publication Data is available

This book has been composed in Archive Chased Black,
Archive Garamond Exp, and Garamond Premier Pro

Printed on acid-free paper. ∞

Printed in the United States of America

1 3 5 7 9 10 8 6 4 2

TO OLIVER,
and the cheerfulness that's always breaking in

Contents

Preface

A book on Martin Luther hardly requires any explanation, least of all in the year 2017, which sees the quincentenary of his *Ninety-Five Theses*. However, given that there are already so many books on Luther, and so many published this year, the appearance of yet another might properly be thought to require some justification.

The reason for this book is quite simple. It is to explain Luther's ideas. There are other stories to tell about Luther. The story of how a thin, anxious young man turned into a fat, complacent old man. The story of how an obscure university professor developed a commercial identity through skillful exploitation of the high-tech media of his day. But all our stories about Luther must be predicated first and foremost on his ideas, on his theology. It was Luther's revolutionary new vision of the Christian faith that changed Christendom, Europe, and indeed the world, forever. The cataclysmic social convulsion that we label "the Reformation" was often characterized in twentieth-century history books as a matter of "great social forces." But "great social forces" are made of people thinking the same thing, or at least of people thinking that they are thinking the same thing (which is pretty much the same thing). In the case of the Reformation, what people were thinking derived primarily from Martin Luther. Other ideas soon proliferated, by extension, imitation, or contradiction. Luther could not control the genie he had let out of the bottle, the spirit of Protestantism. The Reformation was therefore never exclusively Lutheran. But no Luther, no Reformation.

The reason for this book, then, is to explain Luther's ideas—to explain what they were, what was distinctive about them, and how he worked them out. The task is not quite so simple as it sounds. Despite their indisputable historical significance, Luther's ideas have never been that well understood, least of all today, in the context of a European culture busily detaching itself from its Christian roots. And even when Christianity was a more central part of European intellectual culture, Luther's ideas were still widely misunderstood. Lutherans and others in the Protestant tradition, as insiders, were as often as not blithely unaware of what really was distinctive and different about his ideas, while Catholics and other outsiders reckoned the paradoxes that form the deep structure of his thought merely self-contradictory, and found his theology so alien to their own that they settled for at most a superficial caricature of it.

The key to Luther's theology is his notion of certainty. Luther, who might in some ways be regarded as the intellectual progenitor of the "masters of suspicion" (Marx, Nietzsche, Freud), called a great deal into doubt. The early Luther disapproved of this pastime, but the Reformation Luther was a past master of it. Yet doubt was not his default setting. If he called things into doubt, he did so in the name of certainty. Certainty was not simply a quality his mind invested in his own ideas, a common enough foible. It was the explicit focus and priority of his interpretation of the Christian Gospel. The Bible, for him, had to be an utterly certain source of truth. The truth derived from it had, itself, to be utterly certain. And the fruit of that truth in the soul of the believer had to be an unwavering and absolute certainty of the immediate enjoyment of the grace and favor of God. This was the core meaning of his most famous slogan, "justification by faith alone." His heart and soul demanded of Christianity something it had never before given, and to understand Luther and his ideas is to understand how he reshaped the Christian faith to yield this absolute certainty. The purpose of this book is to explain how Luther came to his revolutionary conception of Christian certainty and how that conception contradicted the traditional Christianity in which he had himself been formed.

Historical writing is a sin of omission. To make any sense of the past, one has to leave out an immense amount, and that process is as regrettable as it is inevitable. When the subject is as well documented and as relentlessly researched and commented upon as Martin Luther, then omission will be almost the defining feature of any book, especially a relatively short book. His own published writings are enough to fill a capacious bookcase. The writings of his friends, colleagues, and opponents would furnish a small library. And that is not to mention the massive body of further contemporary evidence that provides the context for the man, his ideas, and his achievement. As for the scholarly literature that has accumulated since his lifetime, it is already of such unimaginable bulk that no single human mind could cope with it in a lifetime of study. It is at least in keeping with Luther's own method that this book is primarily the product of reading in and reflection on his own substantial output—and on the writings of his contemporaries—rather than a distillation from the humanly unassimilable mass of Luther scholarship. Luther spoke of deriving Christian truth from the Bible alone. This was at best an exaggeration, and I do not claim to derive my understanding of Luther from Luther alone. But Luther's own writings are the starting point and reference point for this investigation. Historical writing is, to repeat, a sin of omission. But if, as Luther taught, even the best of human works and actions is still a sin, then perhaps this historian can legitimately hope that his work, however deficient, may nevertheless have some good in it.

It is customary at this point in a preface for authors to remark that, whatever help and advice they might have received from other people in the writing of their book, any mistakes that remain are emphatically their own. In this case, the familiar refrain has even more truth than usual. There really is hardly anyone else to blame. I must therefore do the decent thing and accept full responsibility for what follows. Apart from the two anonymous readers who scrutinized the text on behalf of Princeton University Press, the only other people who have read any of this are my student Jonathan Reimer and my son Oliver. I am deeply indebted to the two anonymous readers, who were generous with both encouragement and constructive criticism, and saved me from myself on numerous occasions. Jon Reimer kindly gave some time, after the successful completion of his doctoral dissertation, to a close reading of the opening chapter, and was especially helpful in tracking down some particularly recondite references. He also compiled the index. Olly heroically worked his way through most of the book in the narrow window of opportunity between completing his education and commencing gainful employment. His cheerful approbation was, as ever, a tonic at a time when stress over a rapidly receding deadline threatened to get the better of me. It is to Olly, therefore, that this little effort is gratefully dedicated.

THE

MAKING

OF

MARTIN

LUTHER

1

WITTENBERG 1517

On 31 October 1517, Halloween, the eve or vigil of the Feast of All Saints, as everyone knows, a young German friar purposefully made his way to the Castle Church in the Saxon university town of Wittenberg and nailed to the door one of the most famous protests of all time—the "Ninety-Five Theses." Within weeks, Martin Luther and his bold challenge to the authority of the Catholic Church were the talk of Germany; before long, the talk of Europe. The *Ninety-Five Theses* themselves, ninety-five pointed and often witty barbs poked into the religious practice of the "indulgence," were originally composed in Latin as the basis of a formal public disputation or debate in the university, but they were soon translated into German and put into print, the medium that enabled them to spread like wildfire.

Bizarrely, there is almost no reliable evidence for this well-known story—though there were ninety-five theses. There is no credible evidence that Luther actually went and nailed them to the church door that day, and every reason to believe that he did not. Not that nailing theses or other papers to a church door was in any sense a bold or unconventional act. Church doors often served as noticeboards, especially in university towns. For example, a few years later, the excommunication of Martin Luther was nailed to the door of Great Saint Mary's, the university church in Cambridge (and someone promptly scrawled some graffiti on it, though that is another story).[1] But, as was first pointed out long ago by Erwin Iserloh, there is no evidence that any disputation on the theses took place in

Wittenberg that day, nor that any was planned in the immediate future.[2] There would therefore have been no point in nailing them up on the noticeboard. Luther himself never refers to such an episode, and there is simply no mention of this story anywhere until after his death. It has all the hallmarks of myth.

Not that this would matter very much if it were not for the fact people are so loyally attached to the legend. When Iserloh first challenged this hallowed centerpiece of Luther hagiography, howls of protest echoed round Germany. All sorts of reasons were put forward for accepting the traditional theory. A blizzard of special pleading broke out, in a classic exemplification of Kolakowski's "law of infinite cornucopia," which states that for any position one is already minded to uphold, "there is never a shortage of arguments."[3] Yet for all the reasons, arguments, and circumstantial evidence adduced, there is still no sign of the story in the historical record until after Luther's death.

The allure of the legend lies, at least for our time, in its image of the romantic rebel, of the individual asserting himself against the system. But this is to misread the man. Luther was indeed a rebel, or became one: a quiet conformist could never have achieved what he did. Yet he was a reluctant rebel, who was drawn from cover only gradually, as circumstances brought him to acknowledge the initially unthinkable idea that the teachings he was deriving from the scriptures were utterly incompatible with the teachings and practices of the church structure of which he had imagined himself to be an obedient servant. He showed unusual courage over the ensuing half a dozen years, during which he emerged as the charismatic leader of a mass movement in Germany and shattered, forever as it turned out, the medieval Christian unity of Europe. His temperamental doubts and anxieties were allayed or repressed by the cast-iron certainties forged in his volcanic intellect: the certainty of faith and the certainty of scripture. But these certainties were not in place in 1517. It was his emerging teachings that gave him the gathering confidence and courage to stand firm against the imposing authority of church and empire. Nevertheless, the legend, like many legends, has an element of truth at its core. Luther was, in the end, an individual, and did assert himself—against almost anything. Yet he was never aware of his own individualism, of what turned into a monstrous egotism. He remained to the end utterly convinced that he was a mere instrument in the hands of God and that his own identity was entirely subordinated to the Word of God.

Luther's own recollections of the events surrounding the *Ninety-Five Theses* suggest a rather different story. When he was in his pomp, in the 1530s and 1540s, holding court in the former house of the Wittenberg Austin Friars, which his sovereign prince, the Elector Duke Frederick of Saxony, had given to him as his family residence once the brethren had all abandoned the communal life, a devoted circle of students and friends gathered daily at his table to catch his words of wisdom. Their gleanings survive in the collections of *Tischreden* or table talk, Twitter-like *obiter dicta* that furnish so many glimpses into Luther's life and character. He discussed the start of the indulgences controversy on numerous occasions, but invariably in terms of writing—never of "disputing"—and without any reference to the crucial details of popular legend. Years later, he remembered it as being "after All Saints" in 1517 that he "first decided to write against indulgences." His recollections of these events show consistency in referring to writing (rather than to a disputation), though not about the precise chronology. On another occasion, setting the matter in a broader context, he said: "In 1517, on All Saints' Day, I first began to write against the pope and indulgences. In 1518 I was excommunicated. In 1519 I disputed with Eck at Leipzig."[4] The formulation is particularly significant: he "disputed" with Eck at Leipzig, but he "began to write" on the Feast of All Saints in 1517. And there is nothing about church doors or hammers and nails.

Nor is there any indication that Luther sent out his theses in a search for instant publicity and notoriety. His letters were quietly dispatched to the episcopal chanceries, where, like so many unexpected and unaccustomed communications that reach busy offices, they sat for a while, as people fitfully wondered what, if anything, should be done about them. According to an account Luther wrote to the Elector Frederick about a year later, some people were saying that he had "started this whole dispute at the elector's instigation, when in fact no one knew of it, not even among my closest friends, except the Most Reverend Lord Archbishop of Magdeburg and Hieronymus, Lord Bishop of Brandenburg." He had "humbly and respectfully notified them before initiating the disputation."[5]

Nor, finally, did Luther actually see himself at the time as challenging papal authority: that came later. The challenge to indulgences set him on a collision course with Rome, but that was not immediately evident. In a more detailed account of these events, in the preface he wrote for the first volume of his Latin *Complete Works* published in 1545, Luther went out of his way to emphasize that his original motives were entirely loyal, in that he felt that abuses of indulgences were detrimental to the honor of the papacy. He even imagined that he would have the pope's support.[6] He was trying to start a debate, not to bring down a system.

What is known for certain about 31 October 1517 is that Luther posted—that is, mailed—his *Ninety-Five Theses* that day, sending copies to nearby bishops in order to call their attention to what he saw as misleading and questionable devotional and pastoral practices relating to indulgences. His cover letter made his intention clear, as Iserloh pointed out. He wanted to secure public correction of what he felt were the misleading claims being made for papal indulgences issued to raise funds for the rebuilding of Saint Peter's in Rome. Beyond that, he probably had some general intention of holding a disputation on his theses, quite possibly in a better known university than the very new institution at Wittenberg, which had been opened barely 15 years before. While it is going too far to suggest that university disputations were like modern sporting contests, the disputation was still the premier academic forum in what was still, for all the growing importance of print, a largely oral culture. The scholar who would emerge as Luther's most effective and best-known opponent, Dr. Johannes Eck, had made his name just a year or two before with well-publicized performances at disputations in the universities of Vienna and Bologna, where, among other things, he had justified the charging of modest rates of interest on loans as a legitimate business practice that did not merit the label "usury"—a position which was then rather radical. When Luther drew up his theses, he may have had no intention of debating them in a backwater like Wittenberg. Ironically, he may even have been indirectly inspired by the example of the man who was to become one of his bitterest foes.[7]

The earliest appearance of the popular legend is found in the preface contributed by Philip Melanchthon to the second volume of Luther's *Complete Works*, published in 1546. The second volume appeared after Luther's death, and Melanchthon, his long-serving right-hand man and close friend, wrote a brief life of his mentor to form the preface. It is in this little biography that we first find the story:

> Luther, burning with pious zeal, issued the propositions on indulgences (which appear in the first volume of his works). And on the eve of the Feast of All Saints 1517 he publicly posted them up on the church that is next door to the castle in Wittenberg.[8]

Of course it is possible to argue that Melanchthon knew Luther well, and could be telling the story on the basis of some personal recollection shared between them over the previous thirty years. But this argument falls down precisely because of the absence of any corroboration in the ample records of Luther's anecdotes. If the nailing of the *Ninety-Five Theses* had been one of Luther's stock tales of his youth, then it would certainly have found its way into these collections. If Melanchthon had heard it from Luther, then others would have heard it too, and even if it had not been written down at the time, once Melanchthon had made the story canonical in his little biography, memories would have been jogged.

Indeed, it is likely that it was precisely because Melanchthon had the *Ninety-Five Theses* without all the related letters and papers which enable us to set that document in context, that he leapt to the erroneous but entirely understandable conclusion that the theses were intended for a university disputation and were therefore posted, as would have been usual, on the church door. It is the letter Luther wrote to the bishops which shows that, at the start, he had a rather different plan in mind. It is moreover quite possible that Melanchthon was conflating an earlier event, a disputation concerning various principles of scholastic theology that had actually taken place in September 1517, with the *Ninety-Five Theses*. For he only came to Wittenberg in August 1518, nearly a year later, by which time the *Ninety-Five Theses* had already made Luther a national and controversial figure.[9] Looking back over a gap of thirty years to a vague recollection of events known to him only by report, Melanchthon seems accidentally to have forged one of history's most enduring myths.

For it is to Melanchthon that we can trace the story back, but no further. This is best seen in a brief analysis of the "new evidence" that was brought forward after Iserloh's challenge in favor of the traditional story. It seemed unimpeachable: a precise description of the event found in manuscript in a printed copy of the New Testament that had been massively annotated by Luther himself:

> In the year of our Lord 1517, on the eve of All Saints, the propositions about indulgences were [   ] posted on the doors of the temples of Wittenberg by Doctor Martin Luther.

There are two features of this text that immediately give rise to doubts. The first is that it refers to "Doctor Martin Luther." Luther was by no means averse to the first-person pronoun, and rarely if ever adopted the Caesarian third person when talking about himself—a subject on which he was always happy to dilate. The second and subtler point is that the words seem partly to echo and partly to embroider the words with which Melanchthon reported the posting of the theses in his brief life of Luther. This is best seen by comparing the two.

> Melanchthon: ... Lutherus, studio pietatis ardens, edidit Propositiones de Indulgentiis, quae in primo Tomo monumentorum ipsius extant, Et has publice Templo, quod Arci Witebergensi contiguum est, affixit pridie festo omnium Sanctorum anno 1517.[10]

> Manuscript: Anno domini 1517 in profesto omnium Sanctorum pr[   ] Witembergae in valvis templorum propositae sunt propositiones de Indulgentiis a Doctore Martino Luthero.[11]

The use of the terms "propositions" and "temples" points towards some dependence of the manuscript note on the printed text.[12] In any case, the decisive information is that while the New Testament in which this note is found was heavily annotated by Luther himself, this particular note is not in Luther's hand but in that of his secretary, Georg Rörer. Moreover, it is found on the last page of the index, a relatively prominent place, and was clearly added by Rörer himself, who almost certainly chose the book as a keepsake of his master when Luther was on his deathbed. (It was common at that time for scholars nearing death to let their friends choose books from their collections as mementos.) Rörer perhaps added the note about the posting of the theses when he read about it later in Melanchthon's little biography. And already we see the accretions of legend forming around the core of truth. In Rörer's version, it is doors, and not just the church, and several churches, not just one. It still gives us no reason to believe that there is any evidence for this best-known "event" in Luther's life prior to the biographical sketch that Melanchthon composed after Luther's death.

Popular and scholarly attachment to this mythic event is astonishing, doubly so in that the event itself, had it indeed taken place, would have been as such entirely routine—the posting of a notice on the noticeboard in advance of a disputation. There is a powerful and deeply ironic will to believe the story (ironic because the story is very much the sort of thing Luther would later denounce as "human tradition"). Andrew Pettegree's recent account of Luther goes to considerable trouble to vindicate the tradition, claiming to offer new evidence in its favor. However, the case made is flawed by the same problem that has bedeviled the discussion ever since Iserloh first challenged the consensus: a confusion between evidence and arguments. Thus it is clear that theses were printed in advance for a disputation that Luther conducted against scholastic theology, in September 1517. But no one has ever disputed the historicity of that disputation, which is manifest from the date of the disputation as given on subsequent reprintings of its theses. As Iserloh observed, the various printings of the *Ninety-Five Theses* never give a date for any disputation: no date, no notice.[13] Evidence relating to the disputation against scholastic theology does not constitute evidence for the nailing up of the theses against indulgences. Far more intriguing is Pettegree's claim that Luther had already had the *Ninety-Five Theses* printed before Halloween 1517. Given Pettegree's status as the foremost historian of the early modern printed book in our times, there is good reason to take his conclusion seriously.[14] But evidence that Martin Luther printed the *Ninety-Five Theses* is still not evidence that he nailed them to the church door, nor even that he proceeded immediately to hold a disputation about them. His approach to the bishops was obviously the result of a plan rather than a whim, and given his intention to hold a public disputation with their permission, having the theses printed was a perfectly sensible way of making it easier to inform people about his aims. That a disputation was held or planned for 31 October that year is improbable in the extreme. The appointed day for disputations at Wittenberg was Friday, and Halloween that year fell on a Saturday.

The *Ninety-Five Theses*, then, were mailed to the Archbishop of Mainz, and perhaps also to one or two other bishops, on 31 October 1517, and proceeded to languish in bureaucratic obscurity for a month or so. In December the archbishop sought advice on them from the local university. Yet at this stage knowledge of the theses still seems to have been relatively limited. It was a matter for discussion in episcopal and ducal chanceries. But the theses did not spread quite as soon as is usually thought. The widely repeated story that the *Ninety-Five Theses* swept through Germany in a fortnight and through Europe in a month was put into circulation thanks to a rather later account penned by Friedrich Myconius, a sometime Franciscan friar turned Lutheran reformer of Gotha.

Before fourteen days had elapsed, these propositions had spread through all Germany, and in four weeks through nearly all Europe, as though the angels themselves were the messengers who set it before everyone's eyes.[15]

But this account is hazy in its details (interestingly, there is no mention of nailing anything to the doors or walls of the Castle Church), and seems to be trying to make sense of rather scrappy information. It is easy to read it as if he meant that this all took place in November, if one starts from 31 October, but Myconius gives no precise dates. The claim about the fortnight was almost certainly derived from Luther himself, who once boasted that his theses had run through Germany within that time.[16] This may well be true—but not in the fortnight following the Feast of All Saints. It was over a fortnight before the archbishop saw them, and he was the first person to whom they were sent. At some point, Luther even explained to Georg Spalatin that he had not sent copies of his theses to the Elector Frederick or his court because he did not want people thinking that the protest against indulgences was some sort of political attack on the archbishop deriving ultimately from the prince.[17]

It was not until January 1518 that people began to find the *Ninety-Five Theses* sufficiently interesting to show them to people other than those directly concerned with the indulgence business. Only at that point did the wildfire ignite. The epicenter seems to have been Nuremberg, where the theses against indulgences were eagerly passed from hand to hand among the city's coterie of fashionable humanist scholars, led by Willibald Pirckheimer. We know a lot about this thanks to a friend of Luther's, Christoph Scheurl, whose correspondence that January is full of references to what was evidently the focus of public attention in the city. Scheurl wrote to Kaspar Guttel on 8 January 1518, telling him that Luther's conclusions on indulgences had aroused considerable interest and approval in

Nuremberg, from Pirckheimer and Wenzel Link among others. Even more interestingly, he added that they had been translated (into German, of course) by Kaspar Nützel, and that he (Scheurl himself) had sent them to Augsburg and Ingolstadt. This would hardly have been necessary if the theses had been known across all Germany by the end of the previous November. In January 1518, then, the theses became known across Germany in weeks. Within months, they were known across much of Europe. Scheurl had posted a copy of the theses to Konrad Peutinger in Augsburg on 5 January, and mentioned them in a letter to Jodocus Trutfetter written that same day.[18] At the abbey of Rebdorf, just a few miles from Eichstätt, a learned monk by name of Kilian Leib, a friend of Gabriel von Eyb, the Bishop of Eichstätt, kept an occasional chronicle of his life and times. Very much a part of the humanist scene despite his life in the cloister, Leib noted the emergence of Luther and the indulgences controversy not under 1517, but under 1518, as the first noteworthy matter that year.[19] January is clearly the key month, not November, in the emergence of Luther onto the public stage. However, it is not enough to know when Luther's *Ninety-Five Theses* became a sensation; it is also necessary to understand why. Theses offered by obscure dons for discussion in new or even old universities did not usually attract such massive attention. To explain why these theses did so requires first understanding what "indulgences" were and then exploring the nature of Luther's critique of them.

"Indulgences" had developed in the Middle Ages as a means of mitigating the rigor and severity of the penitential system that had originated in the early Christian Church to allow for the reintegration into the believing community of serious and notorious, but duly repentant, sinners. As part of this process, penitents in ancient times had to undergo periods of harsh fasting or other ascetic exercises before being admitted once more to communion in the ritual celebration of the Eucharist.

The highly juridical culture of medieval Latin Christianity had elaborated systems of "penitential satisfaction" to a degree that rendered ordinary Christians incapable of performing in a lifetime the accumulated penance for their sins. The doctrine of purgatory, faintly discernible in embryonic form in ancient Christianity, developed in the early second millennium in such a way as to provide for the completion of such penitential satisfaction in the next life. At much the same time, the doctrine of the indulgence developed in such a way as to allow for the amplification or leveraging of penance performed by people in this life. The popes, relying on the juridical interpretation of the "power of the keys" bestowed upon Saint Peter by Jesus (Matt 16:19), and on their consequent power to "bind and loose" in this life and the next, began to allow certain penitential or devotional acts to weigh in at much higher than their intrinsic penitential value. This "indulgence" or "relaxation" of penance was classically associated with the pilgrimage to Jerusalem (from which, of course, many never returned). In time, the range of devotional or charitable acts to which indulgences could be attached extended to charitable donations for purposes of piety (e.g., for the rebuilding or embellishment of a church) or the public good (e.g., the maintenance of bridges and highways), as well as to the recitation of particular prayers or cycles of prayer, such as the rosary.

There was a steady inflationary process visible in the history of indulgences. The scope of the indulgence broadened from the ritual penalties imposed upon repentant sinners under canon law and extended to the broader concept of the "temporal punishment due for sin." Every sin merited two levels of punishment: as an offence against the infinite goodness of God, it merited eternal punishment—hell; but as an offence against a fellow human being it required also some temporal restitution or retribution, something calculated easily for theft, but less easily for lying, fornication, adultery, or murder. Eternal punishment was remitted only by divine grace, mainly through the sacrament of penance. Temporal punishment could be paid by prayer, fasting, or almsgiving, but the full measure of temporal punishment, knowable only by God, was by the end of the Middle Ages assumed to be exacted in purgatory, and was conceptualized in terms of "time" spent there (notwithstanding the logical difficulty of conceptualizing "time" for a disembodied soul). Indulgences were therefore issued in terms of days, months, or years, with the denominations rising until they culminated in the "plenary" indulgence. The plenary indulgence could be issued only by the pope, and was deemed to relieve the beneficiaries from the entire debt of temporal punishment for sin built up in their lifetime.

The theological basis of the doctrine and practice of the indulgence needs also to be appreciated. This was the redemptive work, the passion and death, of Jesus Christ. Christ's sacrifice, as the work of a person who was God as well as man, was of infinite worth. One drop of Christ's blood, according to medieval theologians, was adequate to the redemption of all human sin. His redemptive work, in medieval terms, constituted a superabundance of merits, stocking what came to be called the "treasury of merits," upon which indulgences were drawn like checks on a bank account. (The commercialization of indulgences and of the theological language surrounding them runs very deep.)

Luther's letter of 31 October 1517 explained very clearly what had led him to dash off his theses on indulgences. It was the campaign to raise money for the construction of the new basilica of Saint Peter's in Rome by a grant of a plenary indulgence in return for contributions—generally, if a little misleadingly, called the "sale of indulgences."[20] The chief agent in this campaign, though Luther courteously refrained from naming him, was Johann Tetzel, a Dominican friar with a successful track record in these enterprises. Campaigns such as this, at least in theory, were not commercial but charitable. Although even at that time people (Luther among them) spoke of buying and selling indulgences, indulgences were not tradable commodities or securities. Thus, for example, they could not be resold, although a late development in the practice allowed indulgences to be deployed vicariously, on behalf of other souls already in purgatory. As we have seen, indulgences were granted by way of reward for devotional acts, rather than for cash as such. But the practice of granting them in return for financial contributions undoubtedly commercialized the transaction, rendering it open to economic as well as theological analysis.

Perhaps surprisingly, commercialization was not the focus of Luther's critique (though he did allude to it). What most offended him was that indulgences left their recipients with an entirely false sense of spiritual security. Nothing, he emphasized, not even the "infused grace of God" (available via the sacraments), could give people certainty of grace and salvation.[21] On the contrary, scripture made it clear that salvation was difficult, worked out, as Saint Paul taught, in "fear and trembling" (Phil 2:12). The most remarkable thing about this critique is that it was poles apart from what Luther would be teaching before a year had passed, namely that certainty of grace or salvation was at the heart of faith and the Christian life. In late 1517, Luther was still working within the conceptual confines of Catholic orthodoxy. He was further concerned that indulgences should not be promoted so enthusiastically as to distract Christians from prayer and good works, and that people should not be given the impression that acquiring the indulgence was simply a matter of making the donation, or that it somehow relieved them from the need to repent and confess their sins.

The *Ninety-Five Theses* themselves were a more acerbic document than the relatively emollient letter to the bishops, to which they were appended almost as an afterthought. It would be rash to infer that, in autumn 1517, Luther was necessarily committed to maintaining all his theses. Academic disputations conducted in Latin before select university audiences traditionally licensed a considerable freedom of speech. Paradoxical and provocative ideas could be mooted without committing speakers to defending them come what may. Luther availed himself fully of that academic latitude in a text that gradually works its way from polite questions and modest proposals to rhetorical heights of indignation and sarcasm. Some of his ideas would have been reckoned unarguably true by all his readers. Thus, for example, his insistence that indulgences could not confer certainty of grace (thesis 32) or take away sin (76), as well as his emphasis on actual repentance (1), confession (thesis 7), contrition (36 and 39), and good works (41–44). Others were highly debatable. Luther raises at several points the suggestion that indulgences only freed people from the canonical penalties laid upon offenders by the canon law of the church. This would have represented a considerable narrowing of the scope of indulgences, back towards their historical origins. He also questioned the notion of the "treasury of merits" upon which indulgences were said to be drawn (58). But in the later theses, Luther's prodigious talent for turning a phrase started to make itself felt. There is a real bite to this contrast:

65: The treasures of the Gospel are nets with which people once fished for men of riches.
66: The treasures of indulgences are nets with which now they fish for men's riches.

And his denunciation of the notion that a papal indulgence could even absolve someone of raping the Blessed Virgin Mary (75) combined righteous indignation with the frisson of blasphemy and taboo. No one (as Tetzel himself complained) had ever suggested such a thing, but once the theses were out there, what can only have originated as someone's tasteless joke became a standing charge against indulgences and their peddlers. The string of rhetorical questions (82–89) asking why, for example, the pope did not simply empty purgatory out of sheer good will (82) or pay for Saint Peter's himself (86) added further spice and amusement to the mix. After all of which, of course, Luther added the cautious disclaimer that he submitted everything he had said to the judgment of God and the Church. The *Ninety-Five Theses* were by turns serious, moral, funny, bitter, sarcastic, and shocking, an almost carnivalesque performance. They might have been nothing more than a nine days' wonder, but their sudden vogue is easy to understand.

Johann Tetzel had been busy on the indulgence job since 1516, and by autumn 1517 he was in the principality of Brandenburg, where he matriculated at the new university of Frankfurt an der Oder that winter. He first became aware of the *Ninety-Five Theses* around the middle of December, after the Archbishop of Mainz had referred them to that university for an opinion. Stung by what he regarded as almost a personal attack (although he was not mentioned by name), he held a disputation on indulgences himself at Frankfurt on 20 January 1518.[22] It was probably this event that qualified him for the doctoral degree he was adding to his name later that year. The timing of his response is revealing. It is much easier to believe that he responded to this challenge promptly than that he waited over two full months before taking any action to vindicate his good name.

At some point, Luther may indeed have held his disputation on indulgences at Wittenberg itself, although even this cannot be certain, as there is no definite record of it. There is no reason at all to suppose that he had already done so when he posted his theses to the bishops. There are some later indications that a disputation might have taken place. Konrad Wimpina's edition of Tetzel's disputation theses (they numbered 108) also reprinted the *Ninety-Five Theses*, with the remark that Luther had debated them at Wittenberg before Tetzel held his disputation at Frankfurt an der Oder.[23] But even this is probably an inference rather than a report, and it appears in a book published a decade later. There is also a letter sent to Leo X in the name of the University of Wittenberg, probably in late summer 1518, which speaks of the notorious theses as "having been disputed" there.[24] Luther had compiled his last word on the *Ninety-Five Theses*, his *Resolutions on Indulgences*, by the end of February, although this was not published until late spring.[25] On the other hand, in a letter to Hieronymus Schultz, Bishop of Brandenburg, enclosing a draft copy of the *Resolutions on Indulgences*, Luther voiced his disappointment that nobody had responded to his challenge to a disputation, and his subsequent surprise at seeing his theses (*disputationes meas*) circulated more widely than he had intended, and he explained that it was this which had led him to consider offering his arguments in print. And in 1519 Melanchthon described Luther as having "put forward the theses for disputation," rather than as having actually debated them.[26] So the evidence is somewhat ambiguous. But if a disputation really did take place, then January 1518, when the *Ninety-Five Theses* had become public property and the subject of controversy, is perhaps the likeliest time for it to have been held.

Thanks to the extraordinary diffusion and impact of Luther's *Ninety-Five Theses*, the idea has arisen that indulgences were some sort of widely resented abuse or imposition on the late medieval Christian, and that the "sale of indulgences" was a notorious scandal crying out for reform or more radical treatment. Nothing could be further from the truth. Although concerns about indulgences were being raised by some critics in the years following 1500, indulgences were widely sought and highly valued. Luther himself furnishes us with compelling evidence for this. By his own account, the main attraction for him when he was sent by his religious order on a mission to Rome in late 1510 was the possibility of securing the generous indulgences that were available in the holy city. And he later recalled that one of the things that spurred him to protest in 1517 was the eagerness of the townsfolk of Wittenberg to make their way to the nearby town of Jüterbog at Easter, in order to acquire there the plenary indulgence for the rebuilding of Saint Peter's in Rome, which their prince, the Elector Duke Frederick, would not allow to be preached within his own domains.[27] Indulgences attracted a measure of theological critique not because they were unpopular but because they were too popular. Much of the criticism—even some of Luther's— focused on what would now be called "moral hazard," the risk that the apparently easy acquisition of forgiveness afforded by the indulgence would distract the faithful from the need for contrition and penance and make them casual and careless about the dangers of sin.[28]

The easiest way to appreciate the popularity of indulgences is by reflecting on the founder of Luther's university, the man who over the next few years would become his crucial patron and protector, Elector Frederick of Saxony. The elector had indeed forbidden the special indulgence for Saint Peter's to be made available anywhere within his jurisdiction. But this was not because he had any moral or theological reservations about indulgences. It was because he was the proud owner of one of Western Europe's most impressive collections of relics, enshrined in the Castle Church at Wittenberg itself. That church was dedicated to "All Saints," and Frederick seems to have wanted a piece of all of them. The Saint Peter's indulgence threatened to compete with the ample indulgences available there for visiting and venerating the relics and making appropriate offerings. Frederick was simply protecting his interests. His amazing collection was lovingly itemized in a fully illustrated printed catalogue, *The Index of the Most Praiseworthy Relics of the Collegiate Church of All Saints, Wittenberg* (Wittenberg, 1509).[29] This book consisted of woodcuts depicting the holy images and precious reliquaries in which the thousands of holy fragments were preserved and displayed. The catalogue itself did not enumerate the indulgences that could be acquired through devotions paid at these shrines, but Georg Spalatin, the elector's secretary, later calculated that they were worth around two million years off one's time in purgatory. The day on which they were visited to best advantage was the patronal day of the church itself, All Saints (1 November, the day after Luther sent his *Ninety-Five Theses* to the bishops). Nor had Luther disdained his patron's piety. As late as December 1516 he had lent a hand in an attempt to secure from Cologne yet more relics for his sovereign's collection.[30] The elector's personal investment in this project is summed up by the catalogue's cover: the title page has a twin portrait of him and his brother, Johann; and the back has an ornate woodcut of their heraldic arms. As a young man, Frederick had made the great pilgrimage to Jerusalem and the Holy Land in 1493, travelling on one of the last pilgrimages of its kind before the changing conditions of the rapidly expanding Ottoman Empire and the increasing risks from Muslim piracy in the eastern Mediterranean brought that long tradition for a while to a close. For Latin Christians who made that journey, it was not just the holy places and the relics but also the indulgences attached to visiting them that provided much of the spiritual motivation. An Italian clergyman of modest learning, Pietro Casola, a canon of Milan Cathedral, made the great pilgrimage the year after Duke Frederick, and his account of that voyage enthusiastically reports on the relics and indulgences that were to be found along the way.[31]

Luther's critique of indulgences focused on the notion of easy salvation, forgiveness on the cheap, and to some extent on the moral hazard that must arise from such an offer. Yet the most interesting feature of his original critique of indulgences is the vast gap it reveals between his theological standpoint in autumn 1517 and his new position in spring 1518. For, within a year, he was offering Christians salvation on the cheapest terms ever. From one point of view, the doctrine of justification by faith alone was simply the proclamation of a universal, plenary indulgence, available at absolutely no cost or effort. This is no mere cheap shot. For a start, Luther himself was perfectly clear about the parallel. He himself announced that the only indulgence of any value to Christians was the one issued by God.[32] The critique of moral hazard which he had been willing to deploy against the traditional doctrine of indulgences was therefore, inevitably, deployed still more readily against his new doctrine by his opponents. Luther's superindulgence required absolutely nothing of its beneficiaries, not even a token donation or a perfunctory prayer, let alone the inconvenience and embarrassment of confession to an all too human priest (though Luther left plenty of room for such confession, which he continued to regard as a salutary moral discipline, if conducted in the right way). The very slogan "faith without works" said it all. Luther sought to mitigate the risk by insisting that those people who were genuinely justified by faith necessarily and almost naturally brought forth the fruit of good works in their lovingly Christian lives. But the moral hazard was undeniable, and is evidenced in the extent to which Protestant Reformers throughout the sixteenth century felt the need to counter the intellectual challenge posed by what they described as "antinomianism" or "libertinism."

There is more than this to the parallel, however. It is not merely that there is an ironic coincidence between Luther's doctrine of justification and the scholastic doctrine of the indulgence. It is not even that there is an adventitious historical connection between the doctrine of the indulgence and the origins of his new doctrine. It is on reflection plain that Luther's doctrine of justification could not have been conceived, could not have been imagined, could not have been developed if the scholastic doctrine of the indulgence had not previously been worked out by the theologians of the Middle Ages. By a much deeper irony, Luther's understanding of justification is conditioned by the scholastic theory of indulgences. It might almost be regarded as the logical consequence of that theory, and can certainly be seen as its most extreme formulation. The conception of the infinite superabundance of Christ's merits which underpinned the theory of indulgences was fundamental to the rhetoric of the "passion and merits" of Christ that ran through sixteenth-century Protestant preaching and devotion. Luther's doctrine of justification was not so much a reaction against the theory of indulgences as its culmination. This may be why Luther did not formulate his own theology of justification until, thanks to the furore over indulgences, he had not only started, unknown to himself, to cut his ties with the authority of the Church, but had somehow loosed his imagination from the constraints of medieval understandings of how Christian salvation worked. He had at first thought that the doctrine of indulgences went too far. What he realized later was that it did not go far enough.

2

FROM ERFURT TO
WITTENBERG

Martin Luther, the bright and ambitious son, was sent to the University of Erfurt in 1501 by financially secure artisan parents who hoped to see him make a name for himself by progressing through the arts curriculum to the study of law. For nearly four years he devoted himself not only to the traditional pursuits of logic and natural philosophy which formed the core of the curriculum at the universities but also to the newly fashionable studies of classical Latin literature known at the time as the "humanities" (*studia humanitatis*) or "good literature" (*bonae literae*), and known to modern historians as "humanism." But returning to Erfurt from a visit home in summer 1505, he was overtaken by a ferocious summer storm, and the lightning was so close that he prayed desperately for his life. Reacting to the situation in a typically medieval way, he appealed to a saint for intercession, making a vow to Saint Anne—a favorite late medieval saint, the mother of the Blessed Virgin Mary—that if she preserved him from death, he would devote himself to the religious life.

Vows to saints were commonplace in Catholic Europe, intimately connected with the practice of pilgrimage. Healing and deliverance, along with successful or unproblematic childbirth, were common motives for such vows, which might be made by people of any social status, from cobblers to kings, and indeed were often offered up by entire communities or cities, for example in seeking to avert or survive visitations of epidemic disease. Luther himself, in an earlier brush with death, a deep wound to the leg which he claimed was a self-inflicted injury (an accident with a sword), had twice invoked the assistance of the Blessed Virgin to save him from bleeding to death.[1]

It is not entirely clear why Luther chose Saint Anne, and he never explained his choice. Her feast day was 26 July, but that lay some weeks ahead when Luther found himself in the storm. The shrine of Saint Anne at Düren in the far west of Germany had seen a popular pilgrimage develop in the early years of the sixteenth century, so maybe she was just a little more in the popular mind at that time. She was, by some accounts, a patron saint to those in danger from thunderstorms, but a more likely consideration is that she was the patron saint of miners—his father's profession. In Luther's native town of Eisleben, a new church to Saint Anne would be built in the suburbs in the 1520s, and there may already have been a chapel dedicated to her, or at least plans to erect a church. Saint Anne was, as these examples indicate, an increasingly prominent figure in late medieval piety, as the mother of Mary and therefore the matriarch, so to speak, of the Holy Kin. There is nothing extraordinary in Luther's invocation of this saint at a moment of crisis. His impulsive appeal to her was probably little more than a reflection of contemporary devotional fashion. Such recourse to the saints was entirely normal in medieval Catholicism.

That Luther made a vow in such a moment of terror is not remarkable at all. That he kept his vow is much more revealing. On 16 July 1505, to the astonishment of his student friends, Luther threw over the study of law, upon which he had only just embarked, to enter the Erfurt house of the Order of Hermits of Saint Augustine (the Augustinian or Austin Friars). The day was not without significance. It was the feast day of Saint Alexius, who was himself said to have renounced worldly wealth and prospects to take up the religious life.

According to one alternative account, however, Luther had a very different reason for fleeing from the world into the cloister:

the need to avoid prosecution for homicide after having killed a man in a duel or brawl. This notion, launched upon a rightly skeptical world nearly forty years ago by an amateur historian, Dietrich Emme, has proven surprisingly unappealing to an age which not only delights in finding that heroes have feet of clay and cupboards full of skeletons, but has also been absurdly receptive to quaint ideas about religious leaders (compare, for example, the credulity with which so many respond to the idea that Jesus Christ was married to Mary Magdalene). Luther the homicide, however, has won less of a following than Luther the homicide detective. The idea itself, though constructed with the usual panoply of scholarship, is sadly without merit. Nothing could be more piquant than the notion that the founder of the Protestant tradition joined a monastery because he was on the run, but it will not do. Were there any truth in it, it would make nonsense of Luther's own perfectly straightforward account of how he joined the Augustinians because of his vow to Saint Anne. Luther was capable of misremembering things and misrepresenting things. But he was hardly a barefaced liar, and to represent as the fruit of piety a decision which actually arose from criminal necessity would require some explaining. The weak point of Emme's theory, as so often with dubious historical theories, is that there is no evidence for it. He bases his entire case on a couple of stray remarks from Luther's "table talk," recorded by devoted disciples decades later, but neither of these remarks has anything to do with a homicide.[2] The key text in Emme's theory is one in which Luther attributed his joining the friars to the providential will of God, who brought this about "in case they caught me," adding, "Otherwise I would have been caught really easily."[3] Sadly, this recollection is rather obscure, leading one recent scholar to accept Emme's hypothesis on the grounds that it is difficult to make sense of Luther's comment in any other terms.[4] But there is no context to suggest who "they" might have been, and absolutely nothing anywhere to link this with any supposed homicide. Emme's error is to presume that the risk from which admission to the religious order protected Luther was a risk which pertained at that time. The easiest way to make sense of Luther's comment is to refer it to the time in his life when "they" really were out to capture him, namely the later 1510s, when it is certainly the case that key men in his order, such as Johann von Staupitz, did what they could to protect him, and when his ideas spread very rapidly among his German confrères. As a secular doctor of theology in a similar position, he would have been far more exposed to the machinations of his enemies. As a friar, he benefited from the solidarity that medieval institutions tended to show with their members.

The disproof of Emme's thesis, though an argument from silence, is utterly compelling. Had Luther indeed killed someone in a student brawl, whether by accident or design, and had he then secured legal immunity by joining a religious order, the scandal could never have escaped the eagle eyes of his enemies. Even the whisper of such a rumor could hardly have been missed by Luther's first and most hostile biographer, Johannes Cochlaeus. On the first page of his life of Luther, Cochlaeus, after a brief account of his subject's parentage, birth, and childhood, comes down off the fence by informing us that the future friar, from his first years in the religious life, was already remarkable for weird behavior, which was a sign either of mental illness or of some "occult commerce with the devil."[5] An author so desperate for muck to rake could never have missed something as juicy as a rumor of manslaughter, especially not if it was something Luther himself had spoken of at his noisy and well-reported dinner table. Nor could a scandal of such a kind have passed unnoticed. Luther's theology professor at Erfurt, Bartholomaeus Arnoldi of Usingen (generally known as Dr. Usingen), who joined the Augustinians at Erfurt himself a few years later, could hardly have been unaware of the matter if

Luther really had required his order's protection to elude arrest and justice. The story would have been the talk of both university and friary. Nor would Dr. Usingen have had any motive to let the story languish in decent obscurity. Although originally on good terms with his former pupil, he subsequently became an implacable foe of Luther and his new doctrine, publishing around a dozen pamphlets in defense of the old faith in the last ten years of his life. In the mid-1520s, he had to leave Erfurt because of the triumph of the Reformation there, and he moved to Würzburg, where he died in 1532.[6] It is inconceivable that he would not have known and disseminated such a discreditable story had there ever been so much as a whisper of it.

Had Luther fled to the monastery, or been consigned there, on account of manslaughter, then this fact would in addition have constituted a serious impediment to his ordination, and he would certainly have required a papal dispensation in order to be made a priest. There is no indication that such a dispensation was ever sought or issued. Nor can one take Luther seriously as a swordsman. Emme interprets an earlier episode in his student career, when he nearly bled to death as a result of a self-inflicted sword injury, with typical bravura, seeing in this story a veiled account of another duel.[7] Yet even though Crotus Rubianus remembered the young Luther as handy with his fists—an entirely credible observation, given the unmistakable indications of short temper found all over his writings—it is a big step from there to sword fighting.[8] And a man who almost killed himself with his own sword is unlikely to have been a first-rate fencer. No, Luther the homicide has to be regretfully put away.

At the time, Luther's decision to commit himself to the religious life was seen as both voluntary and providential. His novice-master in the order, Johannes Nathin, saw in his conversion a miraculous intervention by God,[9] and no doubt Luther himself saw things in the same light. (He was always something of a self-dramatist, and had he ended his days in some parallel universe as a respected Catholic theologian and preacher, this story might have had a central place in his hagiography.) It is all the harder, therefore, to know what to make of his later claim that his vow was "forced and necessary" (which plays a key part in Dietrich Emme's curious speculations).[10] His decision, by his own account, was entirely voluntary and indeed positively willful, taken without the knowledge of his father (who would rather have seen his son an affluent lawyer than a mendicant friar) and persisted in despite the urgings of his friends. If Luther saw any coercion here, it had to be the hand of God at work, and at times he writes as if this were the case. But in the light of his later conviction that monastic vows were intrinsically sinful, as breaches of both the first and the fourth commandments (Luther followed the Catholic numbering of the Ten Commandments), it would make no sense to infer that, in his view, God had compelled him to join his religious order: that would be equivalent to God having compelled him to sin—a moral and metaphysical impossibility in the Western theological tradition. What "forced" Luther into the cloister was the same thing that ultimately "forced" him out of it: his conscience, that powerful and unruly organ.

It says something very important about Luther that he kept his vow. Not many people, even then, held themselves bound by hasty vows taken privately in moments of crisis. And there were plenty of pressures brought to bear. His father, in particular, was unimpressed. His friends urged him to reconsider. One of the effects of his theological conversion was to be a total reconsideration of the nature of monastic and devotional vows, thanks to which, twenty years later, he freed himself sufficiently from his former conscience to enable himself not only to abandon the habit and habits of a friar but eventually to take a wife. In the summer of 1521, in hiding at the remote Saxon fortress of the Wartburg, Luther was able to rethink his vows in the light of his new understanding of the "gospel" (as he liked to term his new religious message). In doing so, he recalled a couple of things his father had said to him at the time of his entry into religion. The first was this:

> When, to the great annoyance of my father, I had made my vow, after he had calmed down, he said to me "Let us hope it was not some trick of Satan's!" That saying put down such roots in my heart that I never heard anything from him that I have preserved more tenaciously. It seems to me that God spoke to me as though from afar through his mouth, too late to make a difference, but still enough to constitute a warning and a correction.

This should not be misread (as it is by the translators of Luther's correspondence, who turn "it seems" into "it seemed") as a claim that Luther had been troubled by his father's words from the moment he uttered them.[11] Rather, it was only in 1521, at the very crisis of his life, when, as far as he knew, he had faced death by appearing before the emperor in the Reichstag at Worms, that the full significance of his father's words, echoing down the years, dawned upon him.

The other comment of his father's that stuck in Luther's mind was an invocation of the fourth commandment, "Honor thy father and mother." This recollection, about thirty years later, was focused on his first celebration of mass, which is when he reports his father as having said to him: "Son, don't you know that you ought to honor your father?"[12] This comes across as though his father is already providentially voicing the case against monastic vows that Luther was to work out in the early 1520s. But the comment itself was surely, in its original context, no more than a simple statement of an obvious reproof: the son owed it to his parents to discuss his vocation with them. What the story certainly shows is that Luther took his decision for himself, without consulting his family. His father's evident rage on hearing the news is understandable—a poor friar was much less likely than a successful lawyer to be able to look after his parents in their old age. But it is worth noting Luther's comment that his father's speculation about the diabolical instigation of the storm that had precipitated his son's act was voiced *tarde*—late, that is, too late. Luther had presumably found it wiser and safer to inform his father after the event. Even at the age of 22 a young scholar, however handy with his fists, might have had something to fear from a burly miner.

In 1505 Luther was a medieval Catholic with a strong and lively conscience. So his vow was binding. You could under some circumstances escape from monastic vows, thanks to the supreme jurisdiction exercised within the Roman Catholic Church by the pope. Thus, Luther's renowned contemporary, Desiderius Erasmus, secured a papal dispensation in 1517 releasing him from the monastic vows he had undertaken as a teenager, when consigned to the religious life by his guardians. It was this dispensation that enabled Erasmus to live the wandering life of a freelance scholar, rather than spend his days immured behind the walls of some monastery or on the run as an "apostate" or "gyrovague" monk.[13] But Luther, unlike Erasmus, had taken his vows as an adult, with full knowledge of the implications. The German province of the Austin Friars had just the previous year promulgated revised statutes, under which no one could be admitted to the order under the age of 18. But Luther was already over 21. In the modern world, more discriminating procedures for the assessment of vocations would dismiss a decision taken in haste and under stress, and the analysis of consent in courts of all kinds is far more subtle. Around 1500 it was only manifest duress that would have allowed people to wriggle out of such a promise. Until he felt himself released from his vows by the logic of his new theology (which was only in the early 1520s), Luther neither questioned their binding character nor sought to escape them.

Curiously enough, the Bible offers a tale of a rash vow, and, fortuitously, we have Luther's comments on it, in some lecture notes that survive from the period before his theological breakthrough. The tale is that of Jephthah, who, before going out to make war on the enemies of Israel, swore that if he returned home victorious, he would make a burnt offering to the Lord of whatever should come forth from the doors of his house to meet him. Predictably enough, his triumphant return was marred by the emergence from those doors of his daughter, who herself insisted that he should keep his word to the Lord, as a result of which "he did with her according to his vow" (Judges 11:30–40). Many medieval exegetes, revolted by the idea of human sacrifice, and equipped with a theology that allowed and indeed required the non-fulfilment of rash and illicit vows, found in the euphemistic phrasing of the final verse of that story an excuse for arguing that, rather than actually killing his daughter, Jephthah merely brought about her "death to the world" by dedicating her to a life of virginity—a naively anachronistic application of medieval concepts of the religious life to the very different world of ancient Israel. Luther would have none of that. For him, Jephthah fulfilled his vow to the letter. Much later on, he would criticize Jephthah's vow as "ungodly because it was contrary to charity."[14] But by that time he had utterly changed his entire conception of the place of vows in Christian life. Before his own conversion, he held Jephthah to the same exacting standard as himself.

Living as a friar, under a vow of obedience, Luther was at the beck and call of his religious order, which decided on where he should live and how he should work. So he did as he was told, moving from Erfurt to Wittenberg for the academic year 1508–9 to teach, then back to Erfurt to resume theological study, before being returned once more to Wittenberg, which was to be his home for the rest of his life, to take up the professorship of scripture there. It was his religious order, likewise, which sent him to Rome over the winter of 1510–11, the only time he ever set foot outside his native land, on a sort of business trip. In the 1510s he was entrusted with higher responsibilities, serving for several years as a district vicar, with supervisory responsibility for 10 houses.[15] Luther at this time was hardly famous, but he was certainly a coming man among the Augustinians, and his brethren would have been expecting him to rise at least to the heights of Johann Staupitz as provincial vicar, and maybe higher still. There was no room for doubt about his talent, and though his temperament may have been questioned, he might also have been expected to mellow with age. If anything, Luther was to be one of those whose edges harden with age, but that could not have been foreseen at the time.

Luther entered fully, conscientiously, and at times belligerently into the religious life of the Austin Friars. We have his own word for it that he was a devout and dedicated friar, and there is no reason to doubt him.

> I was a real saint, I celebrated mass every day, and confessing with a pure body and heart I prepared to offer the sacrifice.[16]

After his death, a former confrère from the Erfurt house testified to the young Luther's devotional zeal.[17] He was keen to recite the canonical hours of prayer, and became neurotically anxious in the 1510s when his increasing responsibilities as a university lecturer and a senior member of his order inevitably made it difficult for him to fulfil this obligation, so that he sometimes found himself trying to catch up on a backlog of two or three weeks.[18] The anxieties and scruples which he recalled as an older man are characteristic of a certain type of youthful religious enthusiasm, often seen in the Catholic religious orders or in the more rigorous and exclusive Protestant sects.

It was taken for granted that educated friars would be ordained priests, and Luther was made a priest in spring 1507. He later reported the awe with which he approached the celebration of his first mass, and he was prey to as many anxieties about his celebration of mass and his making of his regular confessions as he was about his recitation of the hours.[19] The intensity and orthodoxy of his devotion are alike evident in his later recollections of occasional experiences of awe in the presence of the consecrated eucharistic wafer of bread. At the Corpus Christi procession in 1515, in which Staupitz was carrying the consecrated host, he was overcome with "horror," as he later put it, at the thought of Christ's presence. It tells us even more about Luther's hypersensitive conscience that he later felt it necessary to "confess" this reaction to Staupitz, who brushed the whole matter aside as wrongheaded.[20] Reports of such powerful emotional responses to the eucharistic presence of Jesus are common in medieval hagiography, interpreted there in a positive light as a sign of divine favor.[21]

Luther's recollection of that curious episode in 1515 casts light not only on his piety but also on his evidently somewhat tense and troubled relationship with Staupitz, his hero and mentor. For all their undoubted closeness, and for all Staupitz's decisive influence on him, Luther's stories about him betray an undercurrent of mutual incomprehension beneath the more obvious mutual admiration and affection upon which biographers usually focus. Thus, although Luther did make confession to Staupitz, there is no sense that Staupitz was what would later be called his "spiritual director." For Luther also made his confession to other priests, in search of a consolation which neither Staupitz nor they proved capable of bestowing. In discussing his peculiar trials and tribulations (which he and his biographers describe as his *Anfechtungen*), he reported that when he asked Staupitz about them, Staupitz replied that he himself had never experienced such things, but that obviously they were meat and drink to Luther.[22] On a similar occasion, he bluntly told Luther that he could not understand him. And later, seeing Luther looking downcast in the refectory and asking what was wrong, he was treated to the classic wail, "Oh, what shall I do?"[23] Luther in these moods must have been a somewhat tiresome presence around the house, and Staupitz's responses, filtered though they are through the rose-tinted lenses of Luther's memory, do not sound uniformly sympathetic. And while Luther subsequently maintained that Staupitz's spiritual advice was particularly important in pointing him towards his new theology, the gist of that advice—that Luther should focus his attention on Jesus Christ—sounds like fairly standard pastoral counsel aimed at overcoming an unhealthy tendency to introspection.

Luther's youthful loyalty to his order was unquestioning. When one of the great German humanists of the day, Jakob Wimpfeling, dared to dispute that Saint Augustine of Hippo had ever really been a monk, and therefore fell into controversy with the Austin Friars, who claimed him as their ultimate founder, Luther had no doubts about what side to take. The Austin Friars traced their origins to Saint Augustine, though the historical connection was at best tenuous. The order which Luther joined had in effect been founded in the thirteenth century by the amalgamation of a variety of religious houses and societies that invoked the patronage of Augustine. And while Augustine certainly had lived some kind of communal religious life, Wimpfeling's reluctance to interpret that life as monastic or mendicant in the formal sense those terms held by 1500 was historically justified. If you belonged to any kind of institution or association in the Middle Ages, you were expected to defend it to the hilt, and Luther knew where his duty lay. An annotation in one of his texts of Augustine, probably from around 1510, excoriated Wimpfeling's stubborn and willful effrontery. And according to one of his more wildly exaggerated reminiscences, Wimpfeling's audacity in this matter almost got him killed.[24] Once Luther began to map out his own theology, his commitment to the religious life in general and to the Austin Friars in particular crumbled rapidly. But he did not renounce his affiliation to the friars until he was well down the road to Reformation.

Friars did not study law, they studied theology, so as a new recruit in 1505, Luther transferred to the study of theology in the scholastic tradition. He later recalled how he had sold almost all his books, including the law books that he had probably only recently acquired. As an arts student, Luther had inevitably been exposed to the new currents of Renaissance humanism. Even in joining the Augustinians, he kept his Plautus and his Virgil so as to have some recreational reading.[25] And we know that he attended the lectures of Hieronymus Emser (later to be one of his fiercest early critics) on the popular classical Latin play *Sergius*, written by Johannes Reuchlin. Emser did proceed with the study of law, developing his interests in the humanities in parallel, and like many of the more talented humanist lawyers, he made a career in service at the court of a prince, in his case the other Duke of Saxony, George, whose capital was at Leipzig. Emser's story perhaps shows us what kind of career Luther might have enjoyed had it not been for the vow in the thunderstorm. Apart from his intense reading in the scriptures, which were now, thanks to print, much more easily available to young scholars than they had ever been before, there was presumably nothing unusual about this theological training. In due course he proceeded to the degree of Bachelor of Divinity, and began teaching as well as studying.

Luther looked back on his time as a theology student at Erfurt without enthusiasm. But he did see in that period the start of his lifelong engagement with the Bible, albeit with no thanks to his teachers. Years later, he shared an unflattering recollection of his theology teacher at Erfurt, Dr. Usingen, who, he claims, warned him anxiously against recourse to the Bible, the wellspring of all factions, urging him instead to turn to the ancient doctors of the Church, who had distilled the truth out of the Bible.[26] His encounter with the Bible, as he recalled it on one occasion, was fortuitous or providential:

> At twenty years of age, I had not so much as seen a Bible, and I thought the Sunday readings were all there was to the Epistles and Gospels. But then I found one in the library, and immediately took it back with me to the monastery, where I read it and reread it, again and again, to the amazement of Dr. Staupitz.[27]

But such comments of his about the condition of theology and his own religious knowledge before the Reformation must be taken with a pinch of salt. They are in effect theological critiques of late medieval Catholicism masquerading as autobiography. Thus, although Brecht solemnly rehearses this remark about the Sunday readings as a statement of fact, we can put down this obvious joke as rhetorical exaggeration. (Need one really point out that even before the Reformation a man with a university education in Christian Europe could not actually have been unaware of the existence of the Bible and of the approximate scope of its contents?[28]) Luther was not on oath in his table talk: on another occasion he recalled coming across a Bible as a boy, and enjoying the story he read in it so much that he hoped one day to have a copy for himself.[29] He added that the monks gave him a copy bound in red leather, a telling detail that carries the ring of truth. The general drift of all these reminiscences is his exposure to the Bible text once he had joined the Austin Friars, and his insatiable appetite for it. This we can believe. Another of Luther's later claims was that through his studies he became so familiar with the Bible that he knew the gist of each chapter, although he added that this was compromised once he began to learn Hebrew, which for some reason confused his memory.[30] Undue reliance on a memory that was perhaps not as reliable as its owner liked to imagine goes a long way towards explaining some of the more startling errors and inaccuracies that vitiate Luther's otherwise often impressive scholarship.

The Bible has a central role in another, lengthier recollection of his Erfurt days. By his own account, as a young Master of Arts he was much troubled with sadness—depression, we would call it today—and found solace in reading scripture. As a result, he maintains, he soon discerned "many errors in the papacy." But convictions about the authority of the pope and the church and doubts along the lines of "Are you alone wise? You might be wrong!" got in the way of these perceptions.[31] His later views about the diametrical opposition of scripture and the Roman Church are clearly reshaping his memories here. The evidence of his early writings, mainly lecture notes and marginalia, which he himself excluded from the edition of his collected works in the 1540s because they were written before he had "discovered the Gospel," gives little reason to believe that his reading of the Bible led him in novel directions until the mid-1510s. Some scrappy notes on his copy of Peter Lombard's *Sentences* (the basic textbook of medieval Catholic theology), which probably reflect his early lecturing as a Bachelor of Divinity at Erfurt around 1509–10, show an entirely conventional approach to the subject. The most that we ever see in his pre-Reformational writings are entirely mainstream criticisms of the notorious institutional failings of the Catholic Church and moral failings of the clergy, expressed with considerably less than the vigor of Sebastian Brandt or Desiderius Erasmus. Reformist critique was an orthodox genre.

Luther's later reminiscences of his time at Erfurt draw our attention to a crucial figure in his development: Dr. Johann von Staupitz, the Vicar General of the Order of Hermits of Saint Augustine in Germany. The importance of Staupitz in Luther's life is well known, largely thanks to the frequency and ardor with which Luther recalled it later on. As vicar general, Staupitz was an exceedingly busy man, often on the road about the business of the order and in high demand as a popular preacher. Academically, in addition, he had responsibilities at the new University of -Wittenberg, where he served as lecturer in scripture for the university's first ten years. Yet few scholars seem to have realized how puzzling it is that Luther credited Staupitz with so great an influence on him. The two men were only rarely in the same place, and the only occasion when they may have been together for any significant period was in 1508–9, when, as we shall see, Staupitz summoned Luther to Wittenberg to lecture in philosophy. They were together again for a while in summer 1515.[32]

Luther first met Staupitz at Erfurt in 1506, and seems to have fallen instantly under the spell of the man whom he was later to regard as one of the formative influences on his life and character. Indeed, with characteristic exaggeration he went so far as to say "I got nothing from Erasmus; I got all my stuff from Dr. Staupitz." He was certainly right in saying that he got nothing from Erasmus. Neither Luther nor Erasmus took long to realize how little they had in common, however much their contemporaries may have tended, for various reasons, to lump them together. But it is not even remotely true that he got everything from Staupitz. The distinctive features of Luther's theology, those features that broke with the medieval Catholic tradition, were all his own work. His exaggeration of his debt to

Staupitz serves chiefly to drive home the real point, namely that he owed nothing to Erasmus. But it does also reflect a very real influence, albeit one that was more personal than theological. Many of Luther's recollections of Staupitz, which mostly date from ten years or more after Staupitz's death, are of pastoral advice about dealing with sin and guilt and conscience. Without seeking to embark on long-range psychoanalysis (always a suspect procedure), one can observe that, as almost all scholars agree, there was something not only neurotic but even morbid about Luther's early anxieties over his spiritual life and state. Staupitz's robust commonsense advice helped preserve the balance of Luther's mind until his development of a completely new theology of sin and grace in the years before 1520 brought him a more permanent resolution.

It was Staupitz, though, who was responsible for pointing Luther towards the study of theology and for deploying him to the new university at Wittenberg, to fill the place he had himself vacated as professor there. The house of Austin Friars at Wittenberg took on a new lease of life thanks to the founding of the university (though it was soon afterwards made redundant thanks to Luther's new theology in the 1520s). A regular stream of Augustinians can be seen on the Wittenberg matriculation registers until around 1520. What is clear is that Staupitz saw talent and promise in the young novice, and marked him out from the start as a coming man, fast-tracking him for high office in the order. It is equally clear that Luther, the common man of humble artisan stock, was bowled over by the attention he received from Johann von Staupitz, the intellectual scion of a noble house of Saxon landowners. Staupitz was extremely well connected: his boyhood friendship with Frederick, the future Elector of Saxony, with whom he had been educated, was to be a determining influence not only in his life but also in Luther's. As Luther's social, academic, and hierarchical superior, Staupitz was in the ideal position to shape the young friar's development, and all the evidence indicates that he added to his social advantages a good measure of personal charisma: he was a popular and effective preacher in an age when the role of the preacher was one of the most influential of all public roles. Luther's subsequent claim that Staupitz "incited" him "against the pope" is simply incredible as it stands, and should at most be read as an interpretation of events rather than a mere recollection.[33] Staupitz certainly offered Luther some encouragement and guidance as trouble swirled about him in the latter part of the 1510s. But there is nothing in his own writings to suggest any kind of hostility towards the papacy. A recent scholar has spoken rather expansively of "Staupitz's anti-Roman sentiments," but on inspection this comes down to a casual description of Christ as the "true pope" (found in a later copy of notes taken down while he preached) and a joke about a papal election, itself known only from Luther's table talk.[34] If this is "anti-Roman sentiment," there is more of it to be found in the writings of John Fisher, who went to the block on Tower Hill in 1535 rather than renounce papal primacy.[35]

Staupitz's emphasis on making satisfaction for one's sins within the context of penance has something in common with Luther's original challenge to indulgences, but nothing at all in common with Luther's subsequent rejection of sacramental penance in general and penitential satisfaction in particular. That Staupitz "incited" Luther against indulgences is more plausible. Staupitz, like many Catholic contemporaries, was disturbed by recent developments in the theory and practice of indulgences. There is no indication, however, that Staupitz had any wish to repudiate the basic doctrine of indulgences (as opposed to its more luxuriant recent developments in theory and practice). Scholarly attempts to trace elements of Luther's theology to roots in that of Staupitz remain deeply unpersuasive.[36] There are perhaps, in the later Staupitz, some echoes of Luther's Reformational teaching, but these are at best faint, and at most they show not his theological influence over Luther, but Luther's theological impact on him. Staupitz's own early work shows him to have been a typical theologian of his religious order. His main original work, *Sermons on Job*, delivered and written up around 1500, stands squarely in the tradition of medieval biblical interpretation. Like the first great commentator on the Book of Job, Gregory the Great, Staupitz finds in Job above all an exemplar, both a "figure" (as medieval theology put it) of Jesus Christ and a model for all good Christians to imitate. Gregory's commentary was often referred to as the *Moralia*, and, as that title indicates, it was decidedly moralistic in tone, concerned with virtue and reward. The mature Luther had very little time for Gregory, but Staupitz knew his commentary well. Staupitz's own commentary was learned in the fashion of its time, citing liberally both from the Latin Fathers of the Church and from selected medieval theologians and spiritual authors. The official theologian of the Austin Friars was Giles of Rome (d. 1316), who had himself been a pupil of Thomas Aquinas, and Giles was indeed the most frequently cited medieval authority in Staupitz's *Sermons on Job*.[37] Augustine, the order's patron, was of course also very obviously present in the work. But the Augustine of the early Staupitz was very much the medieval Augustine, the author of the *Confessions*, the *City of God*, and *On the Trinity*. This was not the Augustine of the mature Luther. Staupitz's Augustine was the Christian philosopher and mystic. Luther was drawn to the narrow-minded polemicist of the interminable tracts against the Pelagians, to Augustine the advocate of a harsh and unyielding doctrine of predestination.[38]

Staupitz and Luther had a meaningful personal relationship, one that had a major influence on both their careers. But this relationship was more personal and spiritual than intellectual, and historical understanding of it has been unduly colored by the roseate glow in which the later Luther bathed his recollections of one of the most important friendships in his life. Only for short periods were they in the same place long enough for Luther to have imbibed much of Staupitz's actual teaching. Occasional conversation and correspondence seem to have formed the substance of their relationship, and Staupitz's influence on Luther is to be seen more in attitudes and commitments than in doctrine: in moral seriousness and pastoral dedication, in a yearning for reform, and in a profound commitment to the study of theology in general, and in particular to the study of the scriptures. Staupitz evidently groomed Luther to be his own successor in the scriptural lectureship at Wittenberg which was to be Luther's lifelong calling. And he certainly encouraged his interest in scripture: perhaps it was thanks to him that the friars gave Luther his red-leather Bible. It was moreover at Staupitz's instigation that Luther took his doctorate in 1512, thus qualifying him for the teaching position at Wittenberg. But in the crucial years of the later 1510s, when Luther embarked on his campaign against indulgences and on his personal theological odyssey, their paths crossed but rarely, and nothing like enough to justify Luther's own claims that Staupitz "incited" him against indulgences and the papacy—unless all he meant by that was that Staupitz offered him encouragement in his quest for truth and reform.

Luther's relationship with Staupitz might at first sight seem to be problematized by one of the most curious episodes in his career, his journey to Rome on business of his religious order over the winter of 1510–11. For Staupitz had in 1510 sought to impose some forceful reforming measures onto the Augustinians of Saxony, and Luther was actually sent to Rome as one of a two-man delegation, seeking to block his program. It says something for both men that this did not lead to a breach between them. However, there is little reason to believe that Luther was heavily invested in the business or outcome of this mission. The mission was unsuccessful, and he is not on record as expressing any resentment about this, which he probably would have done if he had had any real interest in the matter. His fundamental lack of interest is evident in the fact that, while he frequently reminisced in later life about his trip to Rome, he never said a word about his business there. Friars away from their house were obliged, by the rule of the order, to travel in pairs. Although it is not known who the other friar was, the likeliest candidate is Luther's own former novice-master, a leading figure in the Erfurt house, Johann Nathin, who was at the heart of the opposition to Staupitz's plan. When the Staupitz plan was, eventually, triumphant, the Erfurt house became divided, and Luther was with the minority which supported Staupitz.[39] Luther will have been sent along to accompany Nathin and assist with whatever clerical work (writing or copying letters, etc.) had to be done. Brecht does not accept that Luther was necessarily the "junior partner" on this mission, but it nevertheless seems highly likely that this was precisely his role.

Luther's later recollections dwelled not on the business of the mission but on his essentially devotional motives for undertaking the journey.[40] By his own account his personal agenda was one of pure piety, and there is no reason to disbelieve him. He even went so far as to declare that his chief purpose in travelling to Rome had been to make a general confession and thus avail himself of the fullness of forgiveness.[41] Perhaps he had it in mind to acquire the superlative indulgences offered to penitents at the church of Santa Maria Scala Coeli. The acquisition of indulgences was a powerful motive for pilgrimage in the later Middle Ages, as we can see from the surviving narratives of the great pilgrimage to the Holy Land, which often detail the special indulgences available at particular holy sites. Luther also indicates, however, that he was disturbed by the contrast between the holiness of Rome as a place of pilgrimage and the wickedness that he found prevalent there. He was there for only four weeks, but the visit furnished plenty of material for his memory or imagination.[42] Twenty years later, he would often raise a laugh with anecdotes about the moral and spiritual depravity he had observed on this visit, but we need to be a little cautious about taking these stories too literally. They all date from long after his excommunication by Leo X, and reflect a state of mind in which he had come to view the papacy as nothing less than Antichrist. Many of the tales he told are clearly jokes picked up and brought home and ultimately transmuted into historical fact: for example, the Roman priests who consecrated the eucharistic host not with the words of Christ but with the cynical parody "Bread thou art, and bread thou shalt remain." The "words of institution" were pronounced by priests at that time in an almost inaudible undertone, so this recollection can only have been of rumor or humor, if it was not simply made up for comic effect. But there were two Romes for late medieval Christians: the city of pilgrims, abounding in churches, shrines, and relics; and the city of political prelates, swarming with beggars and prostitutes, poorly governed, and racked with poverty. Luther doubtless saw the second, but he went to see the first.

On his way back from Rome in winter 1511, he made a point of calling on the Holy Maid of Augsburg, one Ursula Lamenit, who was reputed to need no physical sustenance beyond the Blessed Sacrament. Figures of this kind were a familiar feature of the late medieval religious scene, and might end up celebrated as saints or condemned as frauds, depending on circumstances. One such fraud was the Holy Maid of Leominster, amusingly described by Thomas More.[43] Another, it turned out, was Ursula Lamenit. But while Luther later noted her subsequent exposure as a fraud, he credited himself with no preternatural insight into the truth back in 1511.[44] His visit to her reflects a characteristically Catholic openness to the possibility of Eucharist miracles, which he retained even after his conversion, observing years later that although some such miracles were presumably Satanic frauds, the genre as a whole confirmed the doctrine of the real presence of Christ in the consecrated materials of the Eucharist.[45] The visit to Rome, then, had no discernible impact on his devotion or his theology. There is no sign of disillusionment or disenchantment in the Luther of the early 1510s. He returned from Rome, as he had departed from Germany, a devout Catholic.

3

THE CATHOLIC LUTHER

It was very much as a devout Catholic that Luther took up his appointment as professor of scripture at the University of Wittenberg in 1512. His intellectual interests were thoroughly conventional. By his own account, his curiosity at this time had been piqued by one of the most widely read of fourteenth-century devotional texts, the *Revelations* of Saint Bridget of Sweden.[1] Bridget's *Revelations*, which had been printed a few times, embodied the deeply Christocentric concerns that mark so much late medieval piety, as well as reformist urges that made as much sense in the context of the Renaissance papacy at Rome as they had in the context of the Avignon papacy of her own time. Luther would later dismiss the reported visions and revelations of nuns such as Bridget as mere ravings, but his interest in them in the early 1510s was very much part of the Catholic mainstream.

In 1513, Luther decided that his main lectures in the coming year would deal with the Psalms. There was nothing untoward in this. The book of Psalms was generally considered by Christian theologians the most obviously "Christological" book in the Old Testament, and was therefore a favored subject for commentary throughout the Middle Ages. Notwithstanding Luther's insinuation that the Bible was unknown to professional theologians, lecturing on a part of the Bible (especially this part) was not at all unusual. The academic pursuit of theology from the thirteenth century onwards had been based on one particular textbook, the *Sentences* of Peter Lombard, on which dozens, if not hundreds, of medieval commentaries and lecture series survive. But this textbook was the starting point for the study of theology, not its be-all and end-all. Scholars lectured on the *Sentences*, as Luther had done, by way of apprenticeship, to prove themselves as theologians, and theology students started by attending lectures on the *Sentences*, but the Bible was by no means ignored.

The invention of print in the fifteenth century permitted a major step forward in the study of theology, by enabling the complete text of the Bible to be made available in far greater quantity and at a far lower price than ever before. "Bibles," as such, were relatively rare until the arrival of print. They were by no means unknown, but it was far more common for the scriptures to be copied and owned and read in discrete portions than to be found as a single book, or even as a coherent set of volumes. The New Testament, the Gospels, the Epistles, even individual gospels, were more common, as were the Pentateuch and the Prophets, often divided between the major prophets and the (twelve) minor prophets, and many individual books such as Genesis, Exodus, or the Psalms (the most widely copied book, because of its devotional use). One-volume bibles, such as Gutenberg's, remained somewhat unwieldy items for several decades, but were common by the close of the fifteenth century. But by the time Luther was teaching at Wittenberg, a standard scholar's Bible was being widely produced in four- or six-volume sets. In these sets, the Latin text of the so-called "Vulgate" (i.e., common) Bible was presented along with a sophisticated body of commentary comprising the ancient interlinear "gloss" (brief explanatory notes, usually presented between the printed lines of the text), the "postils" (or comments) of the fourteenth-century French theologian Nicholas of Lyra, and later annotations by the converted Jew Paul of Burgos and the German theologian Mathias Thoring. These more substantial commentaries were presented in four separate blocks of text printed around a small section of glossed scriptural text that occupied the center of each page. Bibles of this kind, often known as "Lyras" for short, still survive in large numbers, and Luther probably owned one himself. Equipped as they were with excellent indexes, these new printed bibles made it vastly easier to carry out the sort of complex research that Luther practiced, cross-referencing texts across the entire body of the scriptures in order to tease out its full theological significance.

It was the printed Vulgate, not the Greek New Testament of Erasmus or the slowly rising tide of scholarship on the Hebrew Old Testament, that made possible not only Luther's theological achievement but also its wide assimilation by other scholars, who could retrace the steps of his arguments through the pages of their own bibles. It also underpinned the achievements of his opponents, who could thumb through their own bibles in search of the contrary texts and contexts that showed the limitations, biases, and idiosyncrasies of his new doctrines. The impact of this can be seen in the development by the mid-sixteenth century of the new level of division of the Christian scriptures into individual numbered verses, which was fixed thanks to the work of the French Protestant printer Robert Estienne. The division of the books of the Bible into numbered chapters went back to the thirteenth century and to the birth of the universities and of theology as an academic discipline. The scholarly need for a still more precise and direct reference system, to enable scholars to check texts even more efficiently, was itself a product partly of the proliferation of printed bibles and partly of the theological squabbling of the Reformation era.

Luther himself later recalled, perhaps with some element of exaggeration, that when he was a student at Erfurt, not one professor of theology owned a bible.[2] One might legitimately doubt this claim, because printed scholarly bibles survive in very substantial numbers. Nevertheless, his remark points us towards an important truth: the printed Bible changed the basis upon which Christian theologians worked. Thanks to print, for the first time in Christian history scholars anywhere in Latin Europe could have ready access to the entire scriptural text.

Luther took advantage of the new technology in his first major lecture series, commissioning from the Wittenberg printer Johann Grunenberg a cheap printed version of the Psalms, with the text set out in such a way as to leave students (and indeed himself) plenty of white space to write glosses between the lines and fuller notes in the ample margins. His own copy still survives, replete with the notes he made as the basis for his lectures, given between 1513 and 1515. At some time, probably after he had finished that course, he seems to have decided to turn his first lecture course into a more formal commentary, almost certainly intended for publication. This task, to which he alludes in a few letters written in 1516, was never completed, but the substantial albeit unfinished manuscript also survives, and this fuller exposition of the text, supplemented by his earlier rough notes, offers an intriguing insight into his theological views prior to his emergence as a public dissident in the years just before 1520.[3] Although some scholars have sought to find in this work evidence that he had already formulated the crucial insights that characterize his mature teaching, such efforts are misplaced, and depend either on misunderstanding the distinctive character of Luther's mature theology or on misunderstanding late medieval Catholic theology (or both).

Luther's first psalm commentary is nevertheless of considerable interest in assessing his emergence as an original theologian. Although its frame of reference is unmistakably Catholic, it already touches on a number of features, more or less distinctive, that would preoccupy the author throughout his life. And it is also remarkable for what it fails to do. Most medieval expositions of the psalms would expatiate upon familiar theological concepts and categories such as the seven sacraments, the four cardinal virtues, the seven deadly sins, and other such handy enumerations so useful in preaching and teaching. Such topics might not seem at first sight very evident in the texts of these ancient Hebrew songs, but a long tradition of allegorical interpretation licensed theologians to find them there. Luther's overwhelming concern, however, arising from the very first psalm, was with the central theological issue of justice. It was to the understanding and explanation of justice and justification that he returned throughout the commentary—and it is this focus that has led some scholars to conclude that, because the words are there, his later and very distinctive understandings of justice and justification are also already present.

The most striking feature of the commentary, at least to the modern eye, is its stridently anti-Jewish tone. Although there was then a clear Christian consensus that, at the time of Christ, the Jews had (with some exceptions) willfully and culpably rejected his Messianic claims and brought about his crucifixion, calling down upon themselves and their descendants the chastisement of divine providence, and although this consensus underpinned a general hostility towards Jews that ranged from a reluctant and grudging (though highly discriminatory) toleration by way of moral panic to sporadic mob violence and, ultimately, the option of forced conversion or expulsion, anti-Jewish rhetoric did not usually run right through Christian theological reflection. Most commentators on the Psalms did their work without indulging in incessant anti-Jewish polemic. Luther's near contemporary and later opponent John Fisher also produced an unpublished psalm commentary, and he too invokes the familiar ideas and tropes of anti-Jewish rhetoric, blaming the Jews for unbelief and for killing Christ, and classifying them (as Luther does) with tyrants and heretics as the classic triad of the "persecutors" of the Christian Church.

(Christians at the time seem to have been entirely oblivious to the realities of persecution around the year 1500.) But in Fisher's commentaries these allusions are occasional, testifying to an uncomplicated acceptance of widely shared assumptions.[4] In Luther's commentaries, anti-Jewish rhetoric is well-nigh omnipresent, surfacing in almost every psalm, indeed on almost every page. Anti-Jewish ideas are not only endemic, but are systemically integral to the text, in that Luther construes the Jews and their interpretation of the "law" (i.e., the Old Testament scriptures, the Hebrew Bible) as the wrong end of a stark polarity between true and false justice. The Jews and their theology embody a complete inversion of the divine justice that is, for Luther, the crucial theme of the book of Psalms.[5] They seek to justify themselves.[6]

What does most to lend credence to the erroneous notion that Luther was already, so to speak, a "Lutheran" at the time of this early commentary is precisely its overwhelming concern with justice and justification. While these concepts were certainly familiar to late medieval theologians, Luther was already distinctive in focusing so heavily upon them. It is evident that the question of how it might be possible for sinful human beings to be "justified" in the eyes of God, that is, how they could be saved from sin and made fit for the "beatific vision" of God in the world to come, was a cause of far more intellectual perplexity and a matter of far more existential urgency for the young Luther than it was for most other theologians. This, however, is not enough to show that the distinctively Lutheran doctrine of "justification by faith alone" was already in his mind.[7]

That this classically "Lutheran" doctrine had not yet taken shape is evident not only from the absence of any of the lapidary formulae that would encapsulate his later views but also from simple statements of unselfconsciously traditional positions that were utterly incompatible with his mature theology.

Thus the mere passing comment that "we are co-workers with God" demonstrates that Luther was still well within the boundaries of medieval Catholicism.[8] The concept of "cooperative grace" implicit in the claim that the faithful are co-workers (*cooperatores*) is worlds away from the strictly passive or instrumental role ascribed to human action and even volition in Luther's later understanding of salvation. Faith, grace, and justice (three pretty much interchangeable terms) are "given"—*data*—not (as much later) "imputed."[9] Justification is continuous and progressive, not instantaneous. His understanding of salvation is entirely traditional: "The first root of all good is to put one's will into the law of the Lord." Far from believing in "justification by faith alone," Luther's first reference to faith in this commentary is his quotation from the Epistle of James: "Faith without works is dead."[10] Indeed, he censures the "stupid confidence" of those who think that they are saved because they are members of the people of God, because they are baptized believers, without any good works. Faith was a prerequisite for everything.[11] But it was not everything. Christian justice came through faith in Christ, but it was still about works of justice. Christians, unlike Jews, "work towards God and fulfil the works of the Law before God."[12] Salvation for the early Luther, as for the late medieval Church, was ultimately about imitating Christ. The deeds of Christ, and of his saints, done in humility, poverty, and affliction, were examples set before the faithful for emulation.[13]

Justification is, moreover, a process, not—as in Luther's mature theology—an event. It was scalar, not binary: "Those who are just are still to be justified. Those who stand must watch that they do not fall down." Most significantly of all, justice itself was still envisaged, in Aristotle's classical formulation, as "rendering to each their due." This was a definition Luther would later exclude altogether from the domain of theology. For Luther, as for the medieval consensus, Christ had brought a new law to replace the old. Far from being distinct from the Law, the Gospel was nothing other than the Law spiritually understood.[14] Luther's analysis of the problem with the Jews followed conventional lines: they adhered to the flesh rather than the spirit, to the letter rather than the spirit. They therefore clung to a literal and "carnal" understanding of the Law, without penetrating to its true "spiritual meaning."[15] For the later Luther, a series of new dichotomies entirely restructured his understanding of these traditional dichotomies. He would come to identify the "law" with the "letter," a very different perception.

Reliance on their own justice was for Luther the characteristic of the Jews: reliance on God's justice, that of faithful Christians. Taking up a familiar contrast, he argued that "As the just starts out as his own accuser, the unjust starts out as his own defender."[16] The comment has the ring of Lutheran paradox about it, but is a traditional enough idea—familiar from John Chrysostom, and used by many Catholic spiritual writers, as it was easily applied to the practice of sacramental confession. As the commentary progresses, Luther's conception of justice divides increasingly sharply between an illusory human justice, a vain confidence in justification by one's own personal works and merits, and the true justice of God, attained by faith and obedience.[17] But this theological position was squarely in line with the teachings of Augustine, the most widely respected theologian and "authority" of the Latin tradition. And it was widely shared among contemporary Catholic theologians. Salvation was from Christ alone and by grace alone. But for all that, Christians—unlike Jews, he insisted—"worked for God and fulfilled the works of the Law for God."[18] His later theology would offer a very different view.

Showing his hand as a disciple of the "Nominalist" school of theology derived from William of Ockham, he regarded justification by faith and grace as operative not *per se*, but by a divine covenant or contract (*pactum*).[19] On a number of future occasions Luther would avow himself a follower, or former follower, of the Ockhamist school (*Occamicae factionis, meae sectae*). It was Ockham, "without doubt the most ingenious and chief among the scholastic doctors," to whom he affiliated himself, as "my master." Luther thought him supreme among the scholastics, a master of dialectic, albeit devoid of any rhetorical skill.[20] His own frank avowal of his Ockhamist training calls into question more sweeping interpretations of Staupitz's theological influence upon him. Staupitz's favorite scholastic authorities, as we have seen, were Thomas Aquinas and his pupil, Giles of Rome. Luther's encounter with the scholastic tradition was not mediated by Staupitz, however much he may have been affected by Staupitz's personality and pastoral care.

Nor was Luther's Ockhamism without significance for his subsequent theological development. It is a truism that the "Nominalist" philosophical tradition, often known as the *via moderna*, of which Ockham was the most eminent exponent, differed from the *via antiqua*, the so-called "Realist" tradition most eminently represented by the figure of Thomas Aquinas, in the priority it gave to the will over the intellect or being in the understanding of the divine nature and operation. This is too deep a question to explore here, but to skate over the thin ice on top of these depths, one might say that while, for Thomas, goodness and justice were what they were by virtue of the nature of the order that God had created, so that goodness and justice were intrinsically rational, for William of Ockham, that which was good or just was so simply because God said so. The good and the just were extrinsically rather than intrinsically rational. The conceptions of "forensic justification" and "imputed justice" that would be crucial elements of Lutheranism made sense only within the context of the "voluntarist" tradition of Ockham as opposed to the "Realist" or "intellectualist" tradition of Aquinas.

Luther was moreover a solidly hierarchical Christian in these years. By his own account, he was "such a papist that he might have written against Erasmus for disparaging the papacy."[21] The psalm commentary shows him to have been a loyal clergyman who regarded bishops as the backbone of the Church and urged wholehearted obedience to them. "The order of the prelates is the strength of the Church, so the whole heart and intention must be focused on their welfare. If the prelates are safe, then the Church is safe, and vice versa."[22] This was mainstream clerical reformism, the sort of thing being proclaimed the length and breadth of Europe by deans and dons such as John Colet (Dean of Saint Paul's Cathedral in London) or Josse Clichtove (professor of theology at the Sorbonne).[23] Those who called loudest for reform within the late medieval church envisaged reform as starting with and from the episcopate. Of course, like most educated Catholic contemporaries, Luther felt there was a real need for reform. He spoke scathingly of those clergymen who neglected their priestly duties and lusted after women or wealth. "Nowhere today is there anything more pompous, arrogant, and vainglorious than the princes and priests of the Church."[24] He decried the corruption endemic in the system of church benefices and appointments, though he also had harsh words for the laity in the matter of profaning holy days.[25] Likewise, he averred that he had little time for the petty quarrels between and within religious orders.[26]

Luther's position on clerical reformism was thoroughly consistent with his disdain for dissidents and heretics. Those who set themselves up against the church authorities, such as the "Bohemians" (that is, the followers of Jan Hus, who had established an alternative church in parts of what is now the Czech Republic), were puffed up with pride, and were therefore to be shunned as heretics. They came in for particular censure on account of their repudiation of the Church of Rome and of its primacy.[27] Although Luther's commentary was not, as many such late medieval commentaries were, an exercise in tracking and tracing Catholic theology in the Psalms through intricate allegorical interpretation, it was nonetheless transparently founded on an orthodox understanding of the Catholic faith. The Mass was for him a sacrifice, in accord with Catholic teaching.[28] There were seven sacraments.[29] His understanding of the "concupiscence of the flesh" was entirely traditional—in contrast to the radically harsher understanding of that concept that he developed in 1518–19.[30] Good works, however exiguous they might be, and however useless for purposes of salvation without grace, were nevertheless acknowledged as of some kind of good.[31] Although he felt that the use of indulgences perhaps made Christianity seem too easy (this was where he would begin his critique in 1517), he still acknowledged their validity.[32] At some point in these years, probably early on, Luther became entangled in a disputation with Andreas Carlstadt over the latter's claim that the indulgences available in the Castle Church could only be acquired by those who made their confession in that church—a claim that Luther dismantled easily enough, but without for a moment calling indulgences into doubt.[33] Even his concept of preaching was impeccably conventional: every word of the priest, he wrote, should be a judgment teaching that "evil is to be avoided and good to be done."[34] The focus of the preacher was to be on moral instruction in the virtues and vices, just as it said in all the medieval preaching handbooks. The shift from the medieval hermeneutic of virtue and vice to the later Lutheran hermeneutic of "Law and Gospel" was the crossing of a chasm.

There are, particularly in the commentary (as opposed to the lecture notes), some features and traits that would characterize the mature Luther, though these do not represent the core of his mature theology. While he acknowledged his own training in the school of Ockham, he was beginning to voice a modish contempt for the internecine quarrels that preoccupied late medieval theologians, with Scotists and Ockhamists fighting each other tooth and nail. Thus a fairly gentle critique of needlessly subtle theologizing (reminiscent of the critique offered by Thomas à Kempis in the fifteenth-century devotional classic *The Imitation of Christ*) bloomed into a fiercer indictment of the pernicious influence of Aristotle on medieval theology by way of Thomas Aquinas and Duns Scotus.[35] There was an anti-intellectual note to his aside against those who, "these days, prefer the opinions of philosophers and the fables of poets and the wranglings of lawyers to the holy gospel of God, which they disdain along with all study of scripture."[36] With unwitting irony, he also censured "heretics and suchlike," who "call into question everything that has been observed for centuries, and for which so many martyrs have given their lives." Instead, he urges, "humbly learn to be wise; don't be a newfangled author—don't overstep the limits that your fathers have laid down." He warns people that "not to want to believe, but to call everything into doubt and thus to expect a new learning—that is the gravest temptation."[37] It was a temptation that he was yet to face.

Luther's penchant for paradox, which remained with him throughout his life, and is one of the most attractive aspects of his thought and his style, is also evident in this early commentary.[38] All through his life he loved the scriptural tag "Omnis homo mendax," "All men are liars" (Ps 115:11), and he mentions it several times. As yet, though, his purpose in citing it is simply to emphasize that all people are sinners, rather than, as in his later writings, to undercut any possible human or ecclesiastical authority in matters of faith.[39] His theory of obedience is as stern and unbending here as it would be in any of his later writings, though in this text his concern is chiefly with ecclesiastical obedience, particularly to bishops and other prelates, but ultimately to the Bishop of Rome. Not that he ignores the duty of obedience to secular rulers as well, denouncing rebels in no uncertain terms.

The most deeply traditional feature of Luther's early psalm commentary was its unselfconscious fidelity to the medieval and indeed ancient conception of scripture as a peculiar kind of text that, thanks to its divine and inspired character, carried multiple, perhaps even infinite, meanings. The Lutheran Luther was to take a very different view. The very notion of multiplicity or fluidity or uncertainty of meaning in scripture was to become abhorrent to him. Yet in these early years his very approach to scripture was traditional. This went further than the mere affirmation of the "fourfold interpretation" beloved of medieval commentators, which he set out at the very start.[40] Traditional interpretation founded itself on a scriptural text, "the letter kills, but the spirit gives life" (2 Cor 3:6), which was taken, as Luther takes it throughout this commentary, as a charter for searching beneath the superficial meanings of literal statements for deeper spiritual truths. As he put it, "In the holy scriptures, the key thing is to distinguish the spirit from the letter, for it is this that really makes a theologian."[41] By this time, the range of scriptural meanings had been systematized by medieval thinkers into four broad categories: the literal itself; and then the "tropological," the "allegorical," and the "anagogical." These last three represented the "spirit" rather than the "letter," and were all varieties of metaphorical or allegorical interpretation. But "fourfold interpretation" was a cliché of medieval theology, and the Luther of the early psalm commentary was a keen exponent of it.

Later in this text Luther was to set out the doctrine of the multiplicity of meaning in an even more striking way. Suitably enough, he did this in the course of an allegorical exposition of Ps 74: 9, "In the hand of the Lord there is a cup of pure wine." "Everyone," he observed, "who wants to make progress in the Bible and the holy scriptures should ponder this verse as attentively as they can," because, he went on, its point was that scripture was not within the grasp of the human intellect. Because scripture was "in the hand of the Lord," the student needed to approach God in all humility and beg for enlightenment. The holiness of scripture, though, he maintained, was such that it should not be allowed to become the raw material of scholarly rivalry and conflict.

> Holy scripture is not to be handled like Aristotle, where it is fine for one expert to contradict another. There the teacher is like the teaching: both are profane. But here it is a sacred teacher and a sacred teaching. Wheresoever and by whomsoever any interpretation is advanced, if it does not contradict the rule of faith, then no one ought to censure it or to prefer their own interpretation, even if their own is far more obvious and far more consonant with the letter.[42]

Any meaning, in other words, which could be teased out from the text might be allowed to stand, as long as it was not contrary to accepted dogma. This was the polar opposite of his later "literalism."

This Luther, the Luther of the early 1510s, thus permitted a plurality, even a profusion, of meaning, and was hesitant to exclude other people's interpretations. It was a matter of humility to acknowledge that others, too, might uncover truth. The final traditional element in his early theory of scripture was precisely an emphasis on the respective roles of authority and humility in attaining understanding: "Thus the understanding of scripture is not enough for someone unless they also submit themselves to the magisterial authority of some discreet person or superior."[43] The whole point of the later hermeneutic usually summed up as "scripture alone" was to emphasize that truth came only from scripture, that no human authority could mediate that truth (although human means, such as preaching, could and did mediate truth, that preaching itself had to be conditioned and controlled entirely by scripture, not by human authority). Therefore, he later affirmed, any Christian armed with scripture could withstand any authority or interpretation that was not so armed. It is no surprise that the early Luther had an essentially conventional approach to the Bible. But it is remarkable to see, in these words, just how far the early Luther was from his later self. He would always maintain that he was merely a humble interpreter. But that interpretative humility was originally oriented towards human hierarchical superiors. Later on it was oriented solely towards the scriptural text itself, divine rather than human. For Luther this was still humility. But his earlier theory of scripture should help us understand why his opponents saw his later position as arrogance.

It was in the middle of the decade, once Luther had settled into his new role, that more distinctive themes began to appear in his thought. The context for this was his decision to move on from lecturing on the Psalms to lecturing on the Epistles of Paul. This, too, was far from revolutionary in itself. Paul's rich seams of theology had long made him a favorite among scriptural commentators and, since about 1200, among university lecturers. Thomas Aquinas, for example, had produced a major commentary on Paul back in the thirteenth century. Luther's own decision to set to work on Paul may have been immediately inspired by one of the less well known, though still significant, publishing events of a decade which saw the printing of a series of epoch-making books. This event was the publication in 1512 of a new commentary on Paul by the French humanist Jacques Lefèvre d'Étaples. Something of an obscure figure today, Lefèvre was a prominent scholar of that era who continually reinvented and renewed himself throughout an astonishingly long career. Having perhaps helped inspire Luther's theological path in the 1510s, in the 1520s he himself fell to some extent under Luther's spell, and the French humanist became something of an evangelical reformer. Back in 1512 his commentary on Paul was seriously innovative in making some attempt to engage with the original Greek behind the Latin.[44] It sold sufficiently well, despite its considerable bulk, to warrant a second edition in 1515. The chief reason for thinking that Luther took his lead from Lefèvre is that he based his lectures on the slightly revised text of the Vulgate which Lefèvre used in his commentary. For his lectures on Paul (Romans in 1515–16, Galatians in 1516–17, and Hebrews in 1517–18), Luther once more had Johannes Grunenberg run off copies of the epistles in pamphlet form, for the convenience of his students and Luther. His early lecture notes on Paul survive as marginalia on these cheap and cheerful printings.[45]

Like the lectures on the Psalms, the lectures on Romans have been seen by some scholars as the matrix for the gestation of Luther's mature teaching. There is more to be said in favor of this position, because these lectures saw not only a deepening of his earlier concern with justice and an increasing emphasis on the role of faith, but also some crucial advances in his thinking, leading him to challenge the tradition of scholastic theology and on one particular point taking him outside the existing consensus of Catholic doctrine. Luther himself later recalled that through the Epistle to the Romans he had come to "some knowledge of Christ"—some, but not all.[46] Luther's critique of abuses and deviations in the contemporary Church also become a little sharper in tone, especially towards the end. Nevertheless, the lectures on Romans, which remained unpublished and largely unknown until they were rediscovered about a hundred years ago, do not display the new understanding of faith which he would present to the reading public in 1518.

If the context of Luther's development in these years was his wrestling with the letters of Saint Paul, the catalyst was his encounter with the vigorous and voluminous anti-Pelagian writings of Saint Augustine of Hippo. The lectures and other materials on Romans certainly show an increasing engagement with the thought of this patriarch of Latin theology. Luther's reading of Augustine engendered in him a profound alienation from the Aristotelian methodology and assumptions that had characterized scholastic theology since the "christening of Aristotle" by Thomas Aquinas in the thirteenth century. Luther's grappling with the notions of justice and justification in Romans drew him ineluctably to the works of Augustine, whose lengthy and bitter controversy with Pelagius had hammered out much of the vocabulary that was still used to discuss the question of how sinful human beings were "put right" with God. Pelagius, at least as Augustine represented him, taught that human free will was in itself adequate to that task. Thanks to Augustine, all scholastic theologians knew that Pelagius was a heretic, and they were therefore all duly and dutifully "anti-Pelagian"—though some more markedly and successfully than others. But Luther's consuming interest in the subject of justification led him to take on more and more of Augustine's suspicion of human effort and free will, and more and more of his emphasis on the sheer gratuitousness and primacy of divine grace in human salvation. In his scholia on Romans, which amount to a virtually complete commentary and look like a text produced in the wake of the lectures rather than for them, Luther cites from over a dozen separate works of Augustine's. Most of these citations are from just half a dozen of his anti-Pelagian writings. Towards the end, Luther voices his concern that his times are awash with an unwitting but deep-rooted Pelagianism:

> For although there are no professed or avowed Pelagians today, there are a great many in practice and in theory, albeit unwittingly, such as those who think that, unless

they attribute to free will the power to do what lies in it before grace, they are driven to sin by God and therefore sin by necessity.[47]

This growing concern with Pelagianism accompanies a diminution in anti-Jewish comment. For Luther, Jews are still labelled as arrogantly trusting in their own unaided observance of the letter of the law to achieve salvation, in culpable ignorance of the flaws in fallen human nature which render that trust futile. But rather than the simple dichotomy between "us" and "them," between Christians and Jews, that was on show in the psalm commentary, the deeper dichotomy that now concerns Luther is within the Christian body itself: the same arrogant self-reliance which vitiated Judaism has spread throughout Christendom. From this time on, for Luther, the real threat is within the church rather than outside it.

The scholia on Romans have one real sign of things to come: a definite break with medieval tradition over the complex issue of original sin, concupiscence, and baptism. But this discussion takes place within a lengthy digression on Romans 4, in which Luther steps aside to offer commentary on Psalm 31, the second of the so-called "Seven Penitential Psalms," because he notices similar Latin verbs (*reputare* and *imputare*) being used in the Vulgate versions of Romans 4:1 and Psalm 31:2. Here, for the first time, we see Luther working with Augustine on the subject of concupiscence, baptism, and sin in such a way as to conclude that baptism did not take away all sin. This conclusion, as we shall see, was an integral part of Luther's emerging Reformational thought. What is not clear is just how early this insight came to him. There is no sign of it in his early psalm commentary, nor is there any hint of it in the scantier lecture notes on Romans. Nor, finally, is it found in Luther's earliest published work, his little meditation on the Seven Penitential Psalms published early in 1517. This is particularly noteworthy in that

Psalm 31 is one of those seven psalms. Given the importance of this insight in Luther's thought, it is hard to see why it does not appear in this early text if it had already occurred to him.[48]

The root of what might have remained simply a trivial misunderstanding lay in Luther's authentic appreciation of Augustine's conception of human sin and sinfulness as a profoundly systemic problem rather than a mere sequence of regrettable events. Luther, like Augustine and indeed Saint Paul, was more concerned with "sin" than with "sins," with the underlying state of mind rather than with physical or even mental acts. The key scriptural texts here were Romans 6 and 7, especially 7:7, "Nay, I had not known sin, but by the law; for I had not known lust, except the law had said, Thou shalt not covet." Paul, here discussing sin in general but taking adultery as the test case, wanted to make a point similar to that made by Jesus, namely that the thought or desire of committing adultery was just as sinful as the act itself. Paul anchored this observation to the Ten Commandments, which of course stipulated, "Thou shalt not covet thy neighbor's wife." Without this divine revelation, Paul says, the sinfulness of mere unfulfilled desire, as opposed to effectual action, would have been unknown to him. Building on hints in this section of Paul, Augustine further developed this analysis, defining Paul's "infirmity of the flesh" (Rom 6:19) as the "concupiscence of the flesh" (*concupiscentia carnis*), an indwelling liability or predisposition to commit sin rooted in the reality of every person's bodily existence (to use a modern analogy, like a genetic flaw or weakness which would nevertheless require environmental actualization to become a disease). This concept was an integral part of Augustine's elaborate theory of original sin. For him, this "concupiscence of the flesh" was in and of itself sin in every person descended from Adam and Eve.[49] However, in the light of the universal early Christian teaching that baptism washed away all sins, Augustine maintained that in those who had been baptized, while this concupiscence continued to function as an abiding provocation to sin, it was nevertheless no longer properly called sin in and of itself. He acknowledged that Paul sometimes referred to this indwelling weakness in the faithful as "sin," but argued that this usage was figurative rather than literal.[50] Augustine actually developed his sophisticated account of sin and concupiscence in the course of his polemics against the Pelagians, whose main objection to his theory was that it contradicted the dogma that baptism took away all sin. He was therefore very careful to emphasize that he accepted this dogma (to have done otherwise would have been to rule himself entirely out of court), that baptism did indeed take away all sin, but that concupiscence definitely survived baptism even though it was no longer properly to be labelled "sin."

Luther pursued this trajectory one step further. Like Augustine, he was beset by a sense of the permeation of human life by sin. By a simple misreading of one crucial text of Augustine's, however, he came to the conclusion that the concupiscence of the flesh was in and of itself sin both before and after baptism. This misreading is first seen in his scholia on Romans, where it is introduced with becoming modesty, as Luther acknowledges at least the abstract possibility that he might be mistaken in adopting a position which, he realizes, contradicts almost all previous medieval theologians:

> Either I have never got it, or the scholastic theologians have not spoken well enough about sin and grace. They imagine that original sin is wholly taken away, just like actual sin, as if they could both be removed in the blink of an eye, the way darkness is by light. But the ancient Fathers Augustine and Ambrose spoke very differently, according to the manner of scripture, while the scholastics spoke according to the manner of the *Ethics* of Aristotle, who located sin and justice entirely in works and in their presence or ab-

sence. But Saint Augustine put it excellently, saying that "the sin concupiscence is remitted in baptism not so that it does not exist, but so that it is not imputed."[51]

This insight, as Luther realized, was entirely out of line with the understanding of sin and original sin offered by the scholastics. What he did not realize was that their understanding of sin and original sin was entirely in line with Augustine's, and was indeed predicated upon it. By misreading Augustine's claim that concupiscence after baptism remained rooted in the flesh but was no longer counted as sin in itself (though it could become sinful if it received the deliberate consent of the will), he reached the deeply paradoxical conclusion that this concupiscence of the flesh somehow both remained sin after baptism and yet was no longer counted as sin. This small but intricate point represented a radical innovation. When eventually noised abroad, from 1518, it became for his opponents one of the most disturbing elements of his thought. For him a paradox, for them it was a contradiction in terms.

The paragraph just cited, in which Luther first voiced his suspicions about the scholastic understanding of original sin, grace, and concupiscence, simultaneously alerts us to the other crucial, and closely related, development in his thought at this time. Luther's engagement with Romans and Augustine led him to complete disenchantment with Aristotle, whose philosophy was fundamental to the method of scholastic theology. Aristotle, who had been a dominant figure in European intellectual life for nearly three hundred years, was coming under attack from at least two other angles in the early sixteenth century. The quickening stream of thought known to modern historians as "Christian humanism" deprecated the late medieval focus on Aristotelian logic or dialectic as the engine of intellectual inquiry, urging instead that rhetoric, the art of persuasion, was the art of arts. Alongside it ran the gentler and more traditional current of fideism, harking back to the pre-scholastic era of monastic and contemplative learning, allergic to logic-chopping and suspicious of the arrogance of the human intellect. Luther's own anti-Aristotelianism drew rhetorically from both these other veins of thought, but was itself fundamentally theological, rooted in his conviction that naturalistic Aristotelian ethics was utterly incompatible with the Christian understanding of divine grace.

Near the start of his scholia on Romans, where Paul talks of the revelation of the justice of God (Rom 1:17), Luther cites a central text of Augustine's, "It is called God's justice because, by imparting it, he makes people just," and then contrasts this with human justice, which is taken to arise from human effort: "As Aristotle plainly states in Ethics III . . . justice follows and arises from actions." But the human justice defined by Aristotle was, for Luther, a mere sham. True justice, divine justice, did not arise from human good works, but gave rise to them.[52]

By the time Luther had finished with Romans, he had finished with Aristotle, and with the medieval theology that blended Aristotelianism with Christianity. This was openly proclaimed in an event he staged in Wittenberg at the end of summer 1517, the "Disputation against Scholastic Theology." The 97 theses disputed on 4 September 1517 have a fair claim to be more radical in nature than the better known *Ninety-Five Theses* penned a couple of months later. The earlier theses, too, were printed, though presumably for the convenience of those attending the disputation rather than for any serious purpose of publication. Nothing else is recorded of the disputation, but the 97 theses were a pithy summary of themes that had emerged during Luther's engagement with Paul and Augustine over the previous two years.

> 4. The truth is that the human being, corrupted to the root, can neither desire nor perform anything but evil.

41. Almost all of Aristotle's *Ethics* is completely opposed to grace.

43. It is an error to say that one cannot become a theologian without Aristotle.

76. Every work of the law performed without the grace of God appears good outwardly, but inwardly is sin.[53]

The theses are variously labelled as contrary to Duns Scotus, William of Ockham, Gabriel Biel, or "the scholastics."[54] The anti-Pelagian thrust of the whole exercise is spelled out in the first two theses, which uphold Augustine explicitly against Pelagius. The point of what follows is to repudiate scholastic theology as inherently Pelagian. This conviction evidently reflected Luther's increasing exposure to the anti-Pelagian writings of Saint Augustine during his prolonged engagement with the Epistles of Paul. Augustine insisted, against Pelagius, that truly virtuous actions could not be performed by human beings purely by means of their intellect and will. For Luther, Pelagius's emphasis on human will and effort in training for virtue was much the same as Aristotle's theory that one could attain virtue by training and forming habits of virtuous action.

Scholastic theology had gone profoundly wrong, therefore, from the thirteenth century, when Thomas Aquinas had transplanted Aristotle's ethical theories into the corpus of Christian theology. For Luther, this "christening" of Aristotle was not a successful synthesis of nature and grace, but a pollution and profanation of divine truth with a merely human "wisdom." He brushed aside the subtleties with which Thomas Aquinas, Duns Scotus, and the other scholastics integrated the operation of divine grace with the activity of human nature, offering in place of that complex system a sheer dichotomy between divine grace and a human nature permeated with sin thanks to the fall of Adam and Eve.

The Luther in Wittenberg on the eve of All Saints in 1517 was thus a teacher profoundly disenchanted with the scholastic tradition in which he had been trained. In his view, it was vitiated through and through by the unacknowledged Pelagianism that had crept into the Church since the thirteenth century. The emphasis in popular preaching on the Aristotelian virtues and vices obscured from Christians the true reality of sin, which Luther now envisaged in a deeply Augustinian way as an endemic undercurrent of even the holiest life. Indeed, his understanding of sin was already "hyper-Augustinian," in that his misreading of Augustine's conception of the "concupiscence of the flesh" took the debate onto a new level. Moreover, his antipathy to scholastic theology was leading him to misrepresent it. The understanding of justice and justification among scholastic theologians was for the most part formulated with careful attention to the teachings of Augustine, to whom almost all medieval Catholic theologians looked back as supreme among the "Fathers" of the Church. Luther, careless as ever of subtle distinctions, bundled them all together in a box, labelled it "Pelagians," and henceforth paid them even less attention. This antischolastic positioning was over the next few years to help win him friends and supporters from among the Christian humanists, who themselves often expressed suspicion of scholastic theology, albeit on rather different grounds. But Luther's positive new theology of justification was not yet in place. It would emerge only in the wake of the *Ninety-Five Theses*, as the notoriety brought to him by that provocative leaflet encouraged him to pursue his ideas further and emboldened him to believe himself divinely called to the task of purifying theology and renewing the gospel.

4

THE QUEST FOR
CERTAINTY

It was 1518, not 1517, that saw Luther burst onto the scene as a public figure. That year also saw the decisive moment in his theological development. His *Ninety-Five Theses* may have leaked out here or there before Christmas 1517, but it was only in January 1518 that they really hit the market, as they were reprinted in one town after another, in Latin first and then also in German. The Luther phenomenon in this period was very much a German rather than a European phenomenon. The *Ninety-Five Theses* did not appear at this time in any other language. News would reach Rome by spring 1518, but it would be 1519 before the name of Luther was widely known beyond the Germanic cultural sphere. But within it, Luther and his theses were being talked about, in the Netherlands, the Rhineland, Switzerland, and throughout the cultural heartlands of Germany.

Far more important than Luther's graduation to the status of German celebrity was the next, and crucial, step on his theological path. It is not possible to put a precise date on this event, which Luther himself described only later, in varying terms, on different occasions, and for a variety of purposes (none of them including the convenience of future historians or biographers). Long afterwards, though, he dropped one especially helpful hint about the nature and timing of his breakthrough. Preaching on a favorite story from Genesis, that of Abraham (who failed for years to conceive a child with his wife Sara, but found no such problem with his servant Hagar), Luther interpreted

69

the Christian life in general, and his own life in particular, in terms of Abraham's two sons, Ishmael, son of Hagar, and Isaac, born of Sara in her old age. Isaac, as the son of grace, promised by God, was the reward for Abraham's faith, which had never wavered, not even when Sara was long past all apparent hope of motherhood. Abraham's trust in God's promise was, for Luther as for Saint Paul (and indeed for all Christian theologians), the supreme exemplar and pattern of faith. In this particular sermon, Luther wished to draw out another moral or theological lesson from the narrative, namely the contrast between the children of God and the children of this world (and thus of the flesh and ultimately of the devil). In medieval allegory, these two groups, the elect and the reprobate, the sheep and the goats, were respectively symbolized in the persons of Isaac and Ishmael. Such was the interpretative context within which Luther offered the following fragment of autobiography:

> For thirty-five years I was a son of Hagar. I desired to be saved by works through the monastic life. There was no promise there, where I confessed, fasted, and celebrated mass. *I was not certain that I was saved.* . . . But when Sarah became my mother, I grasped the promise, that we are saved without works, by the promise.[1]

The account of the timing and nature of the decisive shift in his theological understanding is more precise here than in any of his other occasional recollections. The distinctively new note in Luther's theology was *certainty*, certainty that he was "saved." Never before in the history of Christianity was such personal certainty, which medieval theologians called "certainty of grace" or "certainty of salvation," deemed normative, rather than exceptional, in Christian life.

For centuries, scholastic theologians, in their inquisitive way, had from time to time addressed the question of whether a

Christian could be certain, at any given moment, of being definitely in a "state of grace"—that is, certain that their sins had definitely been forgiven and that they therefore definitely enjoyed, at that moment, the grace and favor of God. By certainty they meant, as Luther meant, certainty—not near certainty, moral certainty, or any other more or less distant approximation to certainty, but absolute and infallible certainty. Their answer, one and all, was "no," at least in relation to the ordinary course of a Christian's life. The one exception they allowed for was what they called a "special revelation," a direct and unmistakable irruption by God into an individual's life, such as Paul's experience on the road to Damascus. For the scholastics, Paul's own certainty of salvation, which shines through his writings, was not a normative expectation for the Christian life, but a privileged illumination underpinning his providential role as the "Apostle to the Gentiles."

This understanding of certainty of grace as normally impossible was a commonplace across the diverse schools of medieval theology, Thomist, Scotist, and the rest. Thomas Aquinas had summed it up with his usual lucidity.[2] Even while Luther was still an obscure lecturer in Wittenberg the familiar consensus was being restated in university towns such as Cambridge and Cologne. Luther's own mentor, Johann von Staupitz, was as firm as anyone in his exclusion of such a certainty of grace from the normal run of the Christian life.[3] Luther himself knew how unusual his position was, observing in 1518 that certainty of grace was something which his opponents "all deny."[4] Instead of certainty, scholastic theologians and preachers offered hope, trust, and sometimes "moral certainty," a reasonable confidence, a sort of working hypothesis of forgiveness and salvation based on divine mercifulness.

It was with this hitherto complete consensus that Luther broke in 1518, in his thirty-fifth year. There was perhaps an ironic inevitability about this step, though not about Luther's taking it. If enough academics asked often enough whether it was possible to be certain of grace, it was arguably only a matter of time before one of them decided that it might be. The first signs of Luther's *démarche* are found in the lectures he was giving that year, on the Epistle to the Hebrews (which, despite some challenges from humanists such as Erasmus, was traditionally attributed to Saint Paul, an attribution Luther loyally upheld). Expounding the text which declares how Christ "appears in the presence of God for us" (Heb 9:24), he urged upon Christians an absolute certainty regarding the efficacy of Christ's intercession with the Father not merely in general but also in their own particular case:

> For this reason the Christian must be certain, absolutely certain, that Christ appears before God as a priest *for him*.[5]

He buttressed this demand with a clutch of New Testament texts that demanded unhesitating faith (Mark 11:23, Matt 8:12, James 1:6) before turning to address the crucial Old Testament text (from Eccles 9:1) which every scholastic theologian who tackled the question of certainty of grace cited as the clincher. The traditional argument made this the premise of a straightforward syllogism, as in the following formulation by Thomas Aquinas:

> But against this is what is said in Ecclesiastes 9, that "no one knows whether they are deserving of love or hatred." But justifying grace renders a person deserving of the love of God. Therefore no one can know whether they possess justifying grace.[6]

Luther himself had cited precisely the same text in his earlier lectures on Romans (1515–16) to make precisely the same point: "we can never know whether we are justified, whether we believe."[7] In his lectures on Hebrews, however, he read this same text very differently, warning that one must

> treat with the utmost caution the opinion of those who apply this text ... to the circumstances of the present moment so as to make people uncertain about the mercy of God and trust of salvation. *For this is to overthrow Christ and his faith completely.*[8]

Instead, Luther maintained, Ecclesiastes 9:1 should be referred not to present grace but to future perseverance. You could not know that you might not, at some future date, spurn God's grace through some sin: faith, and therefore grace, could be thrown away. But that did not mean that you could not know for sure, in the here and now, that you were in receipt and in possession, by faith, of God's saving grace. This immediate certainty was itself the essence of faith, its defining characteristic.

It is impossible to exaggerate the importance of this move in Luther's theological development. Certainty of grace, based on faith alone, indeed commutable with faith alone, became the acid test by which he judged all Christian doctrine and practice. Certainty of grace conferred upon believers, or at least upon Luther and his disciples, that "peace of conscience" (*pax conscientiae*, another of the slogans with which his mature teaching was summed up for the public) which was the practical fruit and objective of belief and worship, of prayer and preaching. Certainty of grace was the revolutionary concept which would lead Cardinal Cajetan later that year to see in Luther's teaching a new doctrine for a new church.[9] It is much harder to observe and analyze the understanding and impact of this doctrine among converts and followers than it is to trace its emergence and elaboration in the writings of a single individual. But "certainty" (*certitudo, Sicherheit*) and "assurance" would become catchwords of the new "evangelical" or, as it was later known, "Protestant" movement. The offer of certainty dispelled the sort of anxiety over sin and grace that motivated what often seems like the frenetic and almost industrial "ritual performance" of late medieval Catholicism, with its votive masses commissioned in their hundreds and thousands, its indulgences denominated in hundreds of thousands of years, and its complex, protracted, and repeated cycles of prayers.

Putting a precise date on Luther's intuition is impossible. But the range of dates can be narrowed down quite closely. As late as the compilation of the *Ninety-Five Theses* in October 1517, there is no hint of this idea in his writings. One of his greatest objections to the practice and soon also to the theory of indulgences was that they imbued their devotees (or, as he came to see it, their dupes) with a false sense of security, leading them to believe that the acquisition of indulgences entailed in itself the complete forgiveness of sins. In the cover letter with which he had sent his theses to the Archbishop of Mainz, Luther opposed to this false sense of security the *a fortiori* argument that "not even the infused grace of God" could confer the kind of assurance people falsely derived from indulgences.[10] The "infused grace of God" was scholastic jargon for the operation of the seven sacraments, especially those of confession and communion. The sacraments conferred grace upon those suitably predisposed to receive and benefit from them. But indulgences were not among the seven sacraments, and did not confer grace. So if even the sacraments could not give their recipients certainty of grace, there was no way that indulgences could. This is the diametrical opposite of what he was to say in 1518 in his lectures on Hebrews and in various minor publications.

The range of dates can be narrowed down a little further thanks to the appearance of Luther's new ideas about certainty of grace in a couple of his earliest publications, his *Instructions for Confession* and his *Sermon on the Proper Preparation of the*

Heart for the Reception of Communion.[11] While neither of these texts can be precisely dated, both of them had been frequently reprinted by the end of 1518, and their content shows that they were composed for Lent that year (Lent in 1518 commenced on 17 February, Ash Wednesday, and ended on 4 April, Easter Sunday). It was a requirement of the Church that Catholics should go to confession and receive communion at least once a year. Because the real presence of Jesus in the consecrated eucharistic host was believed so firmly by medieval Catholics, taking communion was seen as an awe-inspiring encounter with God, for which full confession of sins to a priest was the indispensable prerequisite. So while Catholics attended mass at least weekly (every Sunday and on all major feast days, such as Christmas or the Assumption of the Blessed Virgin Mary), they were more trepidatious about taking communion. The norm throughout Western Europe was to take communion once a year, at Easter, after one had prepared by going to confession in Lent (usually late in Lent), thus fulfilling the expectations of canon law. Priests routinely instructed their flocks during Lent on how to make their confession and prepare for communion. Luther's two texts of 1518 stand within that tradition and encapsulate the pastoral guidance he was offering that year.

Both the *Instructions* and the sermon emphasize that those who come forward to communion should do so relying not on the fact that they had previously made a good confession, but on the certain confidence that they would indeed receive in communion the grace available therefrom by faith alone. The relevant passage in the *Instructions* follows a passage in the lectures on Hebrews almost word for word in developing an argument that seeks to wean hearers or readers from their traditional reliance on confession *per se* as preparation for communion. Displaying that love of the shocking and paradoxical that would characterize both his theology and his rhetoric, Luther informed them that reliance on confession as such was a preparation not for communion but for damnation. Those who took communion relying on having made a good confession "eat and drink judgment upon themselves" (invoking Saint Paul's sentence upon those who receive the sacrament unworthily).[12] In his sermon, he developed his counterintuitive proposition into a striking paradox:

> The best preparation is none other than that by which you are least prepared. And, contrariwise, you are worst prepared when you are most prepared.[13]

It was essential, he added, that someone who approaches the sacrament should do so in absolute certainty of being without mortal sin:

> Make sure that you come forward with full faith (or at least as full as possible) trusting with complete certainty that you will acquire grace.[14]

The *Instructions* evidently drew upon the lecture notes on Hebrews, as it is far more likely that Luther copied lecture notes into a text designed for publication than that he copied from a published text into his lecture notes. The chances are that the relevant section of his lectures on Hebrews was delivered just before or early in Lent, and that we should therefore see early 1518 as the time when Luther first took a firm grip on the fundamental axiom of his theology—which came to be described as "justification by faith alone."

Notoriously, Luther later described the crucial moment of his career as having occurred *in cloaca*—in the privy, on the bog or crapper, in this shit-hole (one picks one's translation to taste, or lack of it—Luther inclined towards the earthier options: the Latin *cloaca* was a standard term for a latrine, but it had a slangy ring).[15] Quite what he meant by this is not immediately apparent and may never be known for certain. It led in the twentieth century to a rather fanciful "psychoanalytical" interpretation of the man and his work, focused on their allegedly "anal" characteristics, themselves fancifully derived from his supposed struggles with constipation, taken as having led him to spend a good deal of his time at the latrine. This absurd but not unamusing reductionism was popularized in the dramatization of Luther's life by John Osborne.[16]

It is true that Luther was occasionally troubled by constipation, but there is no reason to believe that his digestive afflictions were anything out of the ordinary or had any special place in his life. The best evidence for his sufferings comes from 1521, when, as we shall see, Luther had to go into hiding as an outlaw on the run from the authorities of church and empire. Disguised as a *Junker*, a knightly German landowner, and living among a group of military retainers in the Thuringian castle of the Wartburg, overlooking Eisenach, he may well have found the change of diet and lifestyle, no doubt vastly different from those of the friary, something of a shock to his system. But his letters that year show that the agony abated as his system adapted.[17] Such evidence as survives gives us no reason to surmise that he had problems of this nature in the 1510s, still less that his creative insights came upon him as he was straining for relief or release of a more fundamental kind.

Various alternative explanations have been offered for Luther's allusions to the *cloaca*. The least satisfactory of these is that he was referring to his study, reputedly located in the same corner turret of the friary as the latrine. But this is probably to attribute far too literal a significance to what sounds like a figure of speech. Luther was a plainspoken man who readily resorted to coarseness for effect. He was probably just talking loosely about the world in general, or Wittenberg in particular, as "this shit-hole," deploying such language partly in order to make his listeners sit up and pay attention, but also to highlight the contrast between the purity of the Gospel with which God had illuminated him and the darkness and sinfulness of human life without the life of grace. For Luther, what mattered about his Reformational insight was its content.

What Luther does tell us in later years about this formative period in his life is that he had indeed suffered, not so much physically as spiritually. His *Anfechtungen*, as he called them, his trials or temptations or tribulations, might have been characterized in the modern world as mental illness: depression or some other disorder. For a medieval friar these afflictions were seen as being of a spiritual nature. Luther's troubles seem to have consisted primarily of anxiety over his own spiritual status and condition. He had a profound and abiding sense of sin and unworthiness which found little relief in the usual treatment for such a condition, the sacrament of confession and the sophisticated spiritual direction which, at least in a learned environment such as a religious order, could accompany it. Temptations to despair arising from these feelings had troubled him since his childhood. He would look back ruefully on the way that he had repeatedly pestered his confessors with trivial sins.[18] His career as a friar only fed his anxieties, as his conscience could be troubled by his inevitable failure to live up to the ritual demands of the rule of his order. Neither frequent confession nor fasting to the point of self-harm brought him relief.[19] It was only with the transformation of his theological perspective in 1518 that he realized that true peace was not to be found through such strenuous exertion:

> Works never make someone's soul secure, nor do they render the conscience joyous and at peace with God.[20]

Only after Easter 1518, however, was Luther's new theology brought before a wider audience than the students and parishioners of Wittenberg. Thanks to the controversy generated that year by the explosive dissemination of his *Ninety-Five Theses*, he was invited to give an account of himself before the provincial chapter (or regional assembly) of his religious order, the Austin Friars, which that year was to meet under the supervision of his old friend and patron, Johann von Staupitz, at Heidelberg, seat of one of Germany's oldest and most prestigious universities. The opportunity was framed as a scholastic disputation, in which one of the senior theological students of Wittenberg, Friar Leonhard Beier, would advance a set of theses drafted by Luther, with Luther himself offering the authoritative doctoral resolution or summing up after each thesis had been debated. Provincial "chapters" of this kind were routine administrative meetings, and it was not uncommon to enliven proceedings with an academic disputation when they took place in a university town. In many ways, this appearance at Heidelberg was precisely the sort of opportunity to perform before a more illustrious audience that he had been seeking when he sent out the *Ninety-Five Theses* to the nearby bishops.

The propositions that Luther put up for debate at Heidelberg were startling paradoxes, none more so than the first:

The Law of God, the most healthsome doctrine of life, cannot lead anyone to justice but rather blocks their way.

The next dozen or so propositions set an extremely low value on the "good works" that people strive to perform in accordance with this law, and conclude in effect that even their best efforts remain, in themselves, sins. This paves the way for his second bombshell:

Free will, after sin, exists in name only, and, when it does what it can, commits mortal sin.[21]

The denial of free will was in itself a direct affront to medieval theology, which, even in its most predestinarian modes (as for example in the theology of Thomas Aquinas), insisted that the human will was in some sense irreducibly free. At this moment, Luther's denial of free will was perhaps more rhetorical than literal. Even as he explained himself, invoking biblical and Augustinian testimonies to the "captivity" and "slavery" of the human will (concepts which, of course, assume that selfsame theoretical existential freedom which they proceed to declare enslaved or taken captive) with respect to sin, he observed that "it is not that it is nothing, but that it is not free except to sin." Without grace, he continued, citing Augustine, free will was capable only of sinning. Thomas Aquinas would not have disagreed, but Luther's hyperbolic and provocative formulation of his ideas raised hackles.

The connection between the question of free will and the issue of certainty at the core of Luther's theology becomes apparent in his discussion of the second clause of this article, concerning free will "when it does the best it can." The Latin of this, *dum facit quod in se est* (literally, when it does what is within itself; that is, what is within its power), alludes to a familiar tag in the theology of late medieval Catholicism: *facienti quod in se est, deus non denegat gratiam*—God does not deny his grace to someone doing their best. This was an idea that confessors deployed to comfort and reassure those who became anxious about their spiritual condition, a kind of anxiety to which Luther himself was prey, and which he seems to have believed was normal among Christians. Staupitz may well have used this idea in dealing with Luther. It certainly appears in his own writings.[22] Notwithstanding Luther's opinion, such anxiety does not seem to have been widespread. Indeed, the astonishing vogue for indulgences is testament not so much to spiritual anxiety as to a relative spiritual confidence. For it shows that most Christians were confident enough that they would meet the entry requirement for purgatory, namely, to die in a state of grace, having made the proper deathbed confession and received the last rites. Luther himself complained that indulgences left people unhealthily blasé about their spiritual state. But equally there was enough anxiety around to have elicited *facienti quod in se est* as a strategy for pastoral care.

Luther's objection to *facienti quod in se est* was precisely that it failed as a pastoral strategy, when measured against his novel demand that Christians should experience a "peace of conscience" which only certainty of grace could confer. In a somewhat incoherent but nonetheless revealing statement from Heidelberg we begin to see both the limitations of Luther's logical capacity and the crucial importance to him, in his new world of justification by faith, of the sense of certainty about receiving the grace of God. For, he argues,

> if grace is given to people who do their best, then they can know that they are in a state of grace. This is proved as follows. People either know, or do not know, that they are doing their best. If they know, then they also know that they have grace, since it is generally acknowledged that grace is given to those who do their best. But if they don't know, then the doctrine is handed down in vain and its consolation evaporates, because if, whatever works they have done, people still do not know whether they have done their best, then they will remain in doubt forever.[23]

By the time he reached the end of his chain of reasoning, Luther had lost sight of its start, which was an effort to impale his opponents on the horns of a dilemma. His starting point was his intention to demonstrate that, even on the basis of traditional theology, his principle about certainty of grace was demonstrable. However, his argument led not to that conclusion, but to the conclusion that either one knows one is in a state of grace or one is doubtful about it, a conclusion that hardly requires elaborate demonstration. What matters about this argument is its unstated assumption that doubt on this subject is unacceptable. What Luther showed was simply how much importance he now attached to attaining a sense of certainty about being in a state of grace. For him, any doctrine that did not produce such certainty was pastorally worse than useless. From his point of view, if one could not know one was doing one's best, then the proverb was not in fact offering a solution to the anxiety it was designed to address, namely over whether one was in receipt of the grace of God. Therefore, for him, the doctrine really was "handed down in vain."

Besides introducing Luther's new ideas, the Heidelberg Disputation also recapitulated the anti-Aristotelian rhetoric which he had developed over the preceding three years, most pointedly in the *Disputation against Scholastic Theology* (4 September 1517). His anti-Pelagian insistence that, contrary to Aristotle's ethical principle, "the justice of God is not acquired by the frequent repetition of actions" was complemented by the affirmation that "it is infused through faith," an affirmation buttressed by his favorite text from Romans, "The just person lives by faith." It was all summed up in his proposition 25, "The just person is not the one who works hard, but the one who, without works, believes firmly in Christ." It is not surprising to find Luther reporting that the "opinionated" theologians had largely rejected his ideas. But it is significant that he received a warmer welcome from the younger scholars.[24]

The emphasis placed here on the role of certainty of grace in Luther's thought may perhaps seem misplaced, as it is well known that the core of his theology was the doctrine of "justification by faith alone." There may also be unease over the confident identification of early 1518 as the decisive phase in his theological development, because many critics place the decisive moment earlier (some as early as 1513, most around 1515–16), while a few place it as late as 1519.[25] The reason for these disagreements is that attempts to attain a clear understanding of the nature and timing of the crucial step in Luther's theological development have long been bedeviled, ironically enough, by one of his own most serious attempts to clarify it for us. Towards the end of his life, Luther was paid the supreme academic compliment of seeing a plan to publish his "complete works" in his lifetime, and he lived to see the first fruits of this plan, the first volume appearing early in 1545. He marked this signal distinction by contributing an autobiographical preface in which he looked back on the hectic events of thirty years before.[26]

In the course of these sketchy reminiscences, Luther makes two points about his theological development which seem to point in different directions. On the one hand, he places his discussion of an almost revolutionary transformation in his understanding of justification in the context of an account of his activities in 1519. On the other hand, his account of the content of his theological breakthrough focuses so closely on the concept of *iustitia dei*, the justice of God, that many scholars, especially those within the Lutheran tradition (within which most Luther scholarship has been conducted), have been led to conclude that his fundamental insights had been attained as early as 1515–16 (in the lectures on Romans) or even as early as 1513–14 (in his first lectures on the Psalms). For both those lecture courses, as we have seen, exhibit a profound concern with divine justice.

Many of the conclusions drawn from Luther's comments in this preface, however, misunderstand the distinctive element in his theology and therefore misdate the moment when that distinctive element first took shape.[27] To identify *iustitia dei* as *per se* the crucial element in Luther's thought is liable to mislead. For, as a cursory skim through his early lecture notes makes unmistakably clear, Luther had always been deeply concerned, one might even say obsessed, with divine justice. Even in the early lectures on the Psalms, as we have seen, he had drawn a strong distinction between human justice (or self-justification), the human aspiration to be just or to become just by one's own unaided efforts, on the one hand; and on the other, divine justice, the mysterious and mystical quality by which alone the salvation of the sinner was made possible. Such was the subsequent success of Luther's portrayal of Roman Catholicism as a religion preaching "justification by works," as a religion of "works righteousness"—in stark contrast to his own religion of "righteousness by faith"—that it has been all too easy for scholars, especially those in the specifically Lutheran and generally Protestant traditions, to assume that his early emphasis on divine justice, on grace, on the gratuitous character of salvation, already constituted some kind of radical departure from medieval Catholic theology.[28] This was not the case. Roman Catholicism, especially medieval Roman Catholicism, believed just as firmly as any Protestant tradition in "justification by faith," and insisted just as unequivocally that salvation came by grace.

A more careful reading of the 1545 preface leads to the realization that Luther himself is alerting us explicitly to his longstanding concern with *iustitia dei* precisely in order to emphasize the transformative significance of the new understanding of that concept which he ultimately attained. He gives us a clear *terminus ad quem*, a time by which this transformation had definitely taken place, by telling us that it was only when he was equipped with this new understanding that he turned for a second time to the exposition of the Psalms in 1519. This was, he states, "after" he had lectured on Romans, Galatians, and Hebrews. He then describes in rather general terms his intellectual struggle with the concept of divine justice, which he presents as intimately bound up with his profound personal anxieties over sin, guilt, and confession. This struggle culminated in the insight that this justice was primarily "that by which the just person lives, thanks to God's gift, namely by faith." Putting it another way, he accounts for it as the realization that the justice of God was for human beings something that God gave, and not something that they could win by their own efforts (from about 1525 he would therefore call this justice *passive*). It was not something they did, but something that was done to them. He does not spell out in 1545, as he had so often done before, the contrast between passive and active justice, but his readers would by that time have grasped this intuitively. This distinction, endlessly reiterated in Luther's mature writings, is crucial, for the concept of "passive justice" excluded not only the "Pelagian" theory of an active justice by which human beings might work out their own salvation, but also the Augustinian and Catholic conception of "cooperative" grace, by which sinners were enabled, through grace, to collaborate with that grace in the process of justification and salvation—a conception which Luther himself evidently shared when first lecturing on the Psalms and indeed on Romans.[29]

The key to Luther's breakthrough about justice therefore resides less in the idea of justice itself than in the coda "through faith" (*nempe ex fide*). It is the appropriation of the justice of God by faith, entirely passively, that is what matters, and here faith means—as Luther and his disciples stated on countless occasions—no merely general faith in God nor even a merely "historical" faith (*fides historica*) in the theological facts of the incarnation, passion, death, and resurrection of Jesus Christ, but the specific, personal faith that the saving work of Christ had been made actual and effective in one's own case (*pro nobis, pro me*).[30]

To focus too exclusively on Luther's anti-Pelagian understanding of divine justice therefore risks missing the point. Luther believed right from the start that it was the justice of God that effected the justification of sinners, not some justice that they developed or manufactured by their own efforts and on their own account. But such an understanding was mainstream Catholic theology and entailed no breach whatsoever with medieval Catholic doctrine or practice. Thus it is that, in the early lecture notes on the Psalms and Paul's epistles, an emphasis on divine justice sits happily alongside unhesitating endorsement of the seven sacraments, the ecclesiastical hierarchy, the Mass, the cult of the saints, and prayer for the dead. This is perhaps why those early writings were not included in the *Complete Works*. Luther's increasingly strident anti-Aristotelianism set him on the margins of orthodoxy, but he was not altogether alone there, and he was not outside.

It was his new conception of faith, faith now modulated to the key of personal certainty of grace, that constituted Luther's most important and most original contribution in the field of Christian theology. On this faith, on this certainty, everything else hinges. There is not a trace of this in his writings until 1518. From 1518 it is all over them. This fundamental shift in focus was even reflected in his attitude towards Augustine. At first, Luther remarked, he did not so much read Augustine as devour him. But once he had learned from Paul what justification by faith was, "it was all over with me and Augustine."[31] Augustine, he remarked on another occasion, got closer to Paul than all the scholastics, but he still did not get Paul, and did not adequately explain or understand justification.[32]

Upon his return from Heidelberg (15 May 1518) Luther embarked upon a publishing spree. He was already notorious throughout Germany as the "hammer of indulgences," and he was on the way to becoming, in modern terms, a celebrity brand.[33] Anything with his name on it would sell, and his substantial sermons on the Ten Commandments, preached to the laity of Wittenberg some time before the indulgences controversy, therefore now found their way rapidly into print. The sermons were published in Latin, and were not translated into German until some years later. There is no reason to think that they had not originated as popular preaching, but they had perhaps undergone some level of expansion and editing before they appeared in print. Their largely traditional ethical content and the absence of the main themes of Luther's mature theology (most notably that of certainty of grace) indicate that they were pulled out of the drawer to meet the sudden consumer demand for "Luther." There is a note of moral rigorism about the project which smacks more of medieval Catholicism than of Reformation preaching, though salvation is, as ever in Luther, by grace, and he offers an extremely Augustinian account of justification with occasional attacks on "Pelagians." This relatively heavy text, which ran to four editions and was widely read by clergy and humanists, did much to secure Luther's reputation in the early years of his fame as a sound if demanding Christian teacher.

Among the first fruits of what was to be a heavy harvest was his *Resolutions on Indulgences*, a lengthy written-up version of the *Ninety-Five Theses*, arguing for them in detail, as though in a lecture-hall debate. The *Resolutions* had been in preparation for some months, and were not through the press until mid-August, even though the dedication to Staupitz had been written on 30 May. They give clear indications of Luther's new thinking about faith and personal certainty of the forgiveness of sins, and inculcated his theory that forgiveness depended not on an individual's contrition (as in medieval Catholic pastoral theology) but on their faith and trust in the truth of the words of absolution pronounced in the name of Christ by the priest in confession.[34]

In the dedication of this work, Luther recalled how Staupitz once said to him that true penance began from the love of God and of justice, and that this love was the origin of penance, not its objective. That observation, he added, had always remained with him. Since then, having reflected further on the scriptures, he had found that where once "penance" was bitter to his ears, now no word was sweeter, for he had learned the true meaning of "metanoia" from Grecians and Hebraists.[35] It is not long before the explanation of this change of attitude is revealed. Certainty of grace, founded on an absolute trust in the promise of Christ, is clearly set out, and this is the substance of "faith alone."[36] There had been no hint of such a doctrine in the *Ninety-Five Theses* themselves, so this new theology comes as something of a surprise in what was billed as a defense of those theses. The doctrine is presented under the seventh thesis ("Conclusion VII"), which concerned sacramental confession, the context within which Luther had first formulated his doctrine of certainty. This was its first airing before a sophisticated and potentially international audience, in a treatise intended for scholars: "Faith in Christ, the gratuitous donor of forgiveness, is to be taught first of all."[37] Already some of the implications of this new principle were becoming clear. The power of the priest to forgive sins was traditionally rooted in a clutch of New Testament texts such as John 20:23, "Whose sins you forgive, they are forgiven." Luther's new conception of faith shifted the focus from the action or power of the priest to the faith of the penitent:

> Why did Christ say, "Whose sins you forgive, they are forgiven," if not because they are not forgiven to anyone unless he believes himself to be forgiven by the absolving priest?[38]

> The person seeking absolution must therefore take every care that they should not doubt that their sins are forgiven before God, so that they may be at peace in their hearts.[39]

The traditional understanding of the sacraments was therefore called into question. For Luther, they could no longer be seen as supplying grace to those who put no obstacle in their way. That was a view he now stigmatized as heretical, rejecting a two-hundred-year tradition stemming from the theology of Duns Scotus, the theological guiding light of the Franciscan friars. Instead, for Luther, grace functioned only for those who believed in the faith of the sacrament.[40] This certainty of deriving grace from participation in the sacraments was so essential that anyone lacking it was better advised to abstain from the sacraments completely, for fear of the harm they would do their own soul and the offence they would give to God and his Word.[41] The customary invocation of Ecclesiastes 9:1 against the possibility of certainty of grace now horrified him. If that argument were valid, then it would follow that "I doubt whether the merits of Christ granted and applied to me are adequate to the remission of sins. And what could be more loathsome than such a doubt?"[42] The faith that he taught was, in his view, the essence of the Gospel message, and in the light of his new understanding he faced the awful prospect of the near total corruption of the contemporary Church, for "the Gospel of God is pretty much unknown in the greater part of the Church."[43]

Luther was a moving target in 1518, and his earliest opponents found themselves shooting at shadows as he raced ahead onto new ground. Even as the ramifications of his theology were reaching far beyond the narrow issue of indulgences which had brought him into the public eye, the *Ninety-Five Theses* themselves began to come under hostile scrutiny as far away as Rome. Archbishop Albrecht had sent the theses to Rome around the turn of the year, and they worked their way slowly through the administrative machinery there. Not long after Luther's order had held its provincial chapter at Heidelberg, the Dominican friars, to which Johannes Tetzel belonged, were gathering for their general chapter at Rome. It may have been this event, which brought together Dominican friars from all over Europe, that first drew the serious attention of the Holy See to the indulgences controversy. For it was a

Dominican theologian, the pope's official theological adviser as the "Master of the Sacred Palace" (a post invariably held by a Dominican friar), who made the first recorded Roman response to Luther.

Silvestro Mazzolini, known as Prierias from his place of birth (Priero, in northern Italy), held the office of Master of the Sacred Palace from 1515 until his death in 1527. And it was he who was asked by curial officials to take a view on the *Ninety-Five Theses*. The outcome was a brief treatise printed at Rome in June 1518, which, he claimed, was dashed off in three days, as an unwelcome distraction from his more serious theological work. Prierias brought to the task a mind at once analytical and inquisitorial (he had previously served as an inquisitor, or investigator, into heresy in several regions of northern Italy).[44] His inquisitorial temperament led him to focus on what was wrong with Luther's ideas, and his analytical capacity led him to reduce this to the fundamental issue of papal power. Hence the rather odd but revealing title he gave to his report when it was printed in June: *A Dialogue on the Impertinent Propositions of Martin Luther concerning Papal Power*.[45] His report was anything but a dialogue, and it was Prierias, not Luther, who chose to make papal power the central issue, although Luther's *Ninety-Five Theses* had certainly offered a substantial critique of what he saw as the abuse of papal power. While this could be seen as impressive insight into Luther's theology on Prierias's part, there is more than a hint in his work of a defensive attitude conditioned by the recent experience of the Roman curia, most notably of the Gallican challenge to papal authority launched around 1510, when Louis XII of France sought to convene a general council of the Church with a view to deposing Pope Julius II. (There may also have been memories of Savonarola's defiance of papal authority in the late 1490s.) Thanks to that recent controversy, curial theologians were perhaps too ready to see any criticism as a challenge to

papal authority, and, conversely, to seek to deploy that authority to silence unwelcome criticism.

Prierias evidently found the *Ninety-Five Theses* little more
than a jejune nuisance. The document made little sense to him,
devoid as it was of any contextualizing information. He starts
out equably enough, but evidently read the theses with mounting annoyance, reacting to the increasingly heightened rhetoric of the text itself. At first he managed to reserve his condemnation for Luther's words rather than for Luther himself, but
he gradually worked himself into a splenetic temper in which,
even when Luther expressed a perfectly orthodox (if somewhat
tendentious) view, he responded by trying to find fault. Thus
Luther's thesis 40 stated that "Apostolic indulgences should
be preached carefully, in case people erroneously infer that
they are preferable to other good works of charity." Prierias
could hardly argue with that, and started his response "True
enough." But he had to find fault, so he added, "but similar
caution should be shown in criticizing or curtailing them, to
the prejudice of the apostolic power and of the privilege conferred by God upon Saint Peter."[46] In the end he descended
to vulgar abuse and argument *ad hominem*, denouncing Luther's arguments as vain and puerile, and Luther himself as a
trasher, not a teacher. Luther would talk about indulgences
differently, Prierias claimed, if he had a comfortable bishopric
and a plenary indulgence to rebuild his cathedral.[47] However,
in a telling and unguarded aside he not only conceded that
indulgences rested on papal authority rather than on holy
scripture, but then characterized papal authority as "greater"
than that of scripture.[48]

What Prierias did was to raise the stakes. And Luther was
never a man to fold, but would always raise again. Those conciliatory humanist commentators, such as Erasmus, who later
blamed Prierias for escalating the situation with his snap
judgments about heresy and his reduction of the debate to an

argument about papal authority, had a point: Prierias's response did not help. But Luther himself was already imputing heresy to those with whom he disagreed,[49] and was prompt to outbid his opponents in invective. In his *Resolutions*, going through the press while Prierias was still writing his *Dialogue*, he described traditional penitential theology as little more than the torture of consciences.[50]

Luther received a copy of Prierias's *Dialogue* on 7 August 1518, and the very next day reported that he had already embarked on a rebuttal, which was rushed into print by the end of the month.[51] It certainly reads like something thrown together in a hurry, lacking obvious or sophisticated structure. The *Response* is a hasty and intemperate work. His opponent's occasional intimations of heresy are met with countercharges of heresy, idolatry, superstition, and blasphemy. Almost every page denounces Thomas Aquinas, the scholastics in general, or their forerunner, Aristotle. He was well aware of just how violent his rhetoric was, half apologizing for it when he sent copies to his friend Staupitz.[52] But he could not help himself. Vitriolic vilification and indiscriminate invective were his default reactions to theological disagreement. His focus on Thomas Aquinas, however, was calculated. Prierias was one of the foremost living authorities on Thomas. By making denunciation of Thomism and scholasticism run through the text (to the extent that the *Response* has a theme, this is it), Luther was seeking to cast himself, like the great Johannes Reuchlin, as the innocent victim of mean-spirited and obscurantist Dominican persecutors. Dominican theologians at Cologne and Rome, including Prierias, had been the leading figures in the campaign against Reuchlin, which was still grinding its way through the glacially slow processes of ecclesiastical litigation in the curia. Aligning himself with Reuchlin was a shrewd way for Luther to canvass for the sympathy of the German reading public. It may just be a coincidence, but the month which saw Luther make this move in his reply to Prierias was the same month that saw the arrival in Wittenberg of Philip Melanchthon, who happened to be Reuchlin's nephew as well as a rising star of German humanism in his own right. It may have been this connection that emboldened Luther to write a friendly letter to Reuchlin towards the end of the year.[53]

Discursive and discourteous though it is, the *Response* is not without theological interest. Luther not only reiterated his views on indulgences and purgatory but also took up some of Prierias's objections. In particular he addressed the objection that he had not set out his methodological foundations, in a way which would hardly satisfy his opponent, but which is nonetheless revealing. For Luther, Prierias's theological foundation was Thomas Aquinas. Augustine, he said, would have been a wiser choice, but Luther himself then named Paul as his own "first foundation."[54] That was all he had to say about methodology, a subject on which his views would develop rapidly over the next two years. His opponent's hints aroused his understandable concern about the prospect of a heresy trial, and Luther was quick to repudiate the imputation of heresy, on the somewhat disingenuous grounds that his views had not been condemned by any council of the Church.

But most importantly, Luther returned to his big idea: certainty. His original and uncontroversial denial that indulgences conferred certainty of grace was now modified by an insistence that certainty of the forgiveness of sins was available to believers through faith. Without that certainty, he went on, Christian faith itself was evacuated of all meaning. "What else, I ask, is an uncertain gift, but no gift at all? . . . a Christ who gave nothing certain to the Church would seem to have given her nothing at all."[55] His ensuing rhapsody on certainty and doubt left no room for misapprehension over the crucial role of certainty of faith in his emerging theology. For Luther, doubt as to one's standing before God was tantamount to doubting the very power of God to save sinners. This has often been called a "subjective" doctrine of justification, and there is some merit in this old-fashioned Catholic analysis of Luther's teaching. However, it is fairer to say that Luther collapsed the distinction between the objective and the subjective. For the sense of certainty as to one's own salvation, a sense which it is not altogether unjust to label "subjective," was not to be achieved by the traditionally subjective means of introspection and examination of conscience. He had already stipulated in the *Resolutions on Indulgences* that peace of conscience was not to be attained "by inward experience" (by which he seems to mean the kind of mystical experience that might be sought through the cultivation of meditative prayer).[56] This sense of certainty was attained by an entirely objective and external engagement with the saving promise of Christ. Experience was the fruit of faith rather than its cause.[57] For Luther, the focus of this mental operation was emphatically outside rather than inside the self. The focus was Christ, not self. Through that focus on Christ one attained inner peace by means of the realization that Christ's saving work applied to oneself—and that this work, because it was God's work, was utterly certain and beyond all doubt.

The crucial discovery of 1518 was the decisive turning point in Luther's theological development. That discovery was of a complete spiritual certainty that he was in what Catholics would call "a state of grace," complete spiritual certainty that, in the words of the modern evangelicals, "he was saved." This is not to claim that spiritual certainty *rather than* "justification by faith alone" was the theological heart of Luther's theology. The point is that "justification by faith alone" is itself spiritual certainty. The received wisdom about Luther, that his doctrine is all about "justification by faith alone," is correct as far as it goes. The problem is that it is rarely understood. It is a complex and counterintuitive doctrine, deeply paradoxical, as Luther delighted in emphasizing. Catholic opponents found it not so much paradoxical as self-contradictory (the boundary between paradox and self-contradiction is always awkward to police). For Luther and his followers it was a paradox that brought the troubled soul to the haven of a conscience at peace with God and itself.

5

INTIMATIONS OF ANTICHRIST

Although Luther was now the talk of Germany, he was hardly the center of attention in summer 1518. In the wake of Francis I's crushing victory at Marignano in 1515, which secured him possession of the duchy of Milan, kaleidoscopic conflict between France, Spain, England, and the Holy Roman Empire had subsided into an uneasy peace, which papal diplomacy, as usual, was seeking to consolidate with a view to uniting Europe's Christian princes against the encroaching power of the Ottoman Turks in the Balkans and the Mediterranean. As so often before, Christians were once more prey to Berber slaving raids, as well as to displays of Ottoman might such as the conquest of Otranto in 1480, when hundreds of Christian men were slaughtered, and many hundred more women and children were taken into slavery. Universal peace and crusade against "the Turk" were the big questions of summer 1518, and Luther's little matter was not yet anything more than a nine days' wonder.

However, Prierias's report on Luther at Rome had not been without effect, and Thomas de Vio from Gaeta, known to history as Cardinal Cajetan (i.e., the Gaetan), was sent as a papal legate to the Emperor Maximilian on a diplomatic mission which included a brief to calm down the Luther furore. By the end of August Luther had heard that Cajetan had brought papal instructions designed to turn the German Princes against him.[1] Writing to Staupitz, Luther averred that his own summons to appear before Cajetan at Augsburg did not bother him at all. This was mere bravado. He seems to have been a little more anxious when he got there, and later on he admitted that he had been "very frightened" when he set off.[2] In one of his last gestures of deference to his mentor, Luther made a rare admission that perhaps his polemics were a little violent in tone, though only to disclaim responsibility with the observation that, now they were published, there was nothing to be done.

Luther reached Augsburg on 7 October, and while he waited for his first audience with the cardinal, he was feted by local notables, dining, for example, with Dr. Conrad Peutinger, a lawyer and leading citizen. In general, despite the anxiety with which he had been beset at the start of his journey—for, not unreasonably, he was aware that he might meet the same fate as Jan Hus a century before, at Prague, burned at the stake for heresy—he was heartened by the warmth of his reception along the way. His books, still little more than leaflets and pamphlets, were selling well, and had made Luther a household name. As he told Melanchthon, everyone wanted to see the man who had caused such a fuss.[3] As there was no house of Austin Friars in Augsburg, Luther took lodgings in the house of the Carmelites or White Friars, where the prior was Johannes Frosch, an old friend whom he had known at both Erfurt and Wittenberg (where Frosch had graduated Bachelor of Divinity early in 1516). It was probably thanks to this renewal of their acquaintance that Frosch returned to Wittenberg in November 1518 to take his doctorate. On that occasion, Luther took a close interest in proceedings, even asking Spalatin to ensure that suitably tasty food was provided for the celebratory dinner.[4] Frosch had evidently treated him well, and he wished to reciprocate.

Luther first appeared before Cardinal Cajetan on 12 October, less than a year after starting his campaign on indulgences. Their initial exchanges set the tone for the next few days. The cardinal needed some sort of recantation or climb-down, and

Luther was not that sort of person. Cajetan hoped to stop things from going too far, but even before they met, Luther had been contemplating an appeal to a future general council against whatever might be required of him.[5] Cajetan presented Luther with his demands, namely that he should recant his errors and in future refrain from anything that might disturb the peace of the Church. When Luther asked to be told precisely what was supposed to be wrong with his teaching, he was probably surprised to find the cardinal well prepared. In the weeks before their encounter, Cajetan had read the *Sermon on Penance* and the *Resolutions on Indulgences*, and had compiled some careful briefing papers on the issues they raised.[6] So he was able to point out that Luther's views on indulgences directly contradicted the papal bull *Unigenitus*, issued by Pope Clement VI in 1343, showing him the text and the passage. More importantly, he added that Conclusion VII from the *Resolutions on Indulgences*, which taught that those coming forward to receive the Eucharist should believe for certain that they would thereby attain grace, was a "new and erroneous doctrine"—which from his point of view it certainly was.[7] It says a lot for Cajetan that he got straight to the heart of Luther's teaching. But he had himself specifically considered Thomas Aquinas's discussion of certainty of grace in his own commentary on the relevant section of the *Summa Theologiae*.[8]

Luther answered that the papal bull carried no weight with him because it abused and twisted the words of scripture, which were, in contrast, correctly interpreted in his own writings. Cajetan urged him to consider the authority of the papacy, which Luther later represented as a claim that the power of the pope was "above scripture," picking up on an injudicious comment of Prierias's which, however, does not seem to be paralleled in Cajetan's writings against Luther. We do not have the cardinal's version of this particular exchange, but he was presumably insisting on the final authority of the papacy in deciding upon the interpretation of the scriptures, which is not quite the same thing. After more discussion, Luther asked for a day to consider his position, so Cajetan dismissed him, encouraging him to engage in a little self-examination.[9] Luther returned next day (Wednesday, 13 October) accompanied by Staupitz and various others, and then started to lodge a kind of formal protest, with a notary in attendance. Somewhat bemused by this pomposity, Cajetan cut him short and urged him to make less fuss and simply back down.[10] Luther insisted that he would respond only in writing, as he could not bear the verbal fencing in which the cardinal had engaged the day before. (On more than one occasion Luther seems to have found it hard going when he confronted a skilled debater face to face, though he usually found it easy to win conversational battles.) Again somewhat surprised by Luther's attitude, Cajetan disclaimed any intention of engaging in disputation: he was not there to dispute, but to reconcile Luther to the Roman Church. But Luther, backed by Staupitz, sought to be heard in writing, and Cajetan agreed, but on a private rather than a judicial basis. So Luther went away and returned again next day with a lengthy scroll (which later formed a large part of his account of the proceedings at Augsburg[11]) attacking the papal decree and the pope in disputational style, and adducing a lot of scriptural material to support his view on the sacraments. For Cajetan the paper was nothing more than fatuous observations about *Unigenitus*, interspersed with sniping at the papacy, and rounded off with irrelevant biblical citations that Luther mistakenly supposed to prove his novel position on certainty of grace. For Luther, Cajetan was simply being dense, obstinately refusing to accept the plain truth of scripture and the clear light of reason.

As ever, Cajetan sought to lower the temperature, warning Luther against importing "new teachings" into the Church, and urging him to think to himself and the welfare of his soul.

When Luther saw that Cajetan would not accept his arguments from scripture, he stiffened his own resolve and walked out. Later that day Cajetan met Staupitz and Wenzel Link, along with the ambassador from Montferrat, to try to negotiate a compromise that might induce Luther to back down. Staupitz and Link both urged Luther to submit, but in vain (Luther omitted this intervention from his published account of the affair). Link returned later to lend his support to the solution they proposed, so Cajetan was therefore hopeful. But all he got were some weasel-word letters from Luther, half-apologizing, but leaving the main issues aside without any actual retraction.[12] In the meantime, Staupitz and Link seem to have become nervous about their own exposure to the risk of ecclesiastical sanction, and slipped quietly away. Luther himself did the same, leaving Cajetan furious with an outcome that was as inconclusive as it was unceremonious.

The written response that Luther presented to Cajetan at Augsburg set out his usual array of arguments about indulgences and ecclesiastical authority, but is notable in particular for its invocation of a very curious citation from one of the most influential canon lawyers of the fifteenth century, Panormitanus (Niccolò de' Tudeschi, "the man from Palermo"), the drift of whose voluminous commentaries and legal opinions tended to reflect the interests of his current patrons. A one-time conciliarist who later became a strong advocate of papal authority, Panormitanus offered in one of his later writings an argument to explain why it was that the individual judgment of a pope might lawfully prevail even over the decision of a general council, if the pope was guided by "better reasons and authorities."[13] One of his reasons for this position was the *a fortiori* argument that "in matters concerning the faith, even the statement of a private individual might be preferred to that of a pope if the former is guided by better reasons from the Old and New Testaments than the latter." This evidently somewhat remote contingency was in turn justified by the claim that the Church might, on occasion, subsist solely in the person of a single faithful individual, just as, many theologians then taught, it had survived solely in the person of the Blessed Virgin Mary between the death and resurrection of her son, at a time when all the other disciples, even Peter, had abandoned or denied their faith. Luther's invocation of Panormitanus's authority for the contingency that a single individual might be right about something while the pope was wrong was therefore fair enough (though neither of them explain how such a reductive vision of doctrinal authority might work in practice). The text is possibly the only proposition from the entire corpus of ecclesiastical jurisprudence that Luther really valued. Yet what is little more than a thought experiment in Panormitanus resonated with the diapason of individualism that rang deep within Luther's theology, almost unbeknown to the man himself. Luther never lost that Catholic ecclesiological instinct that yearned to unite the community around a single creed, unequivocally understood. Nobody had less enthusiasm than he for allowing people to think for themselves in matters of religion. Yet individualism lurked in every aspect of his thought. Ultimately, his appeal to Panormitanus licensed anyone and everyone to cast themselves, if they saw fit, as the only person marching in step with scripture.[14]

The confrontation with Cajetan precipitated a crisis in Luther's relationship with his mentor, Johann von Staupitz. Staupitz, as Luther's hierarchical superior and personal friend, was called in to aid the cardinal's strenuous efforts to persuade him to back down. It was probably on this occasion that, as Luther later reminded him, Staupitz had admonished him that he (Luther) had "started the whole business in the name of our Lord Jesus Christ." Luther cited that reminder against Staupitz around the time that the papal bull against him was published, in an effort to induce him to make a stand. Yet even as he quotes Staupitz's words against him, he admits in effect that he is quoting them against their original intention in presenting them as a sort of endorsement of his position.[15] Removed from this interpretative framework, they sound like an attempt to persuade Luther to moderate his tone by reminding him of the one in whose name he claimed to act. But to Luther, comments of that kind could only mean, or come to mean, not just an appreciation of his sense of his own motivation, but an endorsement of his claim that he was indeed acting in Christ's name. Staupitz himself shied away from invective. Many years later, Luther recalled a passing comment of his about the ancient Latin father Jerome, "I'd like to know how that man was saved!"[16] Jerome's quarrelsome and overheated temperament shrieks out from his polemics. While Luther may not have spotted it, Staupitz can hardly have missed the parallel with his protégé.

Exactly what went on between Luther and Staupitz is somewhat obscure. For it is clear that shortly after Luther's refusal to back down, Staupitz abruptly departed, leaving him "alone at Augsburg."[17] Christoph Scheurl, who got his information from Wenzel Link (who left along with Staupitz), believed that this was because he feared that he would be condemned along with Luther.[18] Before he left, Luther recalled later, Staupitz "released" or "excommunicated" him. Both of these terms he expounds as constituting release from his obligations of obedience to the rule of their religious order.[19] Quite what this was, or quite what he or Staupitz thought this was, is deeply puzzling. Some historians and biographers have concluded that Staupitz was releasing him from his religious vows.[20] But Staupitz had no authority to do any such thing (under canon law, that power was reserved to the pope), and that is not what Luther says. Nor can this act have been formal excommunication: Luther seems to use the term analogously in his later recollections, likening the event in some way to his excommunication by Pope Leo X and his outlawry from Emperor

Charles V. There is no sign in anything he said or did at that time to suggest that he felt he had been literally excommunicated, however he might have described it years later. While it is clear that Luther later interpreted what happened as having, in conscience, released him from his obligations to obey the rule of his order, there is equally no sign at all of this at the time. For he continued to live as a friar and to describe himself as such. In other recollections of later years, moreover, he emphasized how difficult it was for him to break free from his sense of his obligations to his religious order.[21] This could hardly have been the case had Staupitz authentically and effectually released him from his obligations in 1518. Luther's report had Staupitz carrying out this action to give himself a plausible excuse for inaction should he ever be required to hand Luther over for trial. In 1518, Staupitz, according to another of his recollections, "abandoned me to God." Staupitz's very words, he reported, were these: "I absolve you from my obedience and commend you to the Lord God."[22] This has more than a touch of the hanging judge's valediction, "May the Lord have mercy on your soul." What actually happened must remain a puzzle, but it is clear that Staupitz, exasperated with his friend's obstinacy, was washing his hands of the whole affair. Equally, Luther seems to have felt that both Staupitz and the Austin Friars let him down at that moment. Looking back, he felt that he had been left isolated, abandoned "by all human supports—emperor, pope, the cardinal legate, his prince Duke Frederick of Saxony, his religious order, and by Staupitz, his closest friend."[23] Early in the following year, Luther felt that Staupitz had cooled towards him because he was not staying in touch.[24]

After Luther's departure, Cajetan wrote to the Elector Frederick with his version of what had happened. Cajetan had shown Luther that his teachings on indulgences were contrary to papal teaching, and that his theory on the role of faith in the sacraments was at variance with the traditions and customs of the Roman Catholic Church.[25] The letter shows that he had taken the measure of Luther's propensity to fly to extremes. He had already been worried by the theological positions that Luther had advanced cautiously and for the sake of argument in his *Resolutions on Indulgences*: now, he lamented, these same opinions were being delivered as dogmatic assertions in his sermons. In conclusion, Cajetan made three points. Firstly, Luther's positions were contrary to Catholic teaching and damnable. Secondly, Frederick ought to dispatch Luther to Rome for formal process, as he refused to submit to paternal correction. And thirdly, Frederick should be aware that Cajetan would now abandon his efforts to achieve a local solution and instead report back to Rome, where the matter would therefore have to be resolved. In a personal postscript he urged the elector not to be taken in by those who maintained there was no harm in Luther's opinions, and not to allow his family's honor to be tarnished by association with this "little friar."[26]

Luther returned home to Wittenberg almost a year to the day since he had dispatched his *Ninety-Five Theses* to the Archbishop of Mainz. In that year the unknown friar had become a national celebrity. His immediate tasks were two: to put together an account of the proceedings at Augsburg, and to draft his appeal to a future General Council against the papal mandate requiring him to submit to ecclesiastical authority. The first he did in record time. The elector was initially reluctant to allow Luther to publish it, but soon relented, and the pamphlet *What Happened at Augsburg* was in press in November and in circulation next month, ensuring that his version of events would shape history.[27] Luther's appeal to a council was completed a few days later, by which time he heard that an ineffectual papal envoy, Karl von Miltitz, was wandering around Germany with a bundle of papers to serve on Luther, requiring him to deliver himself to Rome for a hearing.

This was when Luther made his grand gesture (and not, probably, the year before). On the Feast of Saint Catherine (25 November), he made his way to the Castle Church, All Saints, and there made his public protest, promising that he would "never recant what he had taught, written, and preached," and making his formal appeal to a future council. He repeated this performance the following Sunday (28 November, the first Sunday of Advent, the first day of the liturgical year) at the parish church, and had a notary make an official record of the deed. The substantial audience (which included Melanchthon) was moved to tears. If ever Luther nailed a protest to a church door, it would have been then. The text of his appeal was soon itself available in print.[28]

The drafting of his appeal will have been what drew Luther's attention to a text which, as a theologian, would not otherwise have been at the forefront of his interests—the canon law of the Church. As the Roman net closed around him thanks to the efforts of Cajetan, Miltitz, and others, his suspicions as to the true nature of the papacy darkened, and he pursued these by making a close study of the text which he will have opened to help draft his appeal. By the end of December he was wondering if he was right to feel that the Antichrist foretold by Paul was at work in the Roman curia.[29] By March 1519 he had compiled a detailed set of notes on papal legislation and jurisprudence, and with real trepidation he shared with Spalatin the worrying alternatives that now presented themselves to him: the pope was either the forerunner of Antichrist or, worse still, Antichrist himself.[30]

At Augsburg we first see Luther implicitly investing himself with supreme authority in the name of the Word of God. Cardinal Cajetan, seated before him in the fullness of the hierarchical authority he had brought with him from Rome, backed by the Vicar of Christ, must have found Luther's easy assumption of authority both astonishing and irritating.

Luther shuffled and dealt his usual cards—texts from the New Testament extolling faith in Christ—as though they were self-evident testimonies to what Cajetan had identified as *novam theologiam*—a new theology. As Luther put it later, "When I brought forward scriptures for my position, the man put on his fatherly act and began to make up glosses against me out of his own noddle."[31] After returning to Wittenberg, Luther's easy assumption of dogmatic authority became more conscious, albeit as yet still in essentially parodic style. Cajetan had complained to the elector that Luther's letter had been more self-justification than recantation, so in his account of proceedings at Augsburg Luther sarcastically offered a formal revocation. But this instrument, mocking the terminology of canon law, revoked not his own teachings but the papal decretal *Unigenitus*:

> For which reason I, in this document, solemnly revoke it and pronounce it condemned by myself.... I censure, condemn, and execrate that decretal as false, erroneous, and worthy of reprobation.[32]

When Luther adopted this vantage point, argument became impossible. As he explained to his readers, they were not to think that, in presenting his arguments to Cajetan and professing his submissiveness to the judgment of the pope, he was in any sort of doubt about the question or would ever change his mind: "Divine truth lords it even over the pope."[33] He was simply complying with the formal requirements of the situation. He had such complete confidence in his own judgment that he was unable to recognize it as his own: rather, it was the judgment of God. It was this sublime unselfconsciousness that made his assumption of authority so potent and so plausible. No one could have self-consciously carried off such a feat of intellectual sleight of hand. His utter faith in the complete transparency of scripture kept him from realizing that any reading of a text—not just any other reading of a text—is an act of interpretation.

The failure of Cajetan's mission was a blow to papal diplomacy, and it is revealing that even at this early stage, when Luther was nothing like the celebrity he was to be by 1521, the curia saw a real threat in his teachings. If Luther could not be negotiated with, then the key, from the Roman perspective, was to deal with his patron, the Elector Frederick. Frederick was a man of renowned piety, so Leo X chose this moment to recognize and celebrate his devotion to religion and the Church by conferring upon him one of the papacy's most signal honors, the Golden Rose. This prestigious and expensive ornament was an annual award, dispatched together with papal blessings and indulgences, used to seal and oil relationships with princes and potentates. Luther correctly interpreted news of this accolade as evidence that the Romans were determined to secure his condemnation.[34]

Both at Augsburg and subsequently, Luther expressed his eagerness to defend his views in open disputation. He tried in vain to get Cajetan to dispute with him, and then (according to Scheurl) announced his readiness to submit himself to the judgment of the universities of Paris, Louvain, Freiburg, or Basel. In a letter to the elector, he offered to dispute publicly at Leipzig, Erfurt, Halle, Magdeburg, or wherever else the elector's safe-conduct might hold.[35] At some point in his stay at Augsburg, moreover, he met Johannes Maier von Eck, a young theologian from the University of Ingolstadt, just fifty or so miles away, who had already given some critical consideration to his views on indulgences. In their brief conversation, the prospect of a formal public disputation was first mooted, and it was from this seed that there grew the Leipzig Disputation of summer 1519, which brought Luther and his teachings before a still wider audience.[36]

6

LUTHER AND ECK

On the morning of 27 June 1519, a solemn votive Mass of the Holy Spirit was celebrated in the great gothic church of Saint Thomas in Leipzig. Then a crowd processed a few hundred yards to the Pleissenburg, the ducal palace where Martin Luther and his right-hand man, Andreas Carlstadt, were about to engage in a fortnight of formal academic disputation with Johannes Maier von Eck (1486–1543), a scholar generally (though often reluctantly) admitted to be the most capable debater of his age. An introductory oration was delivered by the University of Leipzig's leading resident humanist, Petrus Mosellanus, who sententiously reminded the participants that Christians disputing with Christians should behave like Christians, expressing themselves modestly and moderately.[1]

Eck, as he was usually known, was not just an academic, but an academic careerist. Before Luther had ever been heard of, Eck, a few years his junior, had worked his way busily up the greasy pole. Educated at Heidelberg, Tübingen, Cologne, and Freiburg, he boasted an exalted academic pedigree. Thanks partly to his role in the Leipzig Disputation, he was to become Luther's most famous and most widely read opponent. His *Handbook of Commonplaces against the Lutherans*, first published in 1525, was reprinted over a hundred times in the sixteenth century, and provided raw material for countless Catholic sermons and pamphlets against Protestantism.

Eck and Luther already had something of a history. They were first brought into contact with each other by a mutual friend, Christoph Scheurl, a minor humanist and former lecturer at Wittenberg who was by the mid-1510s a legal official working for the city council of Nuremberg. In 1517 he effected a remote introduction between Eck and Luther, which led to an exchange of polite epistolary greetings which historians, following a lead set by Luther for rhetorical purposes, have dignified with the label of friendship.[2] At that time, Eck was the more celebrated of the two men. Already a published author, he had attached himself out of motives of study and patronage to such eminent scholars as Conrad Peutinger, Gregor Reisch, and Ulrich Zasius. Peutinger had given him a helping hand to a professorship at Ingolstadt and a canonry at Eichstätt in 1510, ensuring that he had the material security adequate to a life of study.[3]

Through his connection with Peutinger and thus with the mercantile elite of Augsburg, Eck had been drawn into the ethical issues surrounding the lending of money at interest, a transaction execrated as unnatural and immoral through much of the ancient Mediterranean and medieval European world. He became the key figure in an episode sometimes known as the "South German Interest Rate Controversy." He adopted what was then the almost revolutionary view that the charging of moderate interest, up to about five percent, by means of a business loan of a very specific kind (the so-called "Augsburg Contract," which underpinned most of the transactions in that city's flourishing money market), did not amount to "usury." The defense of the "Augsburg Contract" was vital to the interests of the local plutocrat, Jakob Fugger, the grand old man of the imperial money market, who was happy to cover Eck's expenses in travelling to well-publicized disputations on the subject at Vienna and Bologna. Fugger had not only financed Charles V's bid for the imperial throne but also the marketing of the indulgence that had brought Luther into the public sphere in the first place.⁴ So when Eck became one of the *bêtes noires* of the early Protestants, his defense of usury (as they saw it) and his connection with Fugger were a gift for satirists.

Notwithstanding talk of their "friendship," there is nothing to indicate that the introduction Scheurl effected led to any bond of special warmth between Luther and Eck. Their next recorded contact was anything but friendly. As an eminent professor of theology as well as a canon of the cathedral, Eck was the natural choice when, in early 1518, the Bishop of Eichstätt, Gabriel von Eyb, wanted someone to provide informed comment on the *Ninety-Five Theses*, by then the talk of all Germany. The result was Eck's first recorded judgment on Luther, a file of rough notes that were to become known as the "Obelisks." The symbol of the obelisk (or dagger, †) was commonly used by medieval scholars to cross-reference notes to a text, usually critical notes, and in this case Eck's notes were presumably related to a printed copy of the *Ninety-Five Theses* marked up in this way. The *Obelisks* were never intended for publication: they were simply a briefing paper.⁵ Nevertheless they leaked out, and a copy made its way to Wittenberg by way of Bernhard Adelmann, a canon of Augsburg Cathedral who was already a keen supporter of Luther's. By March Luther was fuming at what he saw as Eck's betrayal of their friendship. Whether their polite exchange of letters really amounted to a friendship is questionable, but the thought that it did helped Luther nurture a satisfying sense of grievance.

In reply Luther dashed off his "Asterisks," giving at least as good as he had got. The *Obelisks*, which survive only in Luther's *Asterisks*, are frank criticisms, identifying various of the *Ninety-Five Theses* as erroneous, false, frivolous, illogical, confused, irreverent, or self-contradictory. At one point Eck suggests that there is a sting in the tail, at another that Luther's thinking seems to point towards Hussite conclusions. His tone does rise through the notes, as he reads with evidently mounting incredulity. By the end, one thesis is "a proposition full of poison," another "ridiculous."[6] But Eck confined himself strictly to the text, casting no personal aspersions. To that extent, at least, he scrupulously observed the canons of academic courtesy.

Luther's response betrays that eagerness to take offence, and that identification of oneself with one's writings, so often found among academics:

> He has written these *Obelisks*, in which he calls me poisonous, Bohemian, heretical, seditious, headstrong, and petulant . . . there is nothing in the work but the spite and envy of a frantic mind.[7]

This is a harsh account of a paper which, as Eck was swift to point out in a briefly successful effort to calm things down, was never intended even for circulation, let alone publication. But Luther's view has, as usual, carried more weight with later scholarship. Martin Brecht's account of the *Obelisks* in his magisterial biography of Luther is manifestly indebted not to Eck's words but to Luther's, which it uncritically recycles.[8] But while Luther has cited words that all appear in the *Obelisks*, the revealing thing is that he takes them as applied to himself when they are all, in context, referring to his words rather than to his person. It is not uncommon for authors to take criticism of their writing as personal criticism. But it was one of Luther's foibles to mistake his own personal touchiness for a selfless dedication to the truth. Eck had striven to avoid personalities, but Luther's incapacity to distinguish between theological disagreement and personal enmity was a mark of the man from the start. When harnessed on the one side to his unshakable sense of divine mission and on the other to a prodigious gift for personal invective, this made him a formidable opponent.[9]

If it was Eck who dared to disagree with Luther, it was Luther who turned their disagreement into a bitter and sundering quarrel. The cover letter to his *Asterisks* voiced his amazement at

> the effrontery with which you dare to pass judgment on my opinions before you know or understand them. Such temerity is sufficient and reliable evidence that you think yourself the only real theologian, so much so that you not only think your opinion is to be put ahead of all others, but you condemn whatever you don't understand, so that whatever displeases Eck is damned.[10]

He let himself go early on, deploying the text *omnis homo mendax* ("all men are liars," Ps 115:11), the scriptural shillelagh with which he loved to belabor his opponents, so many of whom were human (he never applied it to himself).[11] Eck's debating style is "childish and girly," he blathers, he is the "Obeliscographer" and "Obeliscophrast," raging at Luther out of jealousy. He is a ranter and a liar, a mercenary, suborned by the foes of true learning, brim-full of contumely and delirium, his mouth spewing out lies and blasphemy, bitterness and cursing.[12] The tone of this reply sets the tears he shed over Eck's breach of their friendship in an intriguing perspective.

Despite raising the temperature of the controversy, Luther respected Eck's good faith to the extent that he, too, refrained from committing his contribution to print.[13] So the *Obelisks* and *Asterisks* remained unpublished until they were included in the first volume of Luther's *Complete Works* in 1545. Andreas Carlstadt, Luther's colleague and the Dean of the Wittenberg Theology Faculty, was not so cautious. While his colleague was away at Heidelberg, Carlstadt rushed into print an absurdly detailed blow-by-blow rebuttal of Eck's notes, the dauntingly entitled *370 Theses*, for a disputation scheduled for 9 May 1518.[14]

Only about a quarter of Carlstadt's conclusions were actually directed against Eck, who was addressed with a mixture of condescension and sarcasm, as though he were an annoyingly obtuse schoolboy, and along the way Carlstadt charged him merely with ignorance, ill temper, and vainglory, only hinting that he was a heretic and a Judaizer (this last perhaps a gibe at his support for the charging of interest on loans).

Once Carlstadt had attacked him personally in print, it was inevitable that a man such as Eck would reply in kind, and his *Response to Carlstadt's Invectives* appeared in August. The title was something of an overreaction, but the text itself was relatively measured. It firmly but inoffensively rebutted a number of positions that Carlstadt had imputed to him, and it ostentatiously avoided name-calling. His sights now fixed on Carlstadt, Eck dared him to put their disagreements to the test in public disputation at Rome, Paris, or Cologne.[15] This was the seed from which the Leipzig Disputation eventually flowered. When Eck reminisced about all this twenty years later, he said that he had offered to debate with Luther and that the latter had come up with Leipzig as a venue. It was nothing like as simple as that. The two men met for the first time at Augsburg, while Luther was attending upon Cardinal Cajetan, and the initial idea was for a disputation between Eck and Carlstadt, with Leipzig as the likely venue (Eck rightly judging that Erfurt, Luther's *alma mater*, would be hostile territory). It is likely that, from the start, Eck had either the impression or the hope that Luther would be drawn in, though Luther at first had no such intention. When Eck published his draft theses at the end of December, they were obviously aimed at least as much against Luther as Carlstadt. The final thesis of the twelve was an assertion of the divine right of papal primacy in the Church, an issue which had nothing to do with Carlstadt and everything to do with Luther, as the latter rather sourly observed in a letter to a friend: "But listen to the cheek of the fellow: he picks up my theses and savages them bitterly, paying no attention to the man his quarrel is with."[16]

Needled by Eck's rather obvious efforts to draw him from cover, Luther could not resist taking the bait. As he found himself being maneuvered into participating in the disputation, he set out to needle his challenger in return. In an open letter to Carlstadt, he accused Eck of publishing his theses only after learning that Leipzig had declined to host the contest.[17] Luther had passed this news on to Eck in a letter of 7 January 1519, but, as Eck pointed out, this had not reached him at Ingolstadt until 8 February, over a month after he had published his theses,[18] though he conceded that he should not have published them before he knew for certain that the Leipzigers would agree to host the event. The authorities at Leipzig University had indeed been unwilling to do this, but their overlord, Duke George of Saxony, overruled them.

Luther was wiser than to be drawn into an argument about the rights or wrongs of his original insinuations against Eck. Instead he opened a new front, with a churlish letter in which, after a barrage of insults, he invited Eck to name the day on which they should meet, or else to allow Luther to do so.[19] He reiterated his preferred image of Eck as an irascible and bombastic sophist, consumed with envy and hatred, and addicted to the flattery of Rome. There was indeed an amusing vein of pomposity and Pecksniffian propriety in the overt moderation and restraint of Eck's contributions thus far, albeit little to justify the portrait Luther painted. Luther, in contrast, gloried in the lively mordancy of his polemics, which he rightly judged were gaining him the upper hand against his challengers.[20] His withering characterization of Eck swiftly captured the popular imagination and has held the field ever since. For Bernhard Adelmann in Augsburg, everything Eck did was "full of boasting and showing off."[21]

This exchange between the two main disputants of the three who would meet at Leipzig completed the prolegomena. Eck took the occasion afforded by the open letters to insert a further proposition into the dozen that he had set out in December 1518. The extra proposition concerned the freedom of the will, which Luther's deepening Augustinianism and anti-Pelagianism had reduced to the level of barely nominal existence. Free will would bulk large in the debates at Leipzig, and would eventually cause the greatest of the humanists, Erasmus, to make a public break with Luther. But in the immediate term it was the last thesis, now "Proposition XIII," which attracted attention that spring, because in it, for the first time, Luther faced the question of papal authority head on.

The anxieties about Rome and the papacy that had started to trouble Luther after his encounter with Cardinal Cajetan had not abated in the intervening months. Rome, he confessed to his closest confidant, Georg Spalatin, might more appropriately be named "Babylon," an image to which he would famously return in 1520. It had never been his intention, he explained, to break with the apostolic see, but he was now finding himself compelled to deny that Rome had any rightful superiority over any other church. Most disturbing of all, and only for whispering even to a friend as close as Spalatin,

> And (I whisper it into your ear) I am not sure whether the Pope is the Antichrist himself, or merely his apostle, so wretchedly is Christ (that is, truth) corrupted and crucified by him in canon law.[22]

This was heady stuff, and Luther's anxiety found expression first in busy research into canon law and church history, and then in a treatise on Proposition XIII that was printed shortly before the Leipzig Disputation.[23]

Luther was more circumspect in public than in private. In public there was barely a mention of Babylon, nor any talk of Antichrist. Rather, there was a cautious acknowledgment of the *de facto* power and authority of the Roman Church, a concession based on Saint Paul's injunction to "obey the powers that be." This was more than perfunctory and far from insincere. But it was also anything but the point. After this brief concession, the treatise systematically takes apart the theological, canonical, and historical case for the claim that the Roman Church exercised by divine right a supreme authority within the universal Church. Starting with the classic scriptural texts on which papal authority leaned (Matt 16:18–19 and John 21: 15–17), Luther set about his task with increasing vigor until he was subjecting the decrees of the medieval papacy to withering criticism. The popes and their supporters are denounced as forgers, babblers, corruptors of God's Word, barbarous Latinists, and ignorant pigs. Papal decrees are "impious and perverse blasphemy," while the blatant contrast between papal pomp and apostolic simplicity furnishes ready material for Luther's rich vein of sarcasm. The papacy had thrown the modern church into a confusion greater than that of Babylon (though Luther stops short at this mere hint of his inner fears). The culmination of a rising tide of impatient expostulation is a ringing indictment of the fruits of medieval canon law:

> Now that the papal decrees are ranked equal to the articles of the creed, and even above them by the toadies, we see the harvest: the overthrow of ecclesiastical order, a horrible tormenting of consciences, ignorance of the gospel, absolute impunity for wickedness, and the loathsome tyranny of the toadies at Rome, with the deserved result that no name under the wide blue heaven is more hateful and noisome than that of the Roman curia.[24]

This devastating polemic was printed just before the Leipzig Disputation, too late to reach Eck beforehand and warn him what he might face there. Luther brought a copy with him and used it as a handbook when he clashed with Eck on this issue.

The disputation at Leipzig had been scheduled to start on Monday, 27 June, and the participants and audience arrived over the preceding week. Looking back, Luther claimed that Eck had made sure everything would be arranged to suit himself, but this was hardly how it seemed in June.[25] Eck had come over 200 miles from Ingolstadt, accompanied by a single servant. Luther and Carlstadt travelled the 45 miles from Wittenberg in a sort of convoy of carts, accompanied by colleagues and books, and escorted by a couple of hundred rowdy students. This may have been intended to afford the Wittenberg speakers some protection, as the rivalry between Electoral and Ducal Saxony was reflected in the sometimes acerbic relations between their respective universities. But it was a precaution at least as likely to precipitate trouble as to prevent it.

The first week was entirely given over to the contest between Eck and Carlstadt, which focused on the relative place of divine grace and human free will in the process of salvation. Luther's only moment came on Wednesday, when debate was suspended for the feast day of Saints Peter and Paul (29 June), for which he was invited to deliver the sermon. Keeping his powder dry for the following week, he ignored the obvious opportunity to discuss papal primacy. But since the gospel for the day was one of the fundamental texts in the justification of papal authority, Matthew 16:13–19 (in which Christ said "upon this rock I shall build my church" and promised Peter "the keys of the kingdom of heaven"), his virtual silence on the subject of Peter was itself eloquent. When Peter was mentioned, his role was explicitly reduced to that of a representative or spokesman for the apostles. And the promise of the keys, usually taken as a sign of the authority which Christ would confer on Peter and his successors, was presented by Luther as symbolizing the forgiveness of sins and therefore as pointing not to papal or ecclesiastical authority but to his doctrine of justification by faith alone. Christians could never know that they were in grace, and that God looked favorably upon them, other than through faith: *glaubt er es, so ist er selig; glaubt er es nit, so ist er verdampt*. This claim was more radical than anything else said in the entire 17 days of the disputation: "believe this, and you are saved; believe it not, and you are damned."[26] Looking back on this sermon a few days after the end of the disputation, Eck described it as "plainly Hussite," but he made no allusion to it in the course of proceedings, though he managed a reply of sorts when he was invited to preach on the Feast of the Visitation (Saturday, 2 July).[27]

Eck has come in for a good deal of criticism in the historical literature concerning the Leipzig Disputation, dominated as it has been by scholars whose commitments to Luther are better described as hagiographical than historical. Much, perhaps most, of that criticism is undeserved. Yet if there is one thing for which he might quite properly be held at intellectual fault, it is this: that he entirely failed to appreciate the revolutionary nature of the claim Luther made in that sermon. Cajetan had seen in Luther's thinking the foundation of a new church.[28] Yet it seems to have passed Eck by, for all his quick wit. This may help explain why the distinctive Lutheran doctrine of certainty of grace, which was to be anathematized by the Catholic Council of Trent nearly thirty years later, was omitted from the first ecclesiastical condemnation of Luther, the papal bull launched against him next year by Leo X. For the theological groundwork of that condemnation was laid largely by none other than Eck, who took his quarrel to Rome some months after the close of play at Leipzig.

It was on Monday, 4 July, that Luther and Eck finally faced each other across the floor of the chamber in the Pleissenburg. Well over half of the subsequent debate was about the already notorious Proposition XIII, Eck's affirmation and Luther's denial of the divine right of the papacy to the primacy it claimed in the universal Church. They spent five days on this, but it might as well have been five minutes, and they could certainly have made all their main points and reached their eventual stalemate within an hour. As it was, their debate spiralled in ever decreasing circles.

Early on, Eck realized that he was at a disturbing disadvantage. Not only was he outnumbered, but he was also outgunned: Luther was armed with his recently printed *Resolution on Proposition XIII*, which Eck had not yet had the opportunity to read: "I came to debate," he complained, "not to publish a book."[29] The etiquette of scholastic debate was that disputants performed without book, relying on a sharp mind and a well-stocked memory. But Luther once more showed his preference for a written brief when facing a difficult public appearance. Despite his evident dexterity in debate, Eck was therefore badly underprepared in comparison with his opponent. His treatise *On the Primacy of Peter, against Luther*, written in the wake of the disputation, put together a plausible case for papal primacy, but his presentation of the case at Leipzig itself was nowhere near as well researched, to his cost. The Catholic defense of papal primacy would become almost a cliché before long, but in 1519 it was still novel ground.

Eck came to Leipzig expecting a typical scholastic disputation, hinging on well-turned syllogisms and on appeals to mutually recognized "authorities" (ranging from writings of the apostolic era to the most recent utterances of councils and popes). What he found was the opening phase of a culture clash. It did not help that Luther's own understanding of theological authority was still in flux. Eck was probably aware of Luther's suspicions of scholasticism, although it is unlikely he realized just how far they already extended.[30]

Eck's opening gambit was brief. Papal monarchy in the Church had been established by Christ himself, and this monarchical principle was endorsed by a series of Christian authors (initially he cited only three). The contrary position had been condemned by the University of Paris (generally regarded in the later Middle Ages as home to Europe's premier theological faculty) and had been anathematized at the Council of Constance among the notorious errors of the fourteenth-century English heretic John Wycliffe. He added a couple more citations from early Christian authors, one of which mentioned the famous scriptural text (Matt 16:18), "on this rock I shall build my church," to which, above all, the Roman Church appealed in vindicating its prerogatives.[31]

Luther's counter was direct, powerful, and effective, and perhaps began to give Eck some idea of the gulf that was opening up between them. He welcomed the contention that the Church was a monarchical institution but, resting his own argument almost entirely on scripture, insisted that Christ alone was its head and that no other head was required. Brushing aside Eck's patristic authorities, he cited one or two of his own, notably a text from Jerome asserting the equality of the apostles and therefore of their ecclesiastical successors. Intriguingly, or perhaps revealingly, he made no immediate response to the objection that his views on the papacy already lay under formal ecclesiastical condemnation.

The subsequent debate never moved far from the ground mapped out that day, though more authorities were introduced, especially by Luther, and the arguments were pursued further, with ever finer distinctions. The interest of the debate lies in two features. First, it shows how much of a Catholic Luther still was and thought himself to be. Although his ideas were tending in difficult directions, he strove not to rush too far ahead. Second, and still more importantly, one of Eck's recurring and developing lines of argument gradually sharpened the methodological focus of the debate for both sides, as the two men started to uncover the still largely implicit assumptions that underpinned Luther's approach to theological reasoning.

The two features were connected. Luther came to Leipzig as a Catholic, subscribing in some way to the authority of the "fathers" or "doctors" of the Christian tradition, whom he cited frequently in the course of debate. He subscribed likewise in some sense to the authority of councils, especially "general councils," when pronouncing judgment on disputed religious questions (he had after all appealed to a general council in the aftermath of his meeting with Cajetan at Augsburg); and he shared a broad trust in the "indefectibility" (or even "infallibility") of the Church, that is, the idea that the Church as a whole could not go seriously astray in interpreting the Christian faith. He certainly still saw some role for the papacy, and he was as hostile as anyone else to schism and heresy. He therefore had no time for the Hussite church of Bohemia, which in the fifteenth century had broken away from Rome in schism over the doctrines of the Czech theologian Jan Hus (who had in turn been deeply influenced by the teachings of Wycliffe). His commentary on Galatians, published that summer, insisted that the Bohemian break with Rome was inexcusable, in that it was ungodly and contrary to charity and all the laws of Christ.[32]

The imputation of "Hussitism" or "Bohemian" heresy came to be the sore point of the proceedings. Eck hit upon it almost by chance in his opening gambit, when he casually observed that denying the primacy of the Roman Church was a Wycliffite error.[33] He pressed it with increasing force as the days wore on, sensing the growing intensity with which Luther was reacting. No doubt noticing how Luther skirted round his initial allusion to Wycliffe and Constance, Eck returned to it next day, urging that Luther's view was not only "among the damnable and pestiferous errors for which John Wycliffe was condemned" but also "among the pestilent errors of Jan Hus."[34] This was nicely calculated, as German Catholics reacted almost neuralgically to the name of the Czech heresiarch. If Eck could make Luther guilty by association with Hus, he would be well on the way to victory. This time the thrust struck home. Luther denied any sympathy with the "Bohemian faction" and their schism, yet now pointed to the Greek Church of the East, which refused to acknowledge papal authority but, he maintained, could hardly be regarded as tainted with Bohemian heresy. Eck's insinuation continued to rankle, however, and Luther complained about it again at the end of that session and at the start of the next.[35]

During the lengthy pamphlet exchanges which followed the disputation, Eck offered a telling comparison of his two opponents. Carlstadt he found inept and unintelligent, a judgment likely to be endorsed by anyone who struggles through his tedious writings. Luther, though, was another matter:

> With a livelier wit and a more tenacious memory, his easy voice and manner were better suited to disputation, except for one thing: when pressed by his opponent or stung by some word, he too quickly became incandescent with rage, so that he himself scarcely understood what he was saying.[36]

Eck got onto this quickly and learned how to rile Luther. He kept on pressing the Hussite button, working up his opponent to such a pitch that he not only angrily interrupted him more than once (another breach of disputational etiquette), but also accused Eck of calling him "a most pestilential heretic"— which he had studiously refrained from doing, although he had equally studiously done everything he could to imply it. Indeed, although Eck is conventionally credited with a hectoring and bullying style in debate, he did nothing at Leipzig to earn such a reputation. He was for the most part rigidly formal, rarely if ever interrupting, and maintaining an icy academic politeness. He reserved his criticism almost entirely for Luther's ideas and utterances, avoiding crudely personal gibes. This carefully modulated goading got under his opponent's skin, with the result that while Luther was undoubtedly on his best behavior and, by his own standards, unwontedly restrained, he burst out from time to time in anger or absurdity. As Eck closed in with the "Bohemian" argument—for there was no escaping that the Council of Constance, in condemning Wycliffe and Hus, had condemned Luther's view of the papacy in anticipation—Luther was understandably reluctant to face up to its consequences. Hence his suggestion (made out of reverence for that council) that the positions of Wycliffe and Hus on the papacy had not been condemned there at all, but had been "interpolated by some impostor."[37] Eck had him cornered, and while Luther's continuing disavowals of heresy and schism may have limited the immediate damage, the realization that he had more than a little in common with the Hussites would slowly dawn upon him over the next couple of years, as his own relationship with the established Church became more problematic.

At this stage, however, Luther's love of paradox and provocation overcame him, and after once more repudiating any Bohemian sympathies, he shocked his audience by announcing that among the beliefs of Hus and his followers were many things that were entirely Christian and evangelical. He at once drew the sting by choosing as his example their belief in the Holy Spirit, the holy Catholic Church, and the communion of the saints—in other words their adherence to the Apostles' Creed, the oldest summary of the Christian faith. But later on he went back on the offensive, maintaining that the Council of Constance had indeed erred in condemning Hus's definition of the Church as the "body of the predestined."[38] The idea that the general council at Constance had condemned Christian and evangelical truths cut at the root of medieval understandings of ecclesiastical authority. Luther was no more a "conciliarist" than a "papalist." The pope was a solitary individual, a general council was a collection of individuals, but they were all human and thus all capable of error: *omnis homo mendax.*

The disputation over the papacy gradually tailed off into tiresome volleys of assertions and denials over the interpretation of a few scriptural texts and early Christian Fathers (notably Augustine, Cyprian, and John Chrysostom). Since most of these early writers could be cited on both sides of the question regarding the nature of the "rock" on which Christ undertook to build his church, the exchanges were necessarily inconclusive. Eck seems to have been taken unawares by the direction of debate over Proposition XIII. It was only in the last couple of days on this subject that he started to produce significant patristic testimony to support his position. One suspects that one or two Leipzigers, such as Hieronymus Emser (who would become a friend and ally of his), stepped in as unofficial research assistants to close the gap between Eck and his better prepared opponent, and at a certain point Eck was obviously able to get a copy of Luther's book. Beyond that, Luther spent a lot of time wriggling off hooks, as when he drew a somewhat disingenuous distinction between impugning the primacy of the Bishop of Rome (which he denied) and disputing that the Roman primacy was a matter of divine right (which he acknowledged). But, ironically, the real significance of the debate over the papacy was that it revealed that Luther had no more time for the authority of general councils than he had for that of popes. He was beginning to move visibly outside the bounds of medieval Catholic orthodoxy.

On 8 July the focus of debate shifted to purgatory, with Luther taking his stand on the plain and indisputable fact that the Bible had "almost nothing" to say on the subject—though, curiously, he still affirmed his conviction that purgatory did indeed exist.[39] There were a few scriptural texts that were routinely invoked in discussions of purgatory, but, as he rightly observed, they none of them specified a place, state, or name. For the rest of that short argument, however, Luther found himself in trouble. Eck wanted to know how he could possibly justify his conviction about the reality of purgatory if he was not satisfied with the scriptural basis offered for it. All he got in reply was bluster (though before long Luther would abandon his residual belief in purgatory). More significantly, Eck widened his attack, challenging Luther's preference for scripture over the authority of general councils. According to that principle, he contended, the heresy of Arianism (the denial of the doctrine of the Trinity) would still be flourishing, since the key technical term of the doctrine as defined at the Council of Nicaea was not to be found in the Bible. Instead, the authority of the Church was as reliable in the interpretation of scripture as it was in the identification of its constituent books.[40]

If the scriptural foundation for purgatory was flimsy, then that for indulgences was frankly nonexistent. In their brief discussion of the issue that had made Luther a public figure, Eck was therefore reduced to constructing a syllogism on the theme of ecclesiastical infallibility. General councils of the Church embodied the universal Church's infallibility in matters of the faith; the general councils of the Lateran (1215), Lyon (1274), and Constance (1414–18) had declared and approved the doctrine of indulgences; therefore the doctrine was true. Luther faced a much easier challenge here, and focused his claims on the reasonable contention that indulgences were not considered "necessary for salvation." From this he inferred that they could not form part of the faith, which was of course universally acknowledged as essential to salvation. Indeed, he agreed, the universal Church could not err in matters of faith. However, from this he concluded not that its teaching on indulgences must therefore be true, but that indulgences themselves could not be a matter of faith, and that councils of the Church had erred in declaring them to be so.[41] Eck seized on the implication that Luther's concept of the universal Church was in effect empty. If the flocking of pilgrims to Rome from all parts of the Church for the special "Jubilee" indulgences available there every 25 years did not manifest the consensus of the universal Church, he argued, then there was no conceivable way to ascertain the mind of the universal Church on anything.[42]

The pragmatic argument from the general custom of the Christian people did not bother Luther. As far as he was concerned, the hordes who traipsed to Rome for indulgences were simply ignorant, mistakenly believing, like Eck himself, that indulgences were necessary for salvation. Eck did not believe that indulgences were necessary to salvation, but Luther's utter conviction that he did opens another intriguing window into the working of Luther's mind. For Luther, only what was necessary to salvation could possibly be good for Christians.[43] Eck was happy to concede that indulgences were not necessary for salvation, but nonetheless insisted that they were beneficial. Luther's mental apparatus seems to have assimilated Eck's insistence that indulgences were beneficial and to have processed it in accordance with the principle that only what was necessary to salvation could be good, resulting in the conviction that Eck believed indulgences necessary to salvation. As Lucien Febvre once observed, with characteristic insight, Luther had (to an even stronger degree than most of us) a tendency to filter any intellectual input so as to align it with his own mental predispositions.[44]

The Leipzig Disputation concluded with a two-day clash on the subject of penance, which could have come closer than anything else to the heart of Luther's theology. But Eck was taking the lead in this phase, and chose to focus on two issues which he saw as quick wins. These were the idea that true repentance for sin started from a proper and salutary fear of God and divine punishment, and the fact that the ancient and constant tradition of the Church regarded the "penances" (or penalties) imposed by bishops or priests upon repentant Christians as owed not merely to the ecclesiastical community in this life (as Luther maintained) but also to God in the perspective of eternity (which Luther denied). The evidence from patristic and medieval tradition very much favored Eck, but this did not sit at all well with Luther's new understanding of faith and salvation. For Luther, true penance arose out of love for justice rather than out of fear of punishment, a position which had place in Christian tradition more as the expression of an ideal than as a description of everyday reality. Eck had no difficulty in amassing a solid body of scriptural and patristic testimony in favor of his more realistic assessment of human and Christian motivation.[45] Luther's response, delivered without a tincture of irony, was brisk:

> Snipping different texts from different places without any reason for connecting or comparing them is no way to get at the proper meaning and interpretation of holy scripture. On the contrary, that is the commonest way to get holy scripture wrong.[46]

Luther was on firmer or at least more favorable ground when he took his stand on scripture. Yet while scripture was already his starting point in addressing almost any topic, he had not, prior to Leipzig, explicitly formulated the "Protestant scripture principle," the claim that only the scriptures, and these taken in their "literal" sense, could be decisive in theological argument. The significance of the Leipzig Disputation lies in the fact that it nudged him towards a clearer appreciation of his own implicit assumptions. Eck's dialectical scalpel pared off more of the Catholic rind that still clung to Luther's emerging theology. By making the problems with the fathers and councils evident to Luther, Eck drove him closer to recognizing the implicit logic of his position. Once the popes, the councils, and the fathers had all been categorized as merely human authorities, as prone to err as the next man or woman, the bare text of scripture was all that was left.

After Leipzig, both sides sought to spin the outcome. The notarized record of the disputation, it had been agreed, would be communicated only to the universities selected for the honor of passing judgment on it, namely Erfurt and Paris. But in the age of print such a confidentiality agreement was already unrealistic. The disputants and their supporters were soon writing to friends setting out the story as they saw it, and some of these letters found their way into print, best intentions to the contrary notwithstanding. Each side in due course accused the other of breach of trust and ridiculed them for "singing the anthem before the win." Luther insisted that it was Eck who first broke the agreement by writing a letter to the Elector Frederick. This letter, which was only published later, by Luther himself, was indeed written as early as 22 July. However, Luther had already sent a similarly private letter to Spalatin on 20 July, and on 21 July Melanchthon had written an open letter about the disputation, addressed to Johannes Oecolampadius (then living in Augsburg). This seems to have been the first of these accounts to be published, for it was printed in Wittenberg, and a copy reached Eck before he had even left Leipzig. The open letter he dashed off in reply was dated 25 July and was presumably published almost at once.[47]

Melanchthon charged Eck with various breaches of disputational etiquette and lapses of intellectual integrity. Thus he declared that the patristic citations that Eck adduced in favor of applying Matthew 16:18 ("You art Peter, and upon this rock I shall build my church") specifically and exclusively to Peter were from dubious or spurious sources (even though the texts of Cyprian and Jerome from which Eck quoted were at that time generally believed to be authentic). In reply, Eck complained that Melanchthon was arrogating to himself the task of adjudicating on the disputation, a task which the parties had agreed to entrust to the University of Paris. Eck tried to defend himself without casting any aspersions on Carlstadt or Luther, instead simply appealing to the academic tribunals to whom the transcripts had been referred for final judgment. He might have done better to jump bodily into the arena with his opponents rather than pose self-righteously on the edge of it. Their representation of him gained traction despite his efforts to the contrary, while he offered his audience no similarly caustic representation of them. Luther and his supporters had certainly got the idea of the "attack ad." The plaintive note of self-pity which Eck struck in his attempt at a dignified reply just did not have the audience appeal of rollicking rhetoric. However, as pamphlets continued to appear he shed his scruples and tried to answer in kind, though he lacked Luther's flair for this style of writing. He had definitely done better in the debate than after it. As Luther remarked later, in a backhanded tribute,

> When Eck is there in person, no one can withstand him, and he can lead anyone right away from the truth. But when it comes to paper, he is quite dead.[48]

By the end of the summer, the gloves were off. Luther wrote a longer account of the disputation in a letter to Spalatin dated 15 August and serving as the dedication of the *Resolutions on the Leipzig Disputation*.[49] On 18 August 1519, Luther laid into Eck with a vengeance in the course of a letter to Spalatin, denouncing him as a liar and an illiberal, impudent sycophant.[50] His letters in the second half of 1519 abound with insults and invective against Eck and also, after a while, Hieronymus

Emser, who entered the lists in support of Eck. The aftershocks of the disputation rumbled on well into 1520.

The aftermath of the Leipzig Disputation was the matrix in which humanist support for Martin Luther took firmer shape. Some humanists, such as Beatus Rhenanus and Jacques Lefèvre, had already been voicing sympathy and admiration for him.[51] But his circle of admirers now widened rapidly, as can be seen from the case of Ulrich von Hutten. Germany's wickedest satirist had originally seen the indulgences controversy as just another pointless quarrel among monks. An avid partisan first of Reuchlin and then also of Erasmus, Hutten was, to some extent, a disciple in perpetual search of a messiah. After Leipzig he came to see Luther as another German humanist on the wrong end of scholastic jealousy and Roman tyranny.[52] Luther's own carefully drawn parallel between his treatment and that of Johann Reuchlin was starting to pay dividends. But his emergence had a divisive impact on German humanism. Eobanus Hessus and Hieronymus Emser, for example, had both contributed commendatory verses in 1514 to an anti-Hussite polemic published by Hieronymus Dungersheim.[53] It is no surprise that Dungersheim himself, a Dominican friar and an essentially scholastic theologian, turned against Luther after seeing him in action at Leipzig. But Hessus and Emser, both with impeccably humanist credentials, now took opposite sides, and Emser was soon under fire from Wittenberg.

Luther, meanwhile, was heartened by messages of support emanating from cities across Germany, from Augsburg to Zurich, and especially from their humanist circles. Conrad Pellican, for example, the humanist friar of Basel who was closely involved in the printing industry there, wrote to Luther in March 1520 with encouraging news of Luther's impact among friars of all orders in that region. Johannes Lüthard of Lucerne was preaching from Luther's texts, while Johannes of Ulm, a friar based in Freiburg, was "consumed with zeal for your writings."

Basel was full of Luther's admirers: a couple of Austin Friars who were doctors of divinity, the prior of the Austin Canons, and all Pellican's own brethren in the Franciscan house.[54]

There was a definite effort by Luther to win humanist support for his teachings. It was discernible in his recurrent allusions to the vicissitudes of Johannes Reuchlin, whose long-running case at Rome had scandalized humanists across Europe. It was even more evident in his commentary on Galatians, largely written before the disputation, but only published in September. Notwithstanding Luther's private reservations about Erasmus, this commentary went out of its way to affiliate itself with the great man. In the preface, Luther modestly explained that he would rather have awaited the commentary promised by Erasmus, "that supreme theologian," than have published his own; and Erasmus was invoked from the very first comment, on Galatians 1:1, where his name was printed in capital letters, as it was wherever it was used.[55] The commentary also reprised Luther's theological development thus far, in relatively unpolemical style. It summed up his new understanding of the "Word of God" in terms of justification by faith alone and was persistent in urging the absolute certainty with which Christians could contemplate their own condition. It was a mere "fable of the scholastics that a person is uncertain whether or not they are in a state of salvation."[56] The contrast between man (every man a liar) and God (alone truthful) was relentless, as was the dismissal of human or philosophical conceptions of "justice," especially that of Aristotle.[57] Luther's teaching was encapsulated in his explanation of Paul's dichotomy between the Law and the Gospel, a dichotomy which, more than anything else, has defined the Lutheran tradition. What Luther took from Paul was the idea that the law not only taught people what to do, but also, paradoxically, taught them simultaneously that they could not do it, in that the law's demand for perfect fulfilment was simply beyond anyone. This natural impossibility of the law, the utter incapacity of fallen human nature to fulfil the law, was one of Luther's most innovative insights. In his commentary on Galatians, he derived some support for this radical interpretation from Augustine, though on other occasions he acknowledged (surely correctly) that Augustine had not grasped the concept as clearly as he himself did. Either way, Luther's concept of the impossibility of fulfilling the law both shocked and intrigued his contemporaries. A sense of his own theological originality stirs in this text from time to time, as when he remarked that "what follows I have never seen explained in any of the doctors—Jerome, Augustine, and Ambrose all pass over it."[58]

The commentary on Galatians also set out at length for the first time one of Luther's most important and appealing theological concepts, that of "Christian liberty." This slogan was Luther's summary of the message that justification by faith freed Christians from the burden of seeking salvation through legal and ritual observance, by providing them instead with the all-important "peace of conscience" which was precisely not attainable by the legalistic performance of good works, and came only through the certainty of grace arising from justification by faith.[59] Luther only hinted at the critique of penitential practice, pilgrimage, and other religious activities that might flow from this new understanding of Law and Gospel, but this added to his appeal to humanists, offering a more solid scriptural foundation for the critique of mechanical ritualism that Erasmus had been voicing for several years. Conrad Pellican told Luther that he had read the commentary through three times, annotating it heavily.[60] The convergence between Erasmus's agenda and Luther's on this issue helped give some of Luther's Catholic opponents the mistaken impression that Erasmus was in some sense responsible for Luther's assault on the Church (a responsibility Erasmus spent the rest of his life disclaiming). Another reason for the success of the commentary on Galatians is probably that this exercise in biblical exposition was very different in tone from Luther's polemics. Criticism there was, some of it potentially very damaging to the established order, such as the passing remark that "Today, indeed, in a large part of the Church, the Gospel has been subverted."[61] But the moderate and inoffensive tone of the criticism placed the commentary more in the humanist mainstream.

As the controversy over Leipzig continued, Eck decided to seek a vindication of the victory he was convinced he had won by taking the matter to Rome. But as he set out, in spring 1520, he was leaving behind him a Germany starting to laugh out loud at two comic pamphlets circulating to his discredit. *The Unlearned Canons* was a spoof letter, addressed to the "Most glorious, super-learned, all-conquering, Master Johannes Eck," which picked up on a comment in a letter of his in which he had dismissed Luther's followers as ignorant backwoodsmen, unscholarly gentlemen occupying lucrative sinecures in German cathedrals (as opposed to hard-working academics such as himself). This ironic epistle was probably the work of Johannes Oecolampadius, a talented young humanist who, after lurching between the old and the new for several years, would eventually become an adherent of Zwinglian theology and a leading figure in the Reformation at Basel. It pointedly contrasted the achievements of the sophisticated intellectual—most notably, his defense of interest-yielding contracts, which was used to depict him as the lackey of the rich—with the honest simplicity of the "unlearned canons" themselves.[62] The other comic effort was the still more damaging *Eccius Dedolatus* (*A Well-Beaten Eck*), a knockabout sketch which showed the great man in a series of surreal encounters that culminated in a severe beating, and presented him in the guise of the scholastic obscurantists who had been made a laughingstock in the *Letters of Obscure Men*.

A Well-Beaten Eck had reached Luther in Wittenberg by March, and he felt that the style betrayed the authorship of Willibald Pirckheimer.[63] There was probably little Eck could have done to limit the damage done by these crudely and cruelly amusing pamphlets, but it did not help that he was hundreds of miles away while his reputation was being shredded. In July 1520, Adelmann passed on a rumor of another dialogue supposedly celebrating the canonization of Eck on account of the manifold wonders he had worked.[64] Still more damagingly, the controversy between Eck and Luther was in the public eye at the same time as a controversy between Erasmus and Edward Lee, which was seen by Europe's humanists as a confrontation between humanist enlightenment and the uncouth carping of an envious self-seeker. And all this was taking place at a moment when the Reuchlin affair was reaching its final crisis (a crisis not unconnected with the furore over Luther, which played into the hands of Reuchlin's enemies). Martin Bucer spoke for many young scholars when, in a letter to Beatus Rhenanus of April 1520, he linked the Reuchlin and Erasmus controversies with the condemnations of Luther recently published by the universities of Louvain and Cologne (which were also leading the charge against Reuchlin).[65] That Luther's foe was now the butt of the same sort of satire as Reuchlin's persecutors sealed Eck's new reputation as one of the "obscure men," despite the high regard he had hitherto enjoyed in Germany's scholarly circles.[66] Luther's affair was thus wrapped up, in the public's eyes, with those of Erasmus and Reuchlin, and this did an enormous amount to legitimize and popularize his cause.

7

ROME AND WITTENBERG

Johannes Eck spent the autumn of 1519 at work on his defense of papal primacy against Luther's Proposition XIII.[1] The text was finished on 7 February 1520,[2] and not long afterwards he set off for Rome to offer a presentation copy to the pope. He arrived in March and formally presented his autograph manuscript to Leo X on 1 April, with a brief speech that charged Luther with heaping up all that the great heresiarchs of the past had thrown up against the apostolic see.[3] A papal commission had been established to consider the Luther affair in late January or early February, and Eck soon found himself added to its number. Early in May he let Johann Fabri know that the commission had completed its work, and that he had been summoned by Leo to a conference at the Villa Manliana with another theologian and a couple of cardinals for a final review of the text and a decision. The outcome was a draft bull condemning 41 statements selected from Luther's oeuvre as variously "heretical, scandalous, false, offensive to pious ears, or contrary to Catholic truth."[4] Many of these propositions had already been picked out for attack by Eck at Leipzig or elsewhere, and it was Eck who showed the pope precisely where the condemned propositions were to be found in Luther's writings. So it was in many ways Eck's Luther whose teachings were condemned in the bull *Exsurge Domine* ("Rise up, O Lord"), formally promulgated on 15 June 1520.[5]

Rome and the papacy were very much on Luther's mind throughout 1520. The suspicion that the pope might be the Antichrist was burgeoning within him, especially after he read

Ulrich von Hutten's edition of Lorenzo Valla's demolition of the "Donation of Constantine," which came into his hands in February.[6] However, he was not yet ready to air his suspicions publicly. It was neither Eck nor Hutten who drew him once more from cover on the subject of the papacy, but a minor Catholic polemicist called Augustin von Alveldt, an Observant Franciscan friar. Alveldt's treatise *On the Apostolic See* made a serviceable case for papal primacy, and was published in both German and Latin in late spring. Like the work of most of Luther's opponents, it is generally brushed aside by those historians who look upon the evidence within the perspective carefully laid out for them by Luther himself.[7] But its merits can be better appreciated from the fact that Wittenberg put out three replies to it in a matter of months. More importantly, it was responsible for a significant, though generally overlooked, development in Luther's thought.

Luther took on the vernacular edition of Alveldt's work in his *On the Papacy at Rome*, dashed off in May and published in June.[8] This characteristically mordant effort, which with unwitting irony censures Alveldt for the bitterness of his invective,[9] is more than mere polemics. It is the first treatise to set out an idea that would become integral to the Protestant tradition, that of the "invisible Church," or, to be more precise, of the distinction between the visible and the invisible Church. An appeal to the authority of the universal Church was and is a fundamental element in the Catholic account of Christianity. The Protestant appeal to the authority of scripture alone is a radical alternative to it. In 1520, the doctrine of the supreme teaching authority of the Church held sway almost throughout Europe. Any serious alternative account of Christianity had to undermine this powerful and deeply rooted consensus. In *On the Papacy at Rome* Luther found an ingenious way to achieve this.

Alveldt's treatise offered a theory of the papacy which resonated with a powerful theme in early modern European culture:

monarchy. His argument came down to three crucial claims: that any human society or organization had to have a single head or leader; that God would not have left his church on earth without such an essential feature as that single head or leader; and that the evidence of scripture demonstrated that Saint Peter, and therefore by extension his successors the bishops of Rome, occupied that position of leadership. Of course Luther contested the claim that Peter and his putative successors exercised any such role by divine right. But he was still ready to allow the pope a measure of worldly authority, provided that it was not employed to compromise the teachings of the Gospel. That much he had already argued at length against Eck the previous year. But Alveldt's framing of the argument within an overall perspective of the naturally established and divinely authorized conception of monarchy provided a context in which the medieval reading of certain scriptural texts as undergirding papal primacy once more became very believable. What Luther did in *On the Papacy at Rome*, therefore, was to tear down Alveldt's elaborate theoretical perspective, a task he performed with elegant simplicity by redefining the whole concept of the church. The argument he constructed instead rendered irrelevant the principal contention, that any human organization requires a single head. Initially, returning to dualist and fideist ideas he had deployed elsewhere, Luther briefly ruled his opponent out of court for invoking nature and reason in matters that concerned grace and faith. But that was just familiar sparring: not even Luther actually thought or sought to exclude nature and reason from theological discussion and reasoning, however useful such statements might be as debating points. He was often led on by such rhetoric, but he was never taken prisoner by it. His masterstroke was simply to remove the church from the world, and thus from the scope of Alveldt's arguments.

The way Luther did this depends to a surprising extent on ideas he borrowed from his opponent. Alveldt had distinguished several possible meanings of the word "church" in his own discussion of Matthew 18:17, "Tell it to the church." Luther picked up these meanings—universal church, local church, and church building—and characteristically proceeded to insist that only one of them was authentically scriptural. His particular conception of the literal interpretation of scripture made it impossible, in his analysis, for a word in scripture to bear two meanings: scripture was to be interpreted in such a way that it always kept "a certain, simple, and indivisible meaning on which our faith may settle itself without wavering."[10] The Bible's "church," for Luther, is the true church, the universal church, the body of the faithful united under the headship of Christ. This church, he announced, "is not of this world." Christ said that his kingdom was not of this world, but Alveldt sought to reduce that kingdom to this world in his argument for the necessity of an earthly head.

Luther at no point in his attack on Alveldt uses the phrase "invisible church." That label was a conceptual or terminological coinage he would mint a little later, in his response to another Catholic polemicist, Ambrosius Catharinus (as we shall see in due course). Yet the concept is already there in his thought. The true church is the body of true believers (not of those who make a false outward profession of faith): but "nobody can see who believes."[11] It is therefore a spiritual and not a physical assembly, and any attempt to transform it into an outward assembly or union represents a fundamental misunderstanding of its nature. The true, universal, Catholic Church, the spiritual community of Christians, has no physical aspects at all. Those who postulate that the Church is an outward community in this world are "really Jews," Luther added, trading once again on the traditional dichotomy between the "carnal" Jews and the "spiritual" Christians.[12] It is indeed blasphemy to conceive the church in such a worldly fashion. Because the true church is wholly spiritual, it cannot have an earthly head, and it needs only its spiritual head, Christ. The spiritual church of true believers cannot be discerned by earthly eyes, and therefore cannot have an earthly ruler: "How can anyone rule something that he can neither know nor recognize?"[13] The corollary is equally explosive. No outward church on earth can be the true church. His syllogism was incisive:

> That which one believes is neither corporal nor visible. We can all see the outward Roman Church, which is why it cannot be the true church.[14]

In effect, for Luther, the "Roman Catholic Church" was a contradiction in terms. The fact that it was "Roman," local— and no one denied that it was Roman: its essential *Romanitas* was unmissable—was in itself what showed it could not be "Catholic," universal, true. It was precisely the local habitation and the name which made it "a" church, which, in consequence, meant that it could not possibly be "the" church. The "Catholic Church," for Luther, was everywhere, but at the same time nowhere. After this, the canter through the usual scriptural texts is mere ornamentation, there to reassure readers that Alveldt's appeal to scripture can safely be discounted. And Luther skirted cautiously around the issue of Antichrist with two teasing hints, implying, without stating, that the Roman Church displayed the same grasping avarice that was expected to characterize the Antichrist.[15] This was a line of argument he would develop soon afterwards at greater length in the *Appeal to the Christian Nobility of the German Nation*. But the real significance of *On the Papacy at Rome* is its redefinition of the church, which was to be fundamental to Protestant Christianity. Luther never wavered from this new understanding. Twenty years later, he was still deploying the notion the same way, to evade the implications of Augustine's famous observation, itself a commonplace of Catholic polemic against "scripture alone," that he would not believe in the Gospel unless the authority of the Church induced him to do so:[16]

> The true church has never had a name or title in this world. It was always the church without a name that was the true church. So it is believed, but not seen.[17]

Luther's reply to Alveldt, then, was the first text to set out the concept of the invisible church. The position was adopted under the pressure of debate, to escape the authority of the visible church. His answer was to spiritualize the church in such a way as to deny it any effective governmental or disciplinary structure. The point of this move was to ensure that there could be no head of the Church functioning on earth, and thus to overthrow the ecclesiastical authority of the papacy. The price was high: the church became an essentially spiritual and invisible reality, known only to God, entirely dependent on Christ in the Holy Spirit. Given Luther's doctrine of certainty, one could at least know if one was oneself a member of this, the only true church. But one could not know if anybody else was. So really it was the self, God, and his Word: there is a profound individualism about Luther's emerging theology. The little-known treatise against Alveldt is essentially occasional in inspiration, a brief polemic against a respectable case for the papacy. But its significance for the tradition of Protestantism is immeasurable.

Undermining the visibility and thus the identity of the church problematized the whole domain of church governance and authority. Luther's ultimate resolution of this new problem would be his doctrine of the "two kingdoms," roughly coterminous with the "spiritual" and the "temporal" spheres of human life.[18] Under this doctrine responsibility for the external governance of the church would be transferred to the temporal sphere. That Luther's thinking might be heading in such a direction is evident from one of his most widely read writings of that year, his *Appeal to the Christian Nobility of the German Nation*, another crucial component of what was becoming a systematic attack on the papacy and the religious system it ruled. The *Appeal*, a call to the "second estate" of the Holy Roman Empire to take in hand the vast task of church reform which Luther now saw as necessary, was in a sense his first explicitly "Reformational" work. Much of it is a litany of grievances old and new. The lengthy denunciations of the ways and means by which the Roman curia filled its coffers from German pockets recapitulated or embroidered familiar complaints. The fees for dispensations and privileges, the charges that the papacy could levy upon new incumbents of major ecclesiastical offices, and the offerings for indulgences and for crusades which never took place, told a familiar tale of corrupt Italians battening upon long-suffering Germans. But the proposal that priests should be allowed to marry in order to put an end to the scandals of "concubinage" (long-term but unlawful quasi-marital relationships) was more novel, as were the calls for cutting back and controlling religious festivals, pilgrimage, religious vows, mendicancy, masses for the dead, and confraternities.[19]

More important than such details, however, was the platform from which Luther launched his manifesto. Part of the story of Europe's Middle Ages was the way that the papacy and the clergy had successfully labored to establish "the freedom of the church"—that is, the effective legislative and jurisdictional autonomy of the church considered as the body of the clergy. One consequence of this was that the responsibility for ecclesiastical reform had been left to the clergy. Luther's appeal to the nobility was thus a direct challenge to established custom, but he took matters further by denying the underlying principle upon which that custom was founded. The very notion of any real distinction between clergy and laity, he argued, was fundamentally unsound and unchristian. All Christians were, by virtue of their one faith and baptism, priests.[20]

The idea that would later be labelled "the priesthood of all believers" was deployed to break down what Luther called the first bulwark erected by the papacy around its usurped privileges. The papacy was by now the chief target. The *Appeal* had been written in June, and was off the presses by August, when he wrote to a fellow Austin Friar at Magdeburg:

> I am issuing a vernacular book against the Pope on reforming the state of the Church. In it I deal with the Pope pretty fiercely, virtually as Antichrist.[21]

His suspicions about the true nature of the papacy were hardening, though he was still cautious about voicing their full extent. For the most part, Luther confined himself in the *Appeal* to dropping broad hints about the Antichrist, affirming that he was indeed at work in Rome, but making adroit use of veiled or conditional statements to suggest and imply, rather than assert, that he was to be identified with the pope.[22] At only one point did he teasingly let the veil slip, arguing that, even in the absence of other evidence, the sale of special spiritual "faculties" by papal legates in Germany "would be" enough to show that the pope really was the Antichrist. It was clear by now what he really thought, but in this, his final discussion of the subject in the *Appeal*, Luther still held back slightly on the question, offering to say more about it another time.[23]

Notwithstanding his time-consuming polemical engagements, Luther continued to develop his new understanding of faith and justification in his preaching and in his devotional and pastoral writings (the works of his that achieved the widest circulation in those early years). His sermons that year recapitulated the emphasis on approaching the sacraments in certain expectation of God's grace, without reliance on one's own preparation or merits.[24] Luther presented his doctrine of certainty not as the dramatic innovation it was but as a plain and simple interpretation of the scriptures. The unselfconscious naturalness with which he wove this idea into his discourses no doubt helped to familiarize it to a widening audience. His renewed campaigns on Lenten confession and Easter communion were arousing widespread interest—putting scruples, as the Bishop of Merseburg saw it, into the consciences of the simple faithful. The bishops called on Luther to write less provocatively—in vain, of course.[25] At the instigation of Georg Spalatin, Luther wrote up much of his pastoral teaching in *On Good Works,* a more formal Latin treatise that was completed towards the end of Lent and was in print by June.[26] The overwhelming importance of believing that one was pleasing to God was emphasized again and again. Such faith was itself only possible by the grace of God, and the message was driven home by the insistence that not to show such faith was to make Christ a liar.[27] Good works could not bring about such faith, such certainty. This was easily verifiable by asking those who devoted themselves to traditional good works, none of whom dared to claim with any certainty that they or their works were pleasing to God. Faith, however, made even inadequate works good in God's eyes, and this was what the faithful were to believe.[28] Such faith was in fact the greatest work that could be done by or in a human being.[29]

Luther's new understanding of justification had originally been formulated in the context not simply of his wrestling with Paul's epistles but also of his ruminations on the practice of sacramental confession. In its first iteration, faith alone was simply faith in the words of absolution, "I absolve you . . . ," pronounced upon the penitent by their confessor. The priest, for Luther as for the medieval Catholic tradition, was speaking here not in his own right but as a spokesman for Christ. The sound was the sound of the priest, but the words were the words of Christ. Luther's doctrine was therefore bound up with the theology of the Christian sacraments from the start;

yet, as it developed further, it compelled him to take a fresh look at the whole idea of the sacraments. If "faith alone" was all that mattered, was there even a need for sacraments? Did they have any point? Such questions almost posed themselves, and it certainly required no unusual intellectual powers to pose them. The idea of "faith, not works" cast doubt on vast tranches of the religious performance that constituted late medieval Catholicism—indulgences, of course, but also pilgrimages, protracted or intricate cycles of prayer, asceticism, and monasticism. There was no immediately obvious reason why the sacraments should be exempted from this acidic critique.

Luther addressed this concern directly in one of the three great tracts he issued in 1520, the *Babylonian Captivity of the Church*.[30] After an amusing preface, with all sorts of jibes at his opponents, whom he dismisses as egged on by an emissary of Satan and motivated by the vain hope of achieving worldly glory through disputing with Luther, he gets down to business abruptly:

> First of all, one must to my mind deny that there are seven sacraments, and for now posit only three: baptism, penance, and the bread. And all these have been taken away from us into miserable captivity by the Roman curia, and the Church has been stripped of all her liberty (although, if I wish to speak as scripture does, I would have only one sacrament, and three sacramental signs, of which more in due course).[31]

This was far and away Luther's boldest challenge to Roman Catholicism, the first frontal assault on a doctrine probably familiar to almost all the Christians of Western Europe.[32] The seven sacraments were, in name at least, as familiar as the ten commandments: you might not be able to remember them all, but you knew how many there were.

The *Babylonian Captivity* is a loosely constructed text, abounding in digressions, but its ultimate achievement is to offer a fresh understanding and definition of the very nature of a sacrament. This objective is attained synthetically rather than analytically, and is not achieved until the closing pages, where Luther concludes that, properly speaking, the name "sacrament" should be restricted to "promises with signs attached to them."[33] But he has been tending to this conclusion from the point when, having attacked the Catholic practice of administering communion in one kind (i.e., under the form of bread, but not of wine) and the Catholic doctrine of transubstantiation, he starts to expound his own interpretation of the Mass as a "testament" or promise. In a manner more mystical or sacramental than strictly logical, Luther identifies the Mass with the promise of Christ, the promise of salvation, happily interchanging the words "promise" and "testament" (the latter, not the former, being the word chiefly used in the Gospels and Epistles). The "Mass is the promise of Christ," "the greatest promise of all," and consists first and foremost in the words of promise which Christ uttered as he gave his disciples the bread and wine. The concept of the promise ties the sacrament very firmly into Luther's theology of justification by faith alone. Justifying faith had already been defined as an unwavering assent to Christ's promise of forgiveness and salvation, envisaged as assent not merely to a general truth but to the specific realization of that promise in the life of the individual believer in question. Assent to this indubitable and indefeasible divine promise generated in the believer that certainty of grace which delivered the necessary peace of conscience. By presenting the Mass as embodying the promise of forgiveness of sins in the sacramental body and blood ("For this is my blood of the new testament, which is shed for many for the remission of sins," Matt 26:28), Luther made the sacrament a sort of visible expression of that promise.[34] As he would later argue, this sacramental embodiment of the promise rendered it easier for people to grasp the promise and thus to believe it.[35]

The focus on faith and promise (or testament) had the consequence of undermining the theoretical basis of the religious use of the Mass that had dominated Catholic culture for nearly a millennium, the celebration of the Mass for specific votive or intercessory purposes, chief among them the speeding of the passage of Christian souls through purgatory to heaven. The key to this lay in the essential individualism of Luther's new understanding of the Mass, itself the concomitant of the essential individualism of his entire theology. As Luther puts it in a crucial passage, the Mass, as a promise,

> can do no good to anyone, cannot be applied to anyone, done for anyone, or shared with anyone except the believer in person and alone, on account of their faith. For who can accept for someone else or apply to someone else the promise of God, which demands faith of each and every person?[36]

Much of the structure of late medieval Catholicism was founded on the celebration of Mass for the sake of goods to be attained in this world or the next. Monasteries, friaries, colleges, and confraternities were largely financed by endowments or donations given in return for the celebration of masses for the dead. If the Mass was, as Luther now emphasized, a testament (or promise) rather than a propitiatory sacrifice, then the basis of this entire ritual economy was swept away. These devastating conclusions were only sketched out in the *Babylonian Captivity*, in which Luther coined the damaging label "private mass" as an alternative to the traditional term "votive mass," but he would set out the argument more forcefully a couple of years later.[37]

Luther was well aware of the corrosive impact of his teaching. Would it not overturn monasticism and the institutions of intercession and charity? It would indeed, and that was the idea: such was the very machinery that had taken the church into its "Babylonian Captivity." The logic of the denial of sacrifice, however, once more led him into repudiation of a millennium of tradition, this time a tradition common hitherto (like monasticism) to all Christendom. Not that this bothered him in the slightest. No human tradition, however venerable, however universal, could stand in the face of the pure Word of God, or at least against Luther's interpretation of it. He rounded off his discussion of the Eucharist by relating faith in the testament to "peace of conscience." "For this is the testament of Christ, the unique remedy for past, present, and future sins. Only adhere to it with undoubting faith and you will believe that what the words of the testament state will be given gratuitously to you." Only this complete faith—certainty, though he does not use the word here—only this complete faith can confer "peace of conscience."[38]

Certainty, lack of doubt, is likewise the core of Luther's doctrine of baptism, the key to which, for him, lay in the "words of promise," which he identified as "Who believes and is baptized will be saved" (Mark 16:16). We Christians, he wrote, should "exert ourselves on this promise, with absolutely no doubt that we are saved after we have been baptized."[39] He attacks contemporary theologians as "wicked men who even assert that no one ought to be certain of the forgiveness of sins, nor of the grace of the sacraments," a position he dismissed as "impiety."[40] Certitude was required alike of the candidate for baptism and of the recipient of communion.[41] His emphasis on the act of faith, of course, posed a problem for a culture in which the baptism of infants was the norm, as by no ordinary use of speech could faith possibly be ascribed to those who had not yet learned even to speak, much less to reason or to believe. Though Luther had no inclination to turn his back on such a venerable tradition, infant baptism was neither explicitly commanded nor even explicitly mentioned in scripture. By the middle of the 1520s an important strand of Protestantism had emerged which rejected the practice on those grounds, but this was not something which Luther himself foresaw in 1520, though some of his opponents already realized that his theological principles could call infant baptism into question.[42]

The central theological message of the *Babylonian Captivity* was the definition of a sacrament as a divinely instituted sign attached to a "word of promise." But this rather subtle redefinition was at the time less eye-catching than two of the more substantial digressions which preceded the main development of Luther's argument. Traditionally minded theologians were more provoked by his blunt attack on the doctrine of transubstantiation. Even though Luther himself did not deny the real presence of the body and blood of Christ in the eucharistic elements, he did not accept the medieval Catholic doctrine that the bread and wine were transformed into that body and blood. For his insistence on accepting the "most plain and simple sense" of scripture wherever possible led him to insist that, since the scriptures referred to the eucharistic elements not only as "body" and "blood" but also as "bread" and "wine," all these names must be true.[43] Luther's ignorance of Wycliffe's teaching is indicated by his dismissal of the charge that his doctrine might be smeared as Wycliffite or Hussite. His doctrine was maybe not far from that of Hus, but his commitment to the real presence was far clearer than Wycliffe's. Wycliffe did not in fact believe that the body of Christ was in the consecrated host, though, like Luther, he insisted that the host was, just as it seemed, bread. But it is very difficult to read Wycliffe as upholding any kind of real presence of the sort maintained by both Lutherans and Catholics.[44] Transubstantiation itself was now falling foul of Luther's revolt against Thomas and Aristotle, as was the virtual mechanization of the Mass in late medieval culture as an instrument of intercession in this life and the next, along with the doctrine of eucharistic sacrifice that underpinned that process.

Luther's concerns extended from sacramental doctrine to sacramental practice, and the other headline issue in the *Babylonian Captivity* was his growing conviction that the customary way of distributing communion within Latin Christendom should be radically changed.[45] For several hundred years, it had been the custom that only the priest who was actually celebrating a mass would partake of the consecrated wine, the blood of Christ. If anyone else took communion, they would receive it only in the form of the consecrated bread, the body of Christ. The celebrant, however, would take communion "in both kinds." In the overwhelming majority of masses celebrated in Western European churches at that time, it should be added, the celebrant would be the only person taking communion at all. That custom would draw Luther's fire later, but his first target was communion "in one kind." Christ's words were straightforward: "When he says, 'Drink it, all of you,' he is not recommending but commanding."[46]

Luther had first raised questions about this traditional practice towards the end of 1519, during the prolonged aftermath of the Leipzig Disputation. In his *Sermon on the Blessed Sacrament* he made the modest suggestion that the church authorities would do well to allow the laity to partake of the chalice when they took communion.[47] The Hussite movement in Bohemia had made access to the chalice one of the main planks in its reform program, and it is possible that Eck's attempt to paint Luther into a corner at Leipzig as a sort of closet Hussite had backfired by causing Luther in his turn to look on the Hussite program with interest and even sympathy. Certainly those who took Eck's side saw this passing comment of Luther's as further evidence of his Hussite credentials. What is more interesting is how little impact this had on Luther's swelling body of supporters. Given the history of hostility between Germans and Czechs (or Bohemians) over religion, one might expect this mudslinging to have damaged his reputation among Germans. But it made little difference: Luther's books kept on selling. Notwithstanding the genuine modesty of his proposal, there was an outcry against his sermon, mainly emanating from Leipzig, where grumpy Duke George fulminated in vain against his cousin's far from tame theologian. As usual, Luther responded to opposition by raising the stakes. A second salvo on the subject urged the case for communion in both kinds more positively and ridiculed the diocesan machinery which had called upon him to withdraw his sermon from circulation.[48] In the *Babylonian Captivity* Luther returned to the subject yet again, developing a powerful case in favor of administering both the bread and the wine to the laity, and adding the incendiary charge that, in denying them the chalice, the pope and clergy had been tyrannizing over them too long.[49]

It was with the *Babylonian Captivity* that Luther graduated from reformer to revolutionary. His theology was already the intellectual groundwork for a new religion, but if his ideas had remained essentially speculative, like so much scholastic theology, it might have done little more than flutter the dovecotes of Europe's universities. But the seven sacraments were the pillars of Catholic society. Stripping them down to two (baptism and the Eucharist)—a position on which all the varieties of sixteenth-century Protestantism concurred—was radical enough, although marriage and ordination continued as social rituals, while confession gave way to spiritual direction (at least for the devout minority) and the disappearance of extreme unction made little difference to the deathbed scenes that remained as much part of Protestant as of Catholic culture. But the repudiation of the idea of the Mass as a sacrifice, the skepticism about transubstantiation, the doubts about religious vows, and the support for communion in both kinds pointed towards a very different future for Christianity.

Many who had sympathized with Luther thus far began to have doubts when faced with this manifesto. It was the *Babylonian Captivity* that shifted Henry VIII's attitude towards Luther from polite academic interest to the loftily dismissive polemics of his *Assertion of the Seven Sacraments*, with which he made his bid the following year to be recognized as the "Defender of the Faith." But many others were exhilarated by Luther's call for faith and his offer of profound peace of conscience rooted in the unshakable certainty of the Gospel's promise of salvation. Inspired by his lively and consoling reading of Saint Paul, they found themselves drawn after him down a hitherto unsuspected path.

That positive message of the Gospel was the theme of Luther's final major work of this astonishingly creative and productive year: the essay on *Christian Liberty*, which offered an escape from the "Babylonian Captivity" that he had earlier diagnosed. Like so many things he wrote, this essay was essentially the product of circumstances. When Karl von Miltitz visited the court of the Elector Frederick in late summer, he managed to bring about a meeting between Staupitz, Link, and Luther, in the hope of persuading Luther to write in conciliatory terms to the pope.[50] That letter, dated 6 September 1520, became the dedication or preface to the essay, though the arrival in Germany the following month of the papal bull against him almost made him change his mind.[51] But a meeting with the emollient Miltitz himself at Lichtenberg, at the Elector's Court, put the plan back on track, and the book was in print by December. Miltitz's hopes were not entirely fulfilled. Luther meant well, politely assuring the pope that his quarrel was nothing personal. But the effect of this mild overture was drowned out by what followed—a torrent of denunciation against Rome as worse than Babylon or Sodom, outdoing the infidelity of the Turks, with vigorous asseverations of Luther's determination to resist Rome as long as he had faith. Perhaps this reflected the arrival of the papal bull.

Luther justified his strong language by the examples of Christ, Saint Paul, and the prophets, loading the blame for controversy onto Prierias, Cajetan, and Eck, and casting himself in the role of the pope's candid friend.[52]

Despite this inauspicious start, the *Christian Liberty* itself was a stirring if unsystematic exposition of Luther's new theology, developing still further the dramatic contrast between the spiritual and the corporal, the visible and the invisible, which had flowed out of his sharp separation of Law and Gospel and into his idea of the essential invisibility of the true church. This contrast made sense of the eye-catching paradox which famously opened his argument:

> The Christian is the absolutely free lord of all, the subject of none.

> The Christian is the most obedient servant of all, the subject of all.[53]

Christian liberty was internal and spiritual, directed towards eternal life, while Christian service or obedience was external and physical, directed towards communal life in this world. What was important, in Luther's view, was to keep these two spheres (in effect, his "two kingdoms") appropriately separate. External and physical service in this world, the fruit of law, was of no consequence to the spiritual liberation from sin and growth in grace and love needful for life in the next. That all came from the gospel. Thus Luther's theory of "Law and Gospel" was for the first time properly expounded here, and justification by faith alone was set out more clearly than ever before, along with the priesthood of all believers.[54] "Christian liberty" was the freedom of the spirit, freedom in the faith of the Gospel, freedom from the external constraints imposed by the law, by that external church which he had already denounced as false precisely because of its externality and its visibility. It led towards not a "law of love"—for Luther would brook no law for the faithful—but a life of love, modelled on Christ and modelling Christ for others. Ceremonies are helpful scaffolding for beginning the construction of the devout life, but Luther felt they end up getting in the way. One should not be ruled and dominated by ceremonies and observances—hence some of Luther's wide popular appeal, for the late medieval Church was laden with ceremonial observance, and the contrast between this and the liberating teachings of Christ could be mercilessly exploited.

Luther's extension of this polemic from ceremonial observances to the observance of the moral law was far more contentious. Recapitulating his repudiation of Aristotelian ethics, Luther dismissed observance of the moral law as any kind of means towards salvation. His denigration of traditional external moral theology was rooted in his reading of Paul and appealed insistently to the words of Christ, but Luther was far happier with Paul's doctrine of salvation by grace than with his forthright moral rigorism, and far happier with Christ's image of the tree and the fruit than with his unmistakable emphasis on righteous moral agency. The rhetoric of the rejection of "good works" tended to focus on the repetitive and often almost mechanized ritual performance of late medieval Catholicism, and in doing so made common ground with the Erasmian critique of "superstition." This has led even acute readers and critics (such as the great Leopold von Ranke) to miss the full extent of Luther's radicalism in the field of ethics.[55] But the logic of Law and Gospel, the denial that there could be in this fallen life any genuinely "good" works, tended in a very different direction from Catholic moralism, whether it was that of Desiderius Erasmus or that of Thomas Aquinas. Luther always repudiated the accusation that he was an "antinomian," that is, someone who believed that justification by faith was so powerful that a believer need no longer bother even trying to observe the moral law. Yet it is revealing that he and his successors found it so often necessary to repudiate that accusation, and it is not evident that their reiterated denial was always an adequate inoculation against the virus, which has flared up more than once in the broad Protestant tradition. Luther's polemic against "good works," his insistence that every good work is in and of itself a sin, put him in a different theological world from both Erasmian humanism and scholastic Catholicism. Their theological world, he concludes in the peroration of *Christian Liberty*, in a fleeting reference to the doctrine that was gradually crystallizing in his mind, was the creation of Antichrist.[56]

Throughout the year 1520 Luther had been toying with the idea that the Antichrist might indeed have arrived at Rome, in accordance with the medieval legend or prophecy. He voiced his thoughts or fears about this a little more decisively in his private correspondence than in his public utterances, but even in public he had dropped hints. That Rome was the seat of the Antichrist became apparent to him a few months before the identification of that figure with the somewhat anodyne and implausible person of Leo X himself. Indeed, in the letter to Leo which served as the preface to *Christian Liberty*, Luther had gone out of his way to avoid making any sort of direct attack upon the person of the pope, even though his suspicions about what was happening in Rome were deepening.

What settled his mind on the subject was the papal condemnation of his teachings that was brought to Germany that autumn by Aleander and Eck. Luther finally got a sight of the bull in October 1520, shortly after Eck had promulgated it at nearby Leipzig, and the effect was, as he put it, liberating. "Now I am much more free, at last made certain that the pope is Antichrist."[57] Within weeks he had completed his initial response, *Against the Execrable Bull of Antichrist*, and he followed this up with a detailed defense of the 41 condemned propositions, *The Assertion of All the Articles* (of which both Latin and German versions were in print early in the new year).[58] There was no theological advance in these squibs, though the *Assertion*, with its prefaces on faith alone and scripture alone (doctrines which were not picked out for condemnation in the bull), offered the nearest thing to a handbook of Luther's teaching then available. It would be supplanted in this capacity before long by Philip Melanchthon's *Commonplaces* (1521), a handy compendium of Lutheran theology which rapidly attained the status of a textbook and commenced the process by which "Lutheranism" emerged as a dogmatic system.[59]

As he had threatened earlier in the year, Luther paid back the pope in kind. His books were being burned on papal instructions in many German cities, so the students of Wittenberg reciprocated. On the second Sunday of Advent, Luther preached against the "papal decretals," "foolish philosophy," and the "doctrine of works."[60] This spurred his students to direct action. As he reported to Spalatin, parodying the formal style of ecclesiastical pronouncements,

> In the year 1520, on the tenth of December, at 9:00 a.m., all of the Pope's books were burned at the East Gate of Wittenberg: the Decretum, the Decretals, the Sextus, the Clementines, and the Extravagantes, and the latest bull of Leo X; together with the *Summa Angelica*, Eck's *Chrysopassus* and other stuff of his and Emser's, as well as other things thrown on by various people.[61]

"So now," he added, gleefully, "the pyromaniac Papists can see that it is no great thing to burn books they can't confute. That will be news!" He was also pleased to see his supporters rallying in the face of the papal challenge. Ulrich von Hutten published a typically caustic edition of the text of Leo's bull, complete with sardonic annotations—which showed almost no interest in Luther's theology, focusing instead on sniping at Rome and the Romans.[62]

Yet another Italian Dominican and Thomist, Ambrosius Catharinus, joined the fray towards the end of 1520. His *Apologia* for the papacy was published in December, and reached Luther early in the new year, probably at about the same time as news of his formal excommunication at the hands of Pope Leo X, which was pronounced on 3 January 1521. Luther dashed off a brisk reply, the *Response to Ambrosius Catharinus*, published just before he departed for Worms. The deft ploy of the reply to Alveldt had now hardened into clear dogma: the church was, and had to be, invisible. He had dealt before with the "rock" and the "church" of Matthew 16:18, but now he spelled out his new understanding of the church:

> Therefore, just as the rock is without sin, invisible and spiritual, perceptible by faith alone, so too it is necessary that the church be without sin, *invisible* and spiritual, and perceptible by faith alone, as it is necessary that the foundation be one with the structure. For we say "I believe in the holy Catholic Church," and faith is a matter of "things unseen."[63]

As the church was invisible, Luther's doctrine of the church did not need to be elaborate, and discussion by theologians of his "ecclesiology" is therefore somewhat misplaced.[64]

Luther wasted little time on Catharinus's arguments. The chief importance of his *Response to Ambrosius Catharinus* was that it set before the public a full exposition of the doctrine of the papal Antichrist. The question was no longer whether the papacy existed, he maintained, but what the papacy was. And that was now clear: Antichrist.[65] The importance of this moment is impossible to exaggerate. It represents Luther's decisive public break with the established church. The suspicion of the true, hidden nature of the papacy had been dawning on him for some time, but he had hesitated to proclaim it boldly before the world. Once the pope had, by condemning his doctrine and excommunicating him, declared open war upon the "gospel," he had unmasked himself. Together with the ritual burning of the canon law and the papal bull, the equation of the papacy with Antichrist represented Luther's definitive response to the ecclesiastical sanctions directed against him.[66]

In justification of his stunning claim, Luther's *Response* embarked upon a lengthy exposition of Daniel 8:23–25, one of the scriptural passages traditionally bundled up with the medieval myth of Antichrist. The distinctive religious customs and devotional practices of the Catholic Church are turned here into the "twelve faces of Antichrist" and variously denounced as iniquity, blasphemy, and hypocrisy. Daniel does not himself label as "the Antichrist" the "king of fierce countenance" whose awful advent he here prophesies, but for Luther it was "obvious that this king was to be Antichrist, the adversary of Christ and his kingdom."[67] The realization of the Antichrist loomed large, then, in Luther's imagination. Characteristically, however, he brought a crucial innovation to the traditional story. While he was aware that he was tying together a catena of widely separate scriptural texts in time-honored fashion, he found a crucial error in the traditional conception of Antichrist. Earlier commentators, he claimed, had failed to understand that the Antichrist was not an individual person, as medieval legend had it, but a corporation:

> Hence they erroneously apply the name Antichrist, which Paul uses for the man of sin and the son of perdition, to a single person, when Paul means by it an entire body and chaos of wicked people and a whole line of rulers.[68]

The incorporation of Antichrist made his identification with the papacy a far more durable and potent theme, and gave

Luther's theory more traction than had been achieved by Wycliffe and Hus, who had also found Antichrist in the papacy. As long as the Antichrist was envisaged as an individual person, the identification was wide open to falsification. For the Antichrist was to be dispossessed of his usurped kingdom only by the second coming of Christ. Therefore any candidates for the role who happened to die before the end of the world would manifestly be disqualified, to the discredit and discomfiture of those who had cast them in that role. Incorporating the Antichrist over time as the institution of the papacy both eliminated the risk of falsification and made the papacy itself more demonic. It was a master stroke, the ingenious culmination of two or three years of relentless reflection on the defining institution of the medieval Catholic Church. That said, it would not do to exaggerate the coherence of Luther's thinking on this subject. There was at least as much raw emotion as rational inquiry at work here. As the years passed, the concept of the papal Antichrist became more and more deeply entrenched in his mind and in the Protestant tradition. In order for Lutheranism, and indeed for most forms of Protestantism, to be true, Roman Catholicism had to be not only false but a sort of ultimate antithesis of the truth. The apocalyptic urges in early modern Protestantism all tapped into this root, with the paradoxical result that the papacy became an integral component in Protestant belief systems. As Luther put it years later:

> I believe that the pope is the devil possessed and incarnate, because he is the Antichrist. For just as Christ is God incarnate, so the Antichrist is the Devil incarnate.[69]

8

WORMS AND
THE WARTBURG

Charles V (only 19 years old when elected Holy Roman Emperor) was not even present for his own election. He voted for himself by proxy and was elected *in absentia* on 28 June 1519, the same week that saw the commencement of the Leipzig Disputation. Charles, who had been brought up in the Netherlands, had at that point been in Spain for nearly two years, getting to know the kingdoms that he had inherited in 1516. There is no evidence that Luther's ideas had yet reached Spain, nor that Charles had so much as heard of the troublesome friar. He set out from La Coruña in May 1520, leaving his subjects seething with resentment at the idea of sharing their king with the Empire while paying handsomely in extra taxes for this dubious privilege. (A rebellion ensued.) He was in Flanders by June. The Holy Roman Empire was deficient in central control at the best of times, but a half-year interregnum followed by a year of absentee government gave Luther the best possible chance for survival and success. The self-important papal agent, Karl von Miltitz, hung around various princely courts, ineffectually seeking some progress or compromise on the Luther business. But nobody was paying much attention. Nor was Charles in any great hurry to get to Germany. He stayed in the Netherlands for several months, making two trips to visit Henry VIII, once at Canterbury and then again at Calais. A political alliance against the French was more important to him than a dissident friar in Saxony. By the time he reached

Aachen for his initial coronation as "King of the Romans" in October, it was almost two years since Maximilian had died. Luther himself acknowledged long afterwards how much the emperor's timely death and the consequent interregnum had assisted the cause of the "Gospel."[1]

The greatest test of Luther's career was his summons to appear before the emperor, princes, and prelates gathered at the Reichstag (or "Diet") in Worms. He had been guaranteed safe-conduct by Charles V, but he was understandably far from secure about it. According to some canon lawyers, there was no obligation to keep one's word with heretics. Just over a hundred years before, the Czech dissident Jan Hus had been summoned under a similar safe-conduct to appear not before the Reichstag but before a general council of the Church, convened at Constance. With his heresies condemned, yet refusing to recant, Hus was arrested notwithstanding Emperor Sigismund's guarantee, and was tried, convicted, and burned alive. The history of Hus was well known, and Luther frequently alluded to it. The heightened excitement of his letters in the approach to the Reichstag betrays a nervous intensity remarkable even by his standards. He was expecting nothing less than martyrdom, and his ultimate departure from Worms in one piece may have come not only as a surprise but even as a kind of disappointment, or at least an anticlimax.

Papal diplomacy was keen to engage with the new emperor over Luther. Girolamo Aleander and Johannes Eck had been appointed to convey the papal bulls against Luther to Germany and promulgate them.[2] They were in the Empire by September, when Eck secured the publication of the bull in Meissen, Merseburg, and Brandenburg. In October, Luther's books were confiscated in Ingolstadt. The bull targeted not only Luther but also his followers and supporters, aiders and abettors, and Eck had been given the discretion to decide who they were. He was prompt to use this power to settle a few scores. Willibald Pirckheimer, widely reckoned the author of *A Well-Beaten Eck*, was picked out by him, as were Lazarus Spengler, who was also thought to have written a satire against him, and Bernhard Adelmann, the outspokenly pro-Lutheran canon of Augsburg who had done all he could to besmirch Eck's reputation. It was no surprise to find the names of Carlstadt and Johannes Doltz (or Dolsch), prominent colleagues of Luther's at Wittenberg, but the almost unknown and essentially inoffensive humanist from Zwickau, Johannes Sylvius Egranus, had done no more than many other humanists to merit inclusion. Pirckheimer and Spengler protested noisily at first, but both sought reconciliation and absolution from Eck, as did Egranus. In Pirckheimer's case, this may have been easier because he found that his mild sympathy for Luther was being characteristically interpreted as enmity by its beneficiary. The fate of this early band is intriguingly diverse. Pirckheimer gradually distanced himself from the Reformer and died a Catholic. Spengler went on to be a key figure in the Nuremberg Reformation—in Luther's view, *the* key figure.[3] Adelmann and Doltz remained in the Lutheran camp while Carlstadt and Egranus, who also became committed Reformers, were both to fall out with Luther over matters of doctrine.

After spending a month or two more in the Netherlands, hearing worsening news of disorder and rebellion from Castile, and delaying his arrival in Germany on account of the epidemics raging that year, the new emperor, Charles V, finally arrived in Cologne on 30 October 1520, where he agreed with the electors to convene the Reichstag in January 1521 at Worms, a major city on the Rhine between Mannheim and Mainz.[4] Erasmus was still in the imperial entourage at this time, and wrote to Reuchlin from Cologne emphasizing that he would have preferred to be an onlooker rather than a participant in the drama. Nevertheless he lobbied busily among the luminaries of the imperial court, urging restraint and moderation on anyone who would listen in an attempt to avert the cataclysm which perhaps only he could foresee.[5]

The Reichstag at Worms opened formally on Sunday, 27 January 1521, with a Mass of the Holy Spirit in the cathedral, at which the emperor was flanked by five of the six other electors. No mention was made of Luther in the opening addresses, but in private conversations it was recognized that the Luther business was both important and challenging.[6] Aleander was under instructions to secure the reception and implementation of the excommunication of Luther and the condemnation of his 41 articles. Once ensconced at Worms, he realized the magnitude of the task, one for which he had little training. A scholar by experience and temperament, Aleander had the scholar's keen perception and stereotypical incapacity for decisive action. He had taught Greek at Venice and Paris before being recruited to the service of Érard de la Marck, Prince-Bishop of Liège, and in 1519 he had been an altogether appropriate if somewhat unexpected appointment as Vatican Librarian. It was presumably his scholarly credentials that led to his nomination as papal nuncio to the Court of Charles V for the purpose of implementing the bulls against Luther. Aleander was certainly well equipped to explain the theological issues, and was happy to do so whenever he was given the opportunity. If Luther had not changed all the rules of the game, this might have been qualification enough. But Aleander's reports from Worms show that it was not a scholar that was needed, but a negotiator: someone more like Cardinal Wolsey. Aleander was not even a cardinal, nor indeed was he empowered to negotiate. Worse still, he had no experience of politics at the papal curia, still at that time a crucible for the refining of political skills. His laments at the situation in Worms and through much of Germany make enlightening reading, but show that he had no plan beyond pressing on relentlessly with demands for the implementation of the bulls.

Aleander had reported at the end of February that the Saxon household of Elector Frederick was serving as a sort of command center for a Lutheran political campaign. They had brought a printing press with them (Worms had not had a press hitherto), and used it to churn out campaign materials. It was raining pamphlets, he said.[7] There was a large painting on display at the elector's lodgings, showing Luther in front with Ulrich von Hutten behind, carrying a box on which were shown two chalices and the slogan "The Ark of True Faith." Before them frisked Erasmus with a harp, like David, and bringing up the rear was Jan Hus. And there were images of Luther everywhere. He was depicted as a saintly friar, sometimes with a halo, or else with a dove—the symbol of the Holy Spirit—hovering above his head.[8] These pictures sold like hotcakes, so that Aleander could not even get hold of one to send to Rome. People venerated them like sacred icons, even kissing them, and the citizens of Worms put them up in the windows of their houses, in what seems to have been recorded history's first picture poster campaign. When Luther did get to Worms, a priest touched his gown three times and went his way rejoicing as though he had touched one of the holiest of relics. Aleander half expected to be hearing of miracles before long.[9]

Aleander reported in particular that the Roman position, which was that Luther should be condemned out of hand, lacked heavyweight support among the secular princes. The ecclesiastical electors (the archbishops of Cologne, Mainz, and Trier) were predictably favorable, but there was a warning sign in the fact that he and Eck had hardly managed to get the bulls against Luther published anywhere other than in ecclesiastical principalities (e.g., Mainz, Liège, and Cologne). Among the secular electors, Frederick of Saxony was of course dedicated to his protégé's cause, while the Count Palatine of the Rhine was silent and something of a cipher. Only Elector Joachim

I (Margrave of Brandenburg and brother of the embattled Archbishop Albrecht of Mainz) was a committed opponent of Luther. But while Aleander saw all this, he did almost nothing about it. He was in close and regular contact with the emperor and Jean Glapion, the French Observant Franciscan who had become the emperor's confessor the year before, but he left all the politics to them. Aleander certainly spoke French, but probably knew little or no German, which was a further impediment.

A still more serious problem was reported by Cuthbert Tunstall, the English envoy to Worms, who realized it as soon as he arrived: the emperor was besieged with conflicting advice from the various interest groups around him. The Spaniards wanted him to return to Spain to suppress the urban unrest convulsing Castile. His chancellor, Guillaume de Cröy, Lord of Chièvres, was at least hesitant about dealing with Luther, perhaps influenced by Duke Frederick, who had considerable influence with Charles in his own right. Charles's next closest adviser, bizarrely, thought the top priority was to head for Italy for his second coronation, the full imperial coronation that could only be conferred at the hands of the pope. But then, Mercurino Gattinara was an Italian.[10] What Tunstall did not mention, perhaps because Charles had spoken with Henry VIII in person on his way to the Netherlands from Spain, was the emperor's other interest in Italy—wresting the duchy of Milan from the grip of Francis I of France, who had seized it after his victory at Marignano in 1515. In circumstances as complicated as these, the papal nuncio had to get into the politicking himself and build up some kind of party around Elector Joachim. Aleander's perceptive correspondence gives no indications that he ever considered any kind of strategy for achieving his goals beyond a nagging insistence on obedience to the Holy See.

Months were spent at the start of the Reichstag deciding just how the Luther affair should be taken forward. Aleander simply wanted the papal bulls read, received, and implemented. But Luther's complaint that he was never given a proper opportunity to defend himself in public—a little disingenuous in the light of what had transpired at Leipzig, and of his astonishing presence in print—had fallen on receptive ears, and there was a groundswell of opinion in favor of allowing him to appear in person. From the Roman point of view, this was not part of the script. Aleander was reluctant to see him granted this sort of opportunity for publicity, but was compelled to give way. For all the risk it entailed, this was a triumph for Luther and his supporters. Aleander did his best to safeguard papal interests by securing undertakings that Luther would be given no scope for publicizing his cause, but instead would be allowed only to answer two questions: firstly, whether he had written the books attributed to him; and secondly, whether or not he was prepared to recant those propositions that had been singled out for condemnation. Such undertakings, however, were more easily given than enforced.

The imperial summons, issued on 6 March, was forwarded to Luther from Worms by Elector Frederick in a letter of 11 March. It probably found him at Wittenberg around the middle of the month.[11] His first instinct was to refuse to attend if all he could do was say yes or no.[12] The only recantation he was inclined to make concerned the papacy. Once, he wrote, he had regarded the pope as the Vicar of Christ. Now, however, he revoked that opinion, because the pope was the enemy of Christ and the devil's disciple![13] The gaps in Luther's surviving correspondence at this point may betray a real struggle with his conscience, perhaps a realization that he was prepared to risk martyrdom and that, whatever the outcome, he might be able to make something useful out of his appearance before the emperor if he obeyed. At any rate, by the end of the month he was making plans to set off in company with the imperial herald who had delivered the summons.[14] Travelling by way of

Leipzig, Erfurt, and Eisenach, he was cheered along his way, and en route he picked up a number of companions and sympathizers, such as Justus Jonas and Martin Bucer.

Luther arrived in Worms on Tuesday, 16 April. Aleander knew instantly, from the clamor that arose throughout the town.[15] The following morning the imperial marshal called on Luther at breakfast to summon him to appear before Charles and the princes later that day. Led in by the back door for fear of popular disturbances, he was warned not to speak until and unless spoken to. Joannes ab Eck (no relation of Dr. Johannes Eck), an imperial official, opened proceedings with the two agreed questions, asking whether the books circulating under his name were his, and whether he wished to retract anything in them. This was followed by a recitation of the titles of his books. In reply, Luther shrewdly seized the opportunity to make his case, rather than simply answer the questions. Acknowledging that they were his and that he stood by them, he nevertheless affirmed his readiness to retract anything that was contrary to scripture, as this would involve matters of faith and the welfare of souls. This specious concession—Luther never did concede that anything he taught had been shown to be contrary to scripture—enabled him at once to insinuate one of his fundamental principles, that scripture alone was sufficient to resolve theological issues. He did not wish to deny Christ before men, he went on, so he sought time for reflection. After some deliberation, the princes decided to allow him a day's grace, insisting that when he returned he would give his answer *viva voce*, not in writing. On his way back to his hostel, there were many voices crying out support and encouragement. According to Justus Jonas, many of these cries of support were scriptural quotations or allusions. This may or may not be true, but it certainly shows how Luther's disciples saw the situation. The overtones of comparison with Christ's appearances before Herod, Pontius Pilate, and the high priest are unmistakable in their retelling of these events. After the fate of Hus a hundred years before, and given the wide currency of the parallelism between the two men, there was a general sense that the whole affair would end in flames.

Next day (Thursday, 18 April) Luther appeared once more before the princes, and was once more asked whether he acknowledged his books and whether he would retract. There was widespread expectation that he would. After bidding for the goodwill of his audience by pleading his inexperience in worldly affairs as a humble friar, he launched into a speech, reiterating that the named writings were indeed his own, "For I frankly acknowledge nothing other than what is mine alone, and written by me, excluding interpretation by the efforts of anyone else." Then he launched into an apologia for his oeuvre, distinguishing different veins of work. Many of his writings, he claimed, were simple pious instruction and exhortation with which even his opponents could hardly find fault. To revoke these, he argued, would be to deny the known truth. Then came his polemical works against the pope and the papists, mention of which enabled him to slip in a brief aside against them as torturers of Christian consciences who plagued Christendom and leeched away the livelihood of Germany with dues and levies. To recant these would be to aid and abet tyranny. Finally he distinguished a third class of his writings, essentially private communications, in which, he conceded, he had expressed himself more bitterly than was becoming for a friar. But even these, it transpired, he could hardly recant for fear of lending support to tyranny. Allowing free rein to his histrionic tendencies, he likened himself to Christ before the high priest, and challenged his enemies, "If I have spoken evil, bear witness of the evil" (John 18:23). He would, he insisted, be the first to cast his books on the pyre if he could be convicted by the scriptures of any error. The discord that had arisen through his teaching was neither his fault nor his problem: as he had observed before, Christ had brought not peace but a sword. Warning the emperor against the temptation of putting facile compromise before the Word of God, he implored the assembly not to condemn him.

He was then asked again whether he recanted or not. His answer rings down across the centuries:

> Unless I am convinced by the evidence of scripture or by cogent reasoning—for I believe in neither Popes nor Councils alone, because it is plain that they have often erred and contradicted each other—I am overwhelmed by the scriptures I have myself quoted, and with my conscience thus taken captive by the Words of God, I neither can nor will revoke a thing, since it is neither safe nor sound to do anything against one's conscience. God help poor little me. Amen.[16]

The imperial spokesman countered by appealing to the authority of former ecclesiastical councils, most notably Constance, asking yet again if Luther would recant. Exchanges continued along these lines, with Luther repeating his contention that, while he was unable to gainsay scripture, church councils often contradicted each other. According to the Lutheran account, it was Charles's Spanish entourage that booed and hissed Luther off the stage. (Even the marginal note, "The man of God is laughed at," hinted at the parallel between Luther and Jesus.[17]) But it is likely that many listeners were unsettled by his outright repudiation of the authority of ecclesiastical councils, which for 1200 years had been the Church's standard means of resolving doctrinal uncertainties and defining orthodoxy. Over the next few days, the assembly debated how to respond to Luther's intransigence.

In the meantime, Luther himself was the cynosure of all eyes, receiving visits from all and sundry, many merely wanting a closer look at the notorious dissident.[18] The following week, Luther was summoned to appear at the lodgings of the Archbishop of Trier on Wednesday 24 April. He turned up, with his supporters and closest friends, to face a select delegation of the Reichstag which included the bishops of Augsburg and Brandenburg, the Marquis of Brandenburg, Duke George of Saxony, and Dr. Conrad Peutinger, among others. Their spokesman was one Dr. Hieronymus Vehe, secretary to the Margrave of Baden, who made one final attempt to persuade Luther to back down. He rebutted Luther's comments about councils from the previous week, and emphasized the ill effects of his books, which were fomenting sedition and disorder. Reminding him not only of the readiness of imperial clemency but also of the imminence of imperial justice, Vehe warned that if he did not relent, he would face outlawry. In reply, Luther repeated his strictures on the Council of Constance, emphasizing his view that in condemning Hus's principle that the Church was the corporation of the predestined, they had condemned the Word of God itself. His final position remained his strict adherence to that Word.

Later that day Luther also received a visit from Johannes Cochlaeus, a humanist scholar just a few years older than himself. Cochlaeus, like many humanists, had initially greeted Luther's reforming initiatives moderately favorably, but the *Babylonian Captivity* had given him second thoughts. Any lingering sympathy between the two men was dispelled by their encounter at Worms. Cochlaeus hoped to get Luther to debate with him before a panel of judges appointed by the emperor. *What Happened at Worms* reports Luther as responding with a handsome and polite demurral, while a lampoon published shortly afterwards had Cochlaeus running scared and refusing a challenge from Luther. Cochlaeus's account, which is highly circumstantial and probably reliable, tells a rather different story. Luther was indeed unwilling to enter into a debate (he later said he had been prepared to consider it, but was talked out of it by a friend), and when Cochlaeus invited him to suggest possible judges, he contemptuously proposed that they select a small boy.[19]

The final throws of the dice came on Thursday, when Peutinger and Vehe called a couple more times to urge Luther to submit either to the judgment of the Reichstag or at least to that of a future general council. They perhaps thought their last offer had elicited some sign of possible compromise from Luther, who was then summoned to one last meeting with the Archbishop of Trier. But when it became apparent that rumors of his submissiveness were somewhat exaggerated, the archbishop dismissed him. Soon afterwards, he received word from the emperor that he had thirty days to get himself to a place of safety. Luther therefore left Worms unscathed and unhindered—much to many people's surprise—on 26 April. A week later, on his way home, he disappeared off the face of the earth. Rumor ran riot. He had been murdered. He had been kidnapped. He had been snatched by papal agents. It was many weeks before the truth leaked out, namely that he had been seized in a pre-planned, phony raid and whisked away into hiding. His refuge, which remained a well-kept secret, was the Wartburg, a medieval hilltop fortress near Eisenach. It would be Luther's home for the best part of a year, until March 1522.

The most remarkable outcome of the Reichstag at Worms was not the famous edict of outlawry against Luther, which made its way onto the statute book over the few weeks following his departure. The astonishing thing was the way that Luther and his followers seized control of the news, getting their account of his appearances into print within days, and adroitly putting together a picture of injured innocence which was unsubtly modelled on the story of Christ's passion. The Edict of Worms was intended to mark the beginning of the end for Luther. But the historical memory of that assembly has been fixed indelibly by its Lutheran representation, *What Happened at Worms*, which hit the presses instantly, taking the imperial and Catholic authorities entirely by surprise. Its impact was enhanced by a superb frontispiece depicting Luther the friar, haloed and cleft-chinned, with a faraway look in his eyes, holding an open bible while the Holy Spirit descended upon him from on high in the form of a dove. Never before had a public event of this kind, in effect a show trial, been so promptly reimagined by its victim for public consumption. Even the Christian account of the passion of Jesus took a generation to establish itself.

The parallel with Jesus, implicit in *What Happened at Worms*, was made painstakingly explicit in the *Passion of Martin Luther according to Marcellus* published soon afterwards, with a fine title page showing the wronged friar's face, chin tilted defiantly upwards, saintly, *contra mundum*. Serious parodies of this kind were by no means original. The ancient lives of the saints, after all, had often modelled their narratives on the events of the Gospels, and medieval parallels can also be found. But the casting as Christ of a hero who was still alive, in a widely reprinted pamphlet that usually included a portrait, gave the *Passion of Martin Luther* far greater importance than its predecessors in the genre.[20] As R. W. Scribner argued many years ago, one of the more curious features of the public image of Martin Luther was the way in which so many of the accoutrements of the traditional cult of the saints became attached to his person, from the haloes on some of the printed portraits to the stories of miracles that began to cluster around his very name. As a humble preaching friar of the Order of Hermits of Saint Augustine, he fulfilled medieval expectations of the holy man—just like recent Italian avatars such as the Observant Franciscan Bernardino of Siena or the Dominican firebrand Girolamo Savonarola. With astrological evolutions heading towards a rarely witnessed concatenation of planetary conjunctions in 1524, those expectations were entangled with millenarian hopes and anticipations of sublunary upheavals. What people thought about Luther was at least as important as what Luther thought about in the heady atmosphere of the early 1520s.[21]

The parallel between Luther and Christ was sharpened still further by the runaway success of another pamphlet launched at that time, the *Passion of Christ and Antichrist*, an early exercise in graphic literature which presented German readers with a stark and shrewdly drawn contrast between Christ and the pope—or the Antichrist, as Luther and his followers now insisted on calling him. A Wittenberg production, with words by Melanchthon and pictures by Lucas Cranach, it was crude and biting irony in the vein of the master.[22] Luther loved it. The implicit logic was clear. If the pope was Antichrist, then Luther was Christ, or at least Christ-like. Variations on the theme ran through Protestant culture across Europe for a century or more.

The theological identification of the pope as Antichrist that Luther had worked out in the context of his own excommunication was the seed of a rapidly growing obsession with Satan and his indefatigable machinations against the "Gospel." Medieval and early modern Christians took the devil much more seriously than their modern successors, and there was nothing strange in Luther's concern to renounce the devil and all his works. Late medieval art often depicts the gates of hell as the mouth of a gargantuan demon, sucking down sinners into endless torment. But the devils and demons were not often named by theologians and writers of that era. Luther himself, in his early commentary on the Psalms, frequently found it necessary to discuss the devil, but almost invariably as "diabolus." Heiko Oberman familiarized us with the general importance of the devil in Luther's thought and psychology.[23] But from about the middle of 1521, Luther's demonology underwent a sharp change. Rather than the more abstract *diabolus* (devil), it was now the far more personal figure of Satan that loomed large in his imagination. This is not to claim that "Satan" never figures in Luther's prose before this time: it does, but only rarely, and mostly in quotations or echoes of specific scriptural texts. And it is important to note that this shift is visible in his Latin writings, but not in his German, in which "Teufel" remained the standard description. In his Latin the shift is striking. As late as the *Appeal to the Christian Nobility*, in the summer of 1520, "Satan" appears only twice, while the term "devil" predominates. Five years later, in *The Enslaved Will*, the ratio is completely reversed.[24] The growing prominence of Satan in Luther's Latin reflected his theological development as well as his psychological response to the tensions and threats of his times. After his flight from Worms, Luther spent most of the next twelve months at the Wartburg fortress, and in later years he looked back on that period as one of particularly direct confrontation with Satan, "who often vexed me with his illusions" there.[25] But it was also during this time that he embarked on his translation of the New Testament, a group of documents that were themselves mostly products of an extremely tense and threatening time, and which use the Hebrew name Satan fairly often. Luther's growing concern with him should therefore be seen as an integral part of his "evangelical" agenda.

The first fruits of Luther's confinement at the Wartburg were seen in a pamphlet against the Louvain theologian Jacobus Latomus. Latomus had been working since the middle of 1520 on a defense of the condemnation of Luther promulgated by his own university, but it was May 1521 before it appeared in print. Luther had a copy by the end of the month, and had finished his own rebuttal by the end of the next. After a now routine disavowal of personal abuse, followed by an equally routine dismissal of his opponent as a model of "disdain, arrogance, pride, malice, wickedness, impudence, superciliousness, ignorance, and stupidity," Luther turned his *Confutation of Latomus's*

Reason almost accidentally into the most substantial exposition thus far of his theological or scriptural method.[26] The *Confutation* focused on just two of the issues that Latomus had raised: Luther's paradoxical contention that every good work was a sin; and his insistence, in defiance of the overwhelming majority of previous theologians, that baptism did not take away all sin from the baptized. Each of these claims rested especially heavily on a single scriptural text, and the discussion turned principally on the interpretation of these texts. Luther's engagement with Latomus therefore had the side-effect of requiring him to explain the basis on which he approached the task of scriptural interpretation, and it is in this that the particular interest of the *Confutation* lies.

The idea that "every good work is a sin" dated back to his defense of the *Ninety-Five Theses* in 1518, and had been picked up not only by the Louvain theologians in their condemnation but also at Rome in the papal bull. Defending it against Latomus, Luther still, just as in 1518, rested primarily on one text, Ecclesiastes 7:21, "For there is no just man on earth who does good and sins not." His interpretation here was counterintuitive. The "natural" or "commonsense" reading of these words is as a fairly anodyne observation to the effect that there is no one on earth, no matter how good, who only does good things and never does bad things. To put it another way, it divides human actions into the good and the bad, and posits that even a good life will not result exclusively in good actions, but will also include some bad ones. This rather laborious statement of the obvious is necessary here precisely because Luther's interpretation of the text is so startling. In his reading, the real meaning of this truism is a profound paradox: that there is no human action, however good, which is not at one and the same time a sin; that no human being, however good, is capable of performing an action, not even a good action, which is not in some degree simultaneously a sin. This amounts to a variation on that principle of Luther's commonly summed up in the phrase *simul iustus et peccator*, "at once just and a sinner." Understandably, those who were unconvinced by his new theology saw his reading of Ecclesiastes 7:21 as absurd. That a good work should be at the same time a sin was, for them, meaningless, a contradiction in terms, while the attempt to derive this from that text was merely willful. Latomus's response is typical of Catholic reactions. It was obvious to him what the text meant, and he could scarcely believe that Luther was serious. He drew parallels between this and other scriptural texts which dilated upon the mixed fruits of a human life, and thought that would be enough to show his opponent the error of his ways. In addition, he cited various early Christian Fathers to emphasize the traditional view that sins and good works were mutually exclusive.[27]

As a rhetorical flourish, Luther's description of good works as sins was intriguing and even appealing, a sharp way to remind listeners of the inevitable imperfections of the Christian's life in a fallen world and fallen flesh. Taken out of context and reduced to a principle, however, a teasing paradox was transmuted into a destabilizing contradiction in terms. After all, as his opponents tirelessly argued, if even the best of good works were sins, why bother trying to avoid sinning? Luther had no intention of pursuing his ideas down the blind alley of antinomianism, but his refusal to give an inch led him to turn paradox into axiom. This led him into exegesis of the kind he imposed upon Ecclesiastes 7:21, as tortuous as anything he or Erasmus ever complained of in the most recondite of scholastic logic-choppers. Oscillating as ever between logical literalism and rhetorical rodomontade, Luther argued himself into an unnecessary corner in his determination to concede nothing to those who took issue with him. It was just one small routine in a larger process by which spiritual and scriptural ideas which might in other hands have become the subject for dialogue and discussion instead metastasized into inflexible dogmatic axiom.

Luther relied almost as heavily on a second text in making his case, Isaiah 64:6, "We have all become like one unclean, and all our righteousness like a menstrual pad." Once more, he had no time for any figurative interpretation of this transparently figurative utterance. Latomus invoked the authority of Jerome to mitigate the rigor of Luther's reading, urging that Isaiah was acting as a spokesman for the Jewish people, rather than making an individual confession.[28] But Luther had tremendous fun "slippery sloping" this response. "If we are allowed to mess about with figures of speech in this way, at our mere good pleasure, without giving any reason, what is to stop everything taking on a new meaning?" And he happily descanted on this with some comical rereadings of well-known texts: "Blessed are all those who trust in Him—that is, some of them."[29]

> In no writing, least of all the divine scripture, is it permissible to seek out figures of speech at one's own mere good pleasure. Rather, they should be avoided and one should strive after the pure, simple, and primary meaning of the words, until the context itself or evident absurdity requires a figure of speech to be admitted.[30]

While Luther was grappling with his enemies in spirit in the Wartburg, things were happening back in Wittenberg. Without the overpowering presence of Luther to stifle him, Andreas Carlstadt could finally come into his own. Luther later looked back on his colleague as something of a copycat.[31] Coattailing on Luther's charisma, Carlstadt was now free to develop his own ideas in new directions. Luther had cast doubt on monastic vows and clerical celibacy in the *Appeal to the Christian Nobility*, and his destabilization of customary certainties and traditional taboos had already led a few priests, by summer 1521, to seek to regularize their situation in life by taking wives (presumably, in many cases, women with whom they were already in *de facto* long-term relationships). Controversy arose over these cases, especially when the Archbishop of Mainz sought to enforce canon law against the priests involved. This led Carlstadt to reflect on the question of clerical celibacy which, in theory at least, prevailed throughout Latin Christendom. In the churches of Eastern Europe and the Middle East, married men could become priests, though monks were forbidden to marry, and in general marriage was not permitted for those already ordained priests (not even for widowed priests). But in the churches under the jurisdiction of Rome, marriage was deemed incompatible with the priesthood. It was certainly not possible to ground such a prohibition on scripture alone: the priests of the Old Testament had been permitted to marry, and while the marital status of the apostles in the New Testament was a matter for debate, it was evident that marriage and the priesthood had been neither always nor everywhere incompatible.

Carlstadt worked all this out, and published his *Axioms on Celibacy, Monasticism, and Widowhood* at Wittenberg in 1521.[32] He rushed at once to the straightforward conclusion that the church's laws on celibacy and clerical marriage were groundless and godless. (He put this into practice in January 1522 when, in his mid-thirties, he married a teenage girl.) Carlstadt's *Axioms* were sent to Luther, who was certainly not unaffected by it. Before he had read it, he saw a big difference between the voluntary celibacy to which monks and friars freely vowed themselves and the celibacy which was required of any man who wished to be ordained a priest. Celibacy was of the essence of monasticism, but not of priesthood. However, after perusing Carlstadt's arguments, Luther found himself tending against the whole idea of vows and celibacy, though he had by no means made up his mind. In isolation at the Wartburg, he reflected on this question through the autumn. His first response was a brief paper, *Theses about Vows*, which he sent to Melanchthon on 1 August 1521, a long list of theses for disputation, which Melanchthon promptly sent to the printer, perhaps ahead of an actual disputation on the subject.[33] A few weeks later he returned to the subject in a further letter to Melanchthon, in which he recalled his father's remark on his own decision to join a religious order: "Let's hope this is not some Satanic delusion!" This was apparently the most memorable thing his father ever said to him, judging by the number of times he mentioned it. He brought it up again in the dedication to his father which prefaced his definitive views on the subject, his *Judgment on Monastic Vows*, completed in November and printed at Wittenberg that winter, with Luther making a brief and unannounced visit to the town to superintend production.[34]

Until impelled by Carlstadt's initiative, Luther had not reflected seriously on the implications of his theology for the "religious life." As soon as he did so, the incompatibility of the voluntary piety of monasticism with his notion of justification by faith alone became apparent to him. But it is curious that he had not drawn the inference before. For with vows, as with everything else, it all came down to certainty of salvation and peace of conscience. Amidst all the monastic authors, Luther wondered whether there was even one who placed any confidence in the value of their own vows: "Give me one who dares to assert that his vow is pleasing and welcome to God." As he saw it, for them to do so would be in their terms "presumption," for they taught that certainty of grace was, ordinarily speaking, impossible to attain.[35] Without the confidence that what one was doing was pleasing to God, however, one simply should not act. It was a universal principle of late medieval moral theology that to act against one's conscience was sin. Luther raised the stakes. Peace of conscience was, for him, the fruit of certainty of grace. Any action which did not result in peace of conscience, any action which was not performed in peace of conscience, was therefore done contrary to conscience and was, by definition, sin:

> That conscience which either does not believe or—which is the same thing—doubts that it and its deeds are pleasing to God, thereby sins at once against itself and faith, doing that which it does not believe is pleasing.[36]

The monastic vow, then, from the mere fact that monks could not be certain that it was pleasing to God, was most definitely displeasing to God. All that can give Christians the certainty that Luther requires is faith in Christ, as he conceives it.

> This is the faith that scripture teaches. No one who has this faith can act against their conscience, for they cannot doubt that they are pleasing to God, because Christ has been given to them. Anyone who does not have this faith cannot but always act against their conscience, because they cannot but doubt whether they are pleasing to God.[37]

Luther put forward numerous other arguments in what was a substantial treatise, concluding that

> Our consciences are fortified by that which we have proved from the evident and certain testimony of scripture, namely that monastic vows are of their nature contrary to the Word of God, the Gospel, faith, Christian liberty, and the commandments—not to mention common sense and self-contradiction.[38]

But the rock on which he founded his judgment was certainty of conscience. Looking back, he saw his role in the downfall of monasticism as providential. When five refugee nuns from

Fribourg turned up at Wittenberg in 1532, he jokingly remarked that God, "who blew away monasticism by means of me," was rewarding him for the work by sending him tithes of it.[39] Quite when Luther had abandoned the common elements of religious life as an Austin Friar is not clear. It may be that right up until his departure for Worms he continued to participate in the communal prayer of his house. But there was no such possibility at the Wartburg, where he was able to reflect on monasticism and perhaps also to grow away from it in the relative freedom of that captivity. It was still to be several years before Luther abandoned the last vestiges of his life as a friar. His tonsure had gone by 1523, having doubtless been abandoned for reasons of disguise during his stay at the Wartburg, and it is not likely that he was any longer trying to keep up with his canonical hours or his fasts. But on his return to Wittenberg he still resided in the friary and wore his habit.[40] Only with his marriage in 1525 were the ties finally cut. All outward signs of his former state of life were renounced, though he and his growing family continued to dwell in the former friary, which a grateful prince eventually made over to him formally in 1532.

The autumn of 1521 also saw Luther reach his final judgment on what he called "the private mass," which is to say the celebration of masses for votive purposes, such as for the relief of souls in purgatory. Luther's new theology was as devastating in its implications for votive masses as it was for the votive life. His conception of the rite of the Eucharist as a "testament" had been developed in 1519–20, initially, in a minor way, in his 1519 commentary on Galatians.[41] It was expounded at some length in a sermon preached on Easter Day (8 April) 1520, in which Luther first aired his view that Christ had only instituted two rituals for Christians—baptism and the Eucharist.[42] Doubtless some of that sermon found its way into the *Babylonian Captivity*, which set out the doctrine of eucharistic testament in some detail. In the *Abrogation of the Private Mass*,

Luther was picking up an interpretation of the eucharistic ritual briefly adumbrated in Galatians and especially Hebrews, in which the concept of the last will and testament was exploited to identify Christ as the testator and eternal life as his bequest to his heirs, the faithful.[43]

The imagery of the Eucharist as a reading of Christ's "testament" to his legatees was especially appealing in a culture in which the last will and testament was such a powerful social symbol and legal instrument. Given Luther's growing attachment to the theory of univocal meaning for scriptural keywords, it is not surprising that his adoption of this unconventional (though scripturally based) "testamentary" interpretation of the Eucharist led him to downplay the "sacrificial" interpretation which prevailed in patristic and medieval theology. The Greek διαθηκη served to render the concept of a pact, treaty, or covenant as well as that of a testament, and the Gospel narratives of the Last Supper clearly presented the eucharistic action in the light of the Passover sacrifice that commemorated the covenant God had made with Moses and the Israelites. Luther, of course, retained a conception of Christ's death on the cross as a sacrifice. But for him the testamentary interpretation of the eucharistic ritual excluded the traditional conception of that liturgy as itself a "sacrifice." It was the ancient doctrine of eucharistic sacrifice which underlay the whole apparatus of votive masses and religious foundations seen throughout Catholic Europe, in which the celebration of the Eucharist was a placatory or intercessory ritual directed towards securing divine assistance for this or that temporal or spiritual goal. This practice, seen preeminently in the celebration of masses for the sake of the souls of the faithful dead, had been a part of Latin Christianity for over a thousand years, and was one of the biggest drivers of the tide of endowment and benefaction which had enriched the Western Church over that period via complex institutional structures ranging from monasteries through confraternities and chantries to "obits" (temporary foundations supporting masses for a limited time) and individual masses. By challenging the conception of the Mass as itself a sacrifice, Luther struck at the very root of this liturgical economy, and laid down a foundation for the social and political processes of "the Protestant Reformation," which entailed widespread expropriation of the church. In the wake of his condemnation at Worms, he started to draw practical conclusions from his theoretical premises, and hence to call for thoroughgoing reform.

The theological value to Luther of the conception of the Eucharist as testament was that it enabled him to connect the Eucharist still more effectively with his core doctrine of justification by faith alone, and thus to interpret the sacrament in terms of the certainty that lay at the heart of his religious vision. The language of testament was far more unilateral than that of covenant, with its implications of agreement between two parties, and therefore sat much better with his conception of the sheer gratuitousness of salvation. The Christian, as a legatee of the testament, merely had to believe that Christ spoke the truth in making his bequest of the forgiveness of sins. You could accept the bequest or reject it—but you could not deserve it. Simple and scriptural, his innovative account of the Eucharist was very potent.

Even in "abrogating the private mass," Luther centered his theology on certainty. Certainty of salvation and the certitude of scripture, powerful coordinating principles in his theology, are here explicitly set in their mutually corroborating relationship:

Conscience will damn you any which way, unless it is altogether established on the certain, mighty, and salvific Word of God, that is, unless it is built upon rock. That is the infallible certitude we seek.[44]

The purpose of Christ's legacy in the eucharistic testament was to leave his followers a tangible guarantee of his promise, the substance of which was the forgiveness of sins.

> So we cling to the Divine Majesty, which is forever firmly bound to us through the priceless token bestowed upon us, expecting with the utmost certainty, with the sweetest and most tranquil confidence, that he will deliver what he has promised.[45]

The anxious multiplication of sacrifices by indefatigable priests could not deliver this ultimate certainty. The sacrificing priests of medieval tradition were themselves lost souls and blind guides, "offering sacrifice always and everywhere, yet never attaining certainty, because, having let go of the promise of the infallible God, they are borne hither and yon by their sacrifices and uncertain works."[46] Luther's conscience clung desperately to a certainty that he felt was under perpetual and imminent threat—from papists and fanatics, from the slippery Erasmus, from those who placed, respectively, institutional church authority, personal divine inspiration, or human scholarly common sense between the naked text and the open mind. To inculcate certainty is to insinuate doubt.

9

THE BEGINNING AND
END OF REFORMATION

What brought Luther back to Wittenberg was Satan. Over the previous few years, Luther had become ever more aware of the insidious activity of Satan in human affairs. He had first sniffed him out at Rome, in his earthly vicar, Antichrist, the pope. But Satan had also been busy among the pope's allies and supporters: Cajetan, Eck, Emser, Catharinus, and the rest. *Exsurge Domine* and the Edict of Worms had brought him out into the open, and from May 1521 Luther saw him everywhere. In summer that year Melanchthon wrote with the happy news that Nicholas von Amsdorf was penning a reply to the indefatigable Hieronymus Emser. Emser, Luther now realized, was "full of Satan," and it was an evil spirit that spoke through him. "If I had known before," he added, "that he was possessed by a demon, I would have harassed that demon good and proper."[1] Satan was also present with Luther at the Wartburg, though not in the same way as with Emser. Emser was his tool, Luther his target. "I have withstood a thousand Satans in this restful isolation," he wrote, "It is so much easier to fight against an incarnate devil—that is, against human beings—than against spirits of idleness in heavenly things."[2]

Although it took Luther some time to realize it, Satan was also busy back at Wittenberg. During Luther's prolonged absence, other, hotter heads were beginning to think through some of the implications of the Word, and were concluding that it needed to be put into action. At first this was very much in line with Luther's thinking. Even as Luther was working out his views on the Mass and on religious vows, two of his most devoted followers back in Wittenberg, Andreas Carlstadt and Gabriel Zwilling, were breaking new ground and aspiring to turn theory into practice. With Luther away, Carlstadt was the dominant figure in the university, and Zwilling the most vocal friar in the Augustinian house. Carlstadt was puzzling over whether or not to proceed straightaway to distributing communion at mass "in both kinds," while Zwilling was denouncing the eremitical life to such effect that the house was emptying. Over a turbulent winter, Carlstadt emerged as the spokesman for change, and on Christmas Day, as he had promised, he offered both the bread and the cup to those attending mass, which he celebrated in German.[3] This bold gesture catapulted him into still greater prominence in the town, which he dominated with his preaching. His new found confidence was expressed most sensationally in his decision to take a wife. His marriage was celebrated on 19 January. Turning his attention to the question of religious images, he concluded that their use breached the ten commandments, and some episodes of iconoclasm ensued in early February. But Melanchthon was not entirely happy with the direction of Carlstadt's reform, while the brief visit to the town of the so-called "Zwickau Prophets" caused further ferment. These prophets were a little group of men from nearby Zwickau who, carried away on swelling tides of religious enthusiasm, felt that they were directly inspired by the Holy Spirit. Even the usually solid schoolmasterly temperament of Melanchthon was sufficiently upset to wonder whether there might not be something in their claims. With the town council nervous over direct action from the mob, and the elector looking on in dismay at divisions within both town and gown, the place was at sixes and sevens.

The situation had worsened dramatically since Luther had made his brief, secret visit to Wittenberg in early December to oversee the printing of his books on vows and the Mass. Defying the express wishes of the elector, he now decided to return to Wittenberg and wrest back control. He was evidently somewhat nervous about this audacity, and wrote explaining himself to Frederick both en route and on arrival.[4] He returned just after Ash Wednesday, and on the first Sunday of Lent (9 March) he commenced a series of sermons, known as the "Invocavit Sermons," which promised to address the issue of the moment, the place of religious images in worship, which had been called into doubt by Carlstadt's pamphlet *On the Removal of Images*, printed about a month earlier. But the chief subject of Luther's preaching was himself and his own authority, which he spent the first three sermons emphasizing at the expense of his rivals. It was Luther himself, he assured his listeners, whom God had sent to them:

> Therefore, dearest brethren, follow me. I have never led you astray. I was even the first whom God set to this task. . . . I was even the one to whom God first revealed that this his Word should be preached to you.[5]

His now familiar slogans, "Law and Gospel" and "Christian liberty," were deployed to discredit the Church Ordinance which the town council had issued at Carlstadt's instigation in January. Law and coercion had no place in the domain of faith. All was to proceed by preaching and example rather than by decree. Christian liberty was to respect tender consciences. By the end of March, Luther was able to sum up his impact pithily: "I have offended Carlstadt because I struck down his ordinances, even though I did not condemn his teachings." The problem with Carlstadt was that he had made people think that merely doing things, such as drinking the eucharistic cup and smashing religious images, made them holy.[6] Luther's slogan of Christian liberty had been employed by Carlstadt and others to justify direct action, such as overt breaches of the Lenten fast.[7] (There was something almost sacramental about the breakfasting, that is, the fast-breaking, of the early Reformation.) Luther, though, turned the slogan back upon them, denouncing such "anti-works" of dissociation from Catholic tradition for representing a "works righteousness" every bit as bad as popery itself.

His discourse oscillated, then, between the invocation of scripture and the invocation of his own authority as, in effect, a chosen vessel of God, an apostle. It was as an apostle, rather than a prophet, that Luther presented himself to the world. Perhaps because of the pretensions of the men from Zwickau, he implicitly disavowed prophetic status. He made this explicit ten years later: "I am no prophet, because God did not give me the gift of prophecy. But I am a preacher."[8] However, it had always been at least as much about Luther as about the Bible, and that now became clear. The virtual "cult" of Martin Luther that Aleander had half recognized at Worms was never properly articulated by scholars until the late R. W. Scribner set it out in his incomparable article, "Incombustible Luther." But Luther himself acknowledged or even asserted his own apostolic status in his addresses to the people of Wittenberg that spring, just as he became increasingly willing to countenance and recirculate the burgeoning stories of miracles that God had worked in his name or honor. The fight against his rivals was dirtier and harder because they fought with the same weapon. It had been relatively easy to deploy the authority of the bare Word of God against Catholics, for they avowedly appealed to the authority of the Church. What they extolled as a divinely founded and guaranteed institution, he denounced as thoroughly human and therefore necessarily fallible. The choice was stark. But when both sides avowed their dependence on the bare Word of God, the choice became trickier, and the situation itself became intrinsically problematic. Either such disagreement was a vindication of the predictions of their Catholic opponents, who had foreseen the rather obvious risks and likely results of the "scripture principle," or else there would be a victory for whoever it was that could shout down, bear down, or simply put down their rivals. Rhetoric and politics decided these outcomes. Carlstadt's scriptural case for his iconoclastic program, by any objective standards, was quite as plausible as Luther's rebuttal. But Luther had both the court connections (through Spalatin) and the pulpit presence to ensure his triumph. When Luther was in town, Carlstadt had always stood in his shadow. Recalling Eck's judgment on the latter's mediocre and stilted performance at Leipzig, one is inclined to doubt that he could compete with his leader in popular preaching.

Although they made little serious impact in Wittenberg, from which they soon moved on, the Zwickau Prophets intensified still further Luther's deepening obsession with Satanic powers. Confronted with a sort of farcical yet awful parody of his own defiant theological originality, Luther responded— rather as his own opponents had done—by seeing in these impertinent challengers the hand and mind of Satan himself. "How Satan rages," he commented habitually that year, insisting on his own determination to strike back hard, provoking Satan still further, with a view to precipitating the final crisis of salvation history, the second coming of Christ. When Henry VIII's famous attack on his theology was finally brought to his attention in May, he saw not only human but Satanic agency behind the royal intervention.

> For Satan busies himself with this, in order to distract us from scripture by means of villainous Henries and sacrilegious Thomists.[9]

Satan recurs obsessively in his letters, and he saw in every obstacle or setback the hidden hand of his foe. One might conceive of such talk as jokey, but it was deadly serious. There is a quickening apocalyptic beat to Luther's writing in 1522. He did not indulge in futile efforts to calculate the date of the second coming (a game that more imaginative reformers would start to play in the 1530s), but he did not think it could be long delayed. (Towards the end of his life, he did not see how the world could last much more than another century.[10]) And his ability to set his own theological work into cosmic perspective did nothing to undermine his confidence in the importance of that work and of his own role in it. This sense of the imminent end may account for the uncharacteristically mild attitude he adopted towards Jews for a few years in the early 1520s. In a short treatise of 1523 entitled *Jesus Christ was a Jew by Birth*, he urged Christians to treat Jews with moderation and kindness. He explained that he now understood why the Jews had resisted Christianity in recent centuries, for he would hardly have adopted Christianity himself given the travesty that it had become under the papacy. But now that the gospel was once more being proclaimed, he was confident that Jews would flock to the truth. His confidence reflected what were then traditional Christian expectations about the conversion of the Jews during the closing stages of salvation history. In the event, his expectations were disappointed. With a few exceptions, Jews remained unimpressed with the new form of Christianity. By the 1540s, despite his continuing sense of the imminence of the end, Luther had given up on the Jews, and unleashed upon them a voluminous and hate-ridden polemic, *The Jews and Their Lies.*[11]

Luther's anxieties in the early 1520s were fuelled by an apparently darkening political situation. Catholic authorities were beginning to get themselves organized against the new challenges, with the result that the preachers they were labelling "Lutheran" now became liable to arrest, trial, and potentially execution—in the grotesquely spectacular form of burning alive, which at that time used to draw together crowds of sightseers. The case of Jakob Probst, the prior of the Augustinian Friary at Antwerp, was close to Luther's heart. Probst was a classic example of how Luther's influence spread along the networks of his own religious order. An established preacher in Antwerp, he started to disseminate evangelical ideas in his sermons there, and was arrested early in 1521, despite the best efforts of his sympathizers and followers, who protested in the streets. Interrogated by the Dutch inquisitor Franz van der Hulst, he was induced to recant his beliefs, and was therefore spared the stake as a repentant first offender. By May this news had reached Luther at Wittenberg, and he was much saddened by the fall of an early and enthusiastic follower. Before long, however, he was relieved by the news that Probst had repented of his capitulation, and, having resumed his preaching, was once more under arrest. Rumor had it that he had been, or was about to be, burned alive, and Luther's letters were tinged with a mixture of sadness and pride. Denial of the known truth was, for any sixteenth-century moralist, worse than death. Luther had known for some time that his followers would be called upon to suffer for their beliefs, and it was for him self-evident confirmation of the truth of those beliefs that real persecution had commenced. It was, of course, Satan who was behind it. Probst himself escaped in the end, and survived to flourish as an evangelical preacher in Bremen. But it was not long before the Inquisition claimed its first Reformation victims, Hendrik Vos and Johann van den Esschen, members of the same house of Austin Friars at Antwerp, arrested in 1522 and burned at the stake in Brussels on 1 July 1523.[12]

After the tumults of March, Luther settled down to serious work on the publication of his German New Testament, his main achievement that year, and one of the greatest achievements of his life. It was a masterly and captivating rendering of the text, influencing not only those who were or soon became

Luther's followers, but even his opponents. Early on, the rival Catholic translations were as likely as anything else to take their departure from his work. For the most part, his translation was not deeply marked by his theological preconceptions, though there were some weighted choices to which Catholic controversialists took exception. In a quiet way, however, he did use the translation to address a minor verbal problem with his doctrine of justification by faith alone. This was the curious fact that the only place in the Bible where the word "alone" was used in connection with faith and justification was in the epistle of James, where, as Catholic controversialists liked to emphasize, the case of Abraham was used to show that a person was "justified by works, and not by faith alone" (James 2:24). Notoriously, Luther balanced this by allowing himself to add the word "allein" (alone) to his rendering of Paul's letter to the Romans: "for we reckon that a person is justified by faith *alone*, without the works of the law" (Rom 3:28). This little insertion has generated interminable polemics and apologetics, and the theological defense of this interpretation of Paul is a commonplace in the Lutheran tradition. But considered strictly in terms of translation, Luther's decision remains indefensible in textual terms, and all the more extraordinary from someone who had remarked, only the previous year, that "not even Augustine, though the greatest of all the fathers, was allowed to change a word of Paul's and make up another."[13]

The bulk of the theological and interpretative work in Luther's New Testament, however, was to be found not in the translation itself, but in the prefaces with which he introduced its various books. Here, too, he addressed the problem of James, arguing in the relevant preface that the contradiction of Paul's teaching by James meant that the latter could not be regarded as genuinely apostolic. The evangelical and Reformed Christian traditions were unwilling to follow Luther in this radical solution, the logic of which would in effect have been to remove

James from the canon of the Bible. The preferred solution in the longer term was to argue that James was using words in a different sense from Paul. But this solution was not available to Luther, who, as we have seen, insisted as far as he possibly could that words were used in scripture in plain, simple, and unequivocal ways. His judgment on this question was unclouded and unsentimental:

> Many people work up a sweat reconciling James with Paul, like Philip [Melanchthon] in his *Apologia*. But it doesn't work: they are contradictory. Faith justifies: faith does not justify. If anyone can bring those together, then I'll take my hat off to him and let myself be called a fool.[14]

One of the more striking consequences of Luther's even closer engagement with the text now that he was translating the New Testament, and perhaps also of his intense experiences of the years 1521–22, was a change in the way he began his numerous letters. He now abandoned the classical phrase "Salutem plurimum dat" in addressing Latin letters, in favor of variations upon "Gratia et pax in domino Jesu Christo," an opening reminiscent of the salutations of Paul's epistles. As time went on, his vernacular translation of the Bible would reshape the speech habits of German evangelicals, as would its avatars in other languages, causing Catholic judges and theologians to expostulate against what they saw as the pretentious parroting of scripture by those they hauled before their tribunals. But Luther took the apostolic persona still further. By spring he was meditating on an "Epistle to the Erfurters," an apostolic letter modelled on those of Saint Paul to the nascent churches of Greece and Asia Minor. He toyed with the idea for some months, but was distracted, chiefly by the protracted labors of printing his New Testament, a project in which he took an exceptionally close interest. He told his friend Georg

Spalatin at one point that three presses were stamping out 10,000 sheets a day, but that even at that rate it would be months before the job was done. However, by autumn the New Testament was nearly ready, and in any case was past the Epistles of Paul, which were for Luther the heart of the book. The Epistle to the Erfurters was eventually dated, and presumably dispatched, in July, and then spread very widely and rapidly in print, with about a dozen editions by the end of the year.[15] The university city of Erfurt was one of the places where Luther's message had made a particularly marked early impact, winning a substantial following but provoking pulpit controversy and a degree of disorder, notably over the cult of the saints. Luther's epistle imitated its Pauline models in urging unity and peace, and it affected to strike a middle way. He emphasized on the one hand that a certain devotion to the saints was tolerable and that there should be no disorderly violence against the practice, but insisted much more firmly on the other that there was no sin in refraining from venerating and praying to saints, and that preachers should focus not on peripheral issues such as the saints but on Christ and the Gospel.[16] As Luther came to inhabit more comfortably the apostolic role he had carved out for himself, he wrote a number of these epistles to evangelical churches over the next few years, to Riga, Antwerp, and Strasbourg among others, and these were even published as a coherent collection in 1525.[17]

The fractious and busy period after Luther's return from the Wartburg was the crucible for his political thought. Although in retrospect historians see in the early 1520s the flash floods of "the Reformation," as cities and princes across Germany stampeded to turn the ideas of Luther and his followers or rivals into reality, the situation at that moment felt much more vulnerable. History is much less clear in the making than in the telling. No one could know then that Charles V would be unable to set his sights firmly on the "heretics" until the 1540s.

He had returned to Spain in 1522, to reestablish royal authority after the suppression of the rebellion of the Comuneros (1520–21), and would remain there for most of the 1520s. In the emperor's absence, the kaleidoscopic politics of the Holy Roman Empire had left the Edict of Worms little more than a dead letter through most of Germany. But persecution had begun, albeit on a limited scale, in the Habsburg territories. It looked very much as though the faithful remnant was to be put to the test. Luther was caught between two conflicting forces. On the one side was imperial authority, seeking to persecute him and his followers in the name of the Catholic Church. On the other was a popular movement of dissent from traditional religion that was frequently exploding into direct action, a movement Luther had inspired but for which he had no intention of being held to account. He therefore faced a dilemma. Depending as he did for his very survival on the patronage of the Elector Frederick, there was no way he could promote a radical account of politics. A message of disobedience and disorder would alienate the man he most needed to propitiate. Yet he could not accept the validity of imperial legislation against him and his doctrine.

This was the context for the potent but somewhat fuzzy notion of the "two kingdoms" which Luther expounded in his pamphlet *On Worldly Government* (1523). The idea of the "two kingdoms" (or "empires": Luther uses the word *Reich*) clearly owed something to the "two cities" famously contrasted in Augustine's ancient classic, *The City of God*, but Luther elaborated his distinction in a new way. The political thought of the two kingdoms was in the first instance tailored to the needs of a faithful remnant rather than to those of an established church, for Luther was still not expecting his Gospel movement to achieve significant worldly success. In distinguishing the kingdom of God from the kingdom of this world, he divided the human race between one and the other. True believers were members of the kingdom of God, and did not need secular power or the fear of punishment to make them conform to canons of legal and moral justice. Returning to his favorite moral analogy, he observed that it would be futile to write laws telling trees how to bear their fruit, because they just did it naturally. Likewise, true Christians kept the law "through the Spirit and faith," by virtue of the renewal of their nature in grace.[18] However, true Christians were for Luther a vanishingly small minority, even among the baptized, among the nominally Christian. The kingdom of the world comprised the vast bulk of humanity, all those who were not Christians. In this rather Hobbesian sphere, sin and self-interest were rampant, and the best that could be attained was the maintenance of a semblance of outward law and order by brute force and rough justice. Luther's actual prescriptions for secular governance were otherwise unremarkable, the anodyne commonplaces of the medieval and Renaissance literary genre of "mirrors for princes." Rulers should aim at the common good rather than their own pleasure, beware of flatterers, punish malefactors, et cetera.

What Luther's doctrine of the two kingdoms emphatically was not, was a modern separation of Church and State, and this notwithstanding the claim that if "worldly power presumes to legislate for souls, it interferes with God's rule and only seduces and ruins souls."[19] For Luther, this meant only that when secular government prescribes as a religious duty that which is either contrary to the Word of God or at least not clearly established by the Word of God, then "worldly power drives souls on to eternal death" in seeking to force them "to believe that such things are right and certainly pleasing to God when they are really uncertain, indeed certainly displeasing, because there is no clear Word of God there."[20] Christians were not only entitled but obliged to disobey the secular power if it commanded acts contrary to God's law, though Luther allowed no right to resist. Yet this did not mean that he felt the State was surplus to requirements in the domain of religion. His observation that the secular power should "attend to its own affairs and permit men to believe one thing or another, as they are able and willing, and constrain no one by force" was not intended to exclude the State completely from the religious sphere. The State could not exercise any jurisdiction over conscience, but it had responsibilities in relation to the outward expression of belief. He had already, with his *Appeal to the Christian Nobility* in 1520, called upon the political authorities of Germany to set about extirpating deep-rooted ecclesiastical abuses. This was not what he saw as "prescribing" laws for the spiritual kingdom: it was merely recognizing and enforcing them. The laws were already there, in the clear and certain Word of God. It most certainly was for temporal authorities, for the rulers of this world, if they were true Christians, to require outward conformity to that law. Matters of the soul as such, however, were beyond their scope. It was for bishops, not princes, to act against heretics: "For one can never counteract heresy with force."[21] It was not the princes' job to save souls. But it was their job to regulate the outward face of the Church itself. The hidden tensions of this account of Christian politics mirror those of the Lutheran theological project as a whole. The thesis that the secular power should enforce only the Word of God presupposed that the secular power had the capacity to judge what was, and what was not, the Word of God. Luther's doctrine left him no room for doubt on the subject: for him, there was neither problem nor even tension. But other rulers could have other certainties.

Luther's personal attitude to secular authority was more submissive in theory than in practice. Shortly after his return to Wittenberg, he showed this in his response to a new theological challenger, Henry VIII of England. Henry's *Assertion of the Seven Sacraments* was a respectable, though hardly inspirational, defense of traditional Catholic doctrine, and its relative success among Catholic polemics against Luther probably had more to do with its royal provenance than with its intrinsic merits.[22] Luther's response was typically robust and outspoken, unhampered by respect for persons. Contrary to what is often said, there was only one reference to human excrement in Luther's reply, when he asserted his right, in defense of his king (namely, Christ), to bespatter "his English Majesty with his own muck and ordure." But he ladled out insults generously to an opponent he defined as an asinine, impudent, and mendacious Thomisticator.[23] Henry was not Luther's sovereign, but he was an ally and uncle by marriage to the emperor, who was. Even Luther's friends were taken aback by the tone of his reply. His enemies were shocked and vindicated, in that they had not expected anything better. Anything but respectful, Luther's response was a reliable measure of its author's essential insubordination.

The irony of Luther's position never became apparent to him, even though his own break with Rome empowered others to break likewise with Wittenberg. All the argumentative ploys he devised against Catholic tradition were to be deployed in turn against his own ideas by those who outbid him in their demands for reform but matched him in their unflinching allegiance to the "pure Word of God." For him this was never an intellectual problem. His démarche was based on the Word of God, theirs on the willful pursuit of individual will-o'-the-wisps. They were dogmatic and wrong: he was dogmatic and right. The divisions which soon emerged within the broad "evangelical" movement were easily accounted for as Satan's counterattack against the resurgent Word. His individualistic theology was at odds with his conformist politics, which ultimately triumphed in his public thinking, and shaped the Lutheran tradition until well into the twentieth century.

As the 1520s progressed, Luther's fire was increasingly directed against those of his enemies who outflanked him, rather than those who made frontal assaults on him. It was Zwingli and the Anabaptists who preoccupied him as the years passed, perhaps because it was more disturbing to be challenged by those who claimed to base their teaching, as he did, on scripture alone. Those who ascribed any magisterial authority to human agents or constructs, whether popes, councils, "Fathers," or "tradition," had from Luther's perspective already ruled themselves out of court. Disagreement on the basis of scripture was meant to have been impossible. Yet still it arose and could not be ignored. It was of course easy to account for: Satan, as usual, was behind it. But it was less easy to suppress. In 1523 and even 1524, the evangelical movement still seemed to many of its leading figures fundamentally united. Luther was seeing danger signs in the wilder departures of Thomas Muntzer and Andreas Carlstadt, but he was still on the friendliest of terms with the reformers of Basel, Strasbourg, and elsewhere. As long as Carlstadt stayed in Wittenberg on sufferance, lecturing but not preaching or publishing, Luther felt in control. But once Carlstadt took his leave, making his way to Basel by way of Strasbourg, with a view to publishing the fruits of two or three years of ruminations, the lid blew off the pot. Luther's sense that Carlstadt had personally ignited the powder train of more radical theology in those cities was deeply misplaced. Once scripture alone was established as the sole authority in matters of Christian doctrine, it was hardly to be expected that no one would draw a contrast between the Old Testament's severe censure of religious images and the profusion of such images in the churches and devotional life of Europe. And if Luther could challenge the traditional doctrine of transubstantiation in the name of a fuzzier notion of a real presence, then it was open to others to question whether, given the physical characteristics of the eucharistic wafer, Christ's words "This is my body," repeated by the priest, were really to be taken literally. Carlstadt reached both these positions fairly promptly, but others likewise reached them without any help from him, even though Luther liked to regard him as the wellspring of these ideas. Once the hierarchical church was stripped of the moral authority to decide upon the meaning of scripture, the way was open to an interminable and irresoluble exegetical wrangle. The guiding principle of Protestantism proved incapable of delivering the certainty it was designed to establish.[24]

Luther's rock-solid commitment to a sort of scriptural literalism or fundamentalism was never as straightforward or unproblematic as he liked to believe and maintain. To describe his hermeneutic as "fundamentalist" is perhaps anachronistic and misleading, as the anti-intellectual overtones of that twentieth-century term are too redolent of a sense of the conflict between "religious" and "scientific" worldviews. To call his hermeneutic "literalist," however, is reasonable enough. He insisted that his opponents were unable to ground their doctrines in the literal text of scripture and that his own doctrines were all so grounded. When his opponents invoked the idea that the same word might be used in various senses, he invariably poured scorn upon their arguments as twisting and distorting the text, although he himself routinely proposed distinctions between senses of the same terms when appropriate. Thus when Cochlaeus deployed against him the standard argument that justification was not by faith alone because it also depended on charity, Luther answered that, on the contrary, charity was the fruit of justifying faith, not a cause of justification, grounding his claim on Galatians 5:22, "The fruits of the Spirit are charity, etc." Cochlaeus queried Luther's sweeping use of "etc" by pointing out that Paul's extensive list of the fruits of the Spirit included "faith" itself, which rendered Luther's argument at best circular and at worst irrelevant. But Luther had already established to his own satisfaction that "faith" in this case meant not belief but faithfulness or honesty (though in his own translation he still rendered it *Glaube*).[25]

Likewise he objected profusely to attempts by his opponents to explain difficulties or evade his conclusions by appealing to the use of figures of speech in the scriptures. Yet he frequently had recourse to figures of speech in dealing with difficulties or challenges raised on the basis of scripture. In the 1520s he found himself in increasing difficulties as other reformers outflanked him. Thus he insisted that Christ's injunction that Christians should not go to law was indeed a commandment (and not a "counsel of perfection," as traditional interpretation had it) but he was not prepared, as the so-called Anabaptists were, to regard Christ's prohibition on taking oaths in the same light. There is nothing in the text to justify Luther's confident explanation that the Christian should take oaths for the sake of others and at their desire, though not for his own sake or at his own wish.[26] Among that loose grouping of believers who were soon labelled "Anabaptists," the more challenging "counsels," thus transformed by Luther into "commandments," were taken as practical guides to behavior. Anabaptists often refused oaths of any kind, thus putting themselves effectively outside every established civil community in Europe. Every institution, from a parish religious confraternity to the courts of a king or emperor, was regulated by oath. The oath, for early modern Europe, was the equivalent of the signature and the identity card or passport in the modern world, a token of commitment and belonging without which it was almost impossible to act in the public sphere. The fate of the Anabaptists, hunted out almost everywhere and almost universally execrated, shows how wise Luther was to rein in his scriptural interpretation at this point. But it was only a combination of Luther's charismatic status and the support of political authorities, rather than any obvious logical cogency, that made his interpretation of Christ's more challenging ethical propositions socially convincing.

Luther himself was never profoundly troubled by these developments, however, because he remained so secure in his own unshakable certainty. The fragmentation of his evangelical opponents demonstrated their disunity and thus their underlying lack of his own crystalline certitude: "Unless there is certainty, there can be no unity."[27] As his own certainty was based on the infallible truth of the Word of God, their disagreement manifestly had to reflect a lack of certainty. In the lectures on the epistles of Peter that he delivered in 1523, he argued that, according to Peter, no one should dare to teach or preach unless they were certain that what they taught was the Word of God.[28] In his later comments on foes such as Zwingli and Oecolampadius (who disagreed with him over the eucharistic presence of Christ), he ruminated repeatedly on evidence, real or presumed, for their inner doubts. Oecolampadius had prayed, before he disputed with Luther over the real presence at Marburg in 1529, that if his cause were not the truth, God should not prosper it in the debate. For Luther, such a prayer betrayed doubt of a kind to which he himself was not prey. Such doubt was in itself a demonstration that Oecolampadius's doctrine was not of God: there was "no room for perplexity or doubt in theology, there should only be certitude with regard to God."[29] Muntzer, he likewise insisted, had been tormented with doubt on his deathbed, desperately clutching a Bible and professing that he believed all that was contained in it—an expression of general or implicit faith which did not measure up to Luther's exacting standards.[30]

The crisis of the evangelical movement came early, and it provoked the last important developments in Luther's thought. The crisis had three elements: the showdown with Erasmus; the break with Carlstadt and Zwingli and what would become the Reformed tradition; and the cataclysm of the German Peasants' War (1524–25), which for Luther was inextricably bound up with the rise of other Reformation splinter groups, such as the followers of Muntzer and those who would come to be called Anabaptists.

In the immediate aftermath of Worms, it was still possible to believe in a broad-based evangelical movement that represented enlightenment and renewal in opposition to the sclerotic corruption of a papist and scholastic establishment. Events at Wittenberg in 1522 showed that the ice was beginning to crack, but it took two or three years for the cracks to become visible. Confidence in the salutary power of scripture alone was still sufficient to persuade reformers that sensible discussion of divergent opinions within the evangelical movement would preserve consensus. Faith would illuminate and pacify conscience, and conscience would in turn recognize, in the spirit, the Word of God in scripture. What could go wrong? Luther found himself acting now as a spiritual guide not just to Saxony but to Germany and the Empire, and even beyond. People from as far apart as the Netherlands and the Baltic States sought his advice on the appointment of pastors or preachers (no longer of "priests") or on the disposition of ecclesiastical property for education or poor relief.[31] People bought into Luther's self-image as a new apostle. The city of Riga wrote begging for a letter, since they could not hope for a visit from Luther in person: "We want you to be our Paul, and we want to be Christ's."[32] His letters to the various churches, such as that to the Estates of Bohemia in July 1522, were transparently modelled on those of Paul.[33]

Luther was anxious to maintain as far as possible the linkage between the "Gospel" and humanism that he had worked so hard to establish in the late 1510s. He reassured Eobanus Hess, the humanist poet of Erfurt, that there was no reason to fear that the rise of the Gospel would jeopardize the revival of classical learning, though even to address the possibility indicates his awareness of a degree of tension. Luther's own unguarded denunciations of "the universities" in the early 1520s, though largely precipitated by the condemnations issuing from Louvain, Cologne, and Paris, offered some justification for this interpretation, as did some of the wilder ideas aired at Wittenberg in 1521–22, such as the abandonment of academic degrees on the grounds that they were not found in scripture. But Luther reminded Hess that "pure theology cannot survive at all without expertise in literature" and that "there had never been any great revival of the Word of God unless the way had been prepared by a revival and efflorescence of languages and literature."[34]

Continued respect for humanism, though, no longer meant paying homage to the name of Erasmus. When Luther heard in 1523 that Oecolampadius had thrown off the monastic habit which he had only assumed in 1520, he sent a letter of hearty congratulations which sought to wean him from his dependence on Erasmus, who had been offended by Oecolampadius's lectures on Isaiah at Basel. Luther urged him to continue, with a strong though discreet critique of Erasmus's credentials as a spiritual guide. Erasmus's oeuvre showed his limitations in this area, he maintained, and he felt stung by some his barbs, though as long as Erasmus pretended he was not Luther's enemy, Luther would likewise pretend that he did not really see through Erasmus's cunning. Erasmus should stick to what he was good at: the study of languages and the assault on scholasticism.[35] At much the same time, Luther manifested his dissatisfaction by removing all praise of Erasmus from later versions of his commentary on Galatians. The tension between the two men ratcheted up steadily, especially thanks to the controversy that erupted between Erasmus and Ulrich von Hutten in 1523. Hutten, who always tried to mince his opponents rather than his words, had launched a splenetic attack on Erasmus in his *Expostulation*. Erasmus's *Spongia*—the "sponge," to wipe from his face the traces of his enemy's spluttering—appeared very shortly after Hutten's death at the end of August, and it was taken by evangelicals as a particularly unfair attack on someone who could no longer reply (though it had been written before his death). Luther was especially scathing: if that was wiping with a sponge, he remarked, what would railing and cursing be like?[36] Luther took a certain malicious pleasure in seeing Erasmus, the self-appointed voice of moderation, go over the top, and his intervention was published as an open letter.

Erasmus himself, meanwhile, was coming under pressure from the other side to clarify his position. It had indeed become increasingly obvious that he was not in sympathy with Luther and the new theology. But his pronouncements thus far had been moderate and even equivocal, and he had found himself embarrassed more than once when private letters to figures on either side had been published. His efforts at mediation could easily be represented as double-dealing. From mid-1523, he received a series of letters from friends in England urging him to rally to the defense of Henry VIII and the Church against Luther's outspoken response to the king's *Assertion*. Famously, he chose to make his break with Luther over the issue of the freedom of the will, which Luther had flatly denied. He worked on this over the winter of 1523–24, and his *Diatribe on Free Will* was on sale from September 1524. Yet although this storm had been brewing the longest, Luther left it a year before giving it his attention. Two other threats seemed more pressing.

By mid-1524, Luther was sensing the fragmentation of the evangelical front. Satan, he realized, was building up a sect which accepted neither the papists nor "us."[37] But the cracks were still not apparent to everyone. When the veteran Catholic humanist Jakob Wimpfeling took up the pen that year to defend the Mass and prayers for the dead, he addressed himself to both Luther and Zwingli.[38] Of the three threats Luther faced in 1524, it was to the danger of fragmentation that he turned first, eventually spurred to action by a letter from the seven reformers of Strasbourg seeking his advice on the theology of infant baptism and of Christ's presence in the sacrament of the Eucharist. Disagreement over the "real presence" had been brewing for some time, but a crisis had, in Luther's view, been ignited by the arrival in Strasbourg of Andreas Carlstadt, whom he blamed as the source of erroneous teachings about the Eucharist.[39] His *Epistle to the Strasbourgers*, published as an open letter, defended infant baptism and the real presence against the views that were now gaining ground in many cities of Switzerland and the Rhineland. Almost at the same time he issued the first part of a book on which he had been at work for some months, a monumental refutation of Carlstadt entitled *Against the Heavenly Prophets*, in which the doctrine of the real presence was defended at considerable length.[40] Luther developed his arguments at even greater length over the following years, but at bottom his case came down to two claims. First of all, the "Sacramentarian" doctrine (as it came to be known) was "contrary to the plain words of Christ, by which he commands us to eat his body." And secondly, denial of the real presence failed the test of certainty, as did the deniers themselves: "this doctrine is not certain, and therefore it cannot render consciences certain."[41]

The first stirrings of the peasants' revolt, focused purely on agrarian grievances, were felt in July 1524, but disorder spread gradually through late summer before erupting in autumn. As the flames of rebellion were fanned, Luther responded first with relative moderation in his *Admonition to Peace*, calling for a cease-fire and recommending that the grievances of the peasants be heard and redressed. But continued violence led him only a month later to expand that work with a section that soon took on a new life of its own as the pamphlet *Against the Thieving, Murderous Hordes of Peasants*, which sold throughout Germany in numerous editions from summer 1525 onwards.[42] Where the *Admonition* had acknowledged the somewhat misdirected evangelical aspirations that lay behind some aspects of the peasants' demands, and gently reminded them that the true evangelical way was that of peace, the second installment denounced their campaign as a rank betrayal of the Gospel. The rhetoric of ruthless repression to which Luther urged the secular authorities shocked friends and foes alike, though of course it made little practical difference to politics. The peasants were always going to be repressed ruthlessly once the princes and nobles put together suitable concentrations of troops.

Luther's almost gleeful cheerleading was vital to the continuing credibility of his religious position, for the eruption of the Peasants' War was the climax of the mounting social and cultural tensions of the early 1520s. It might have spelled disaster for the still few and scattered Reformation movements that had actually taken root. Voices aplenty took up the hackneyed cry that heresy bred sedition. If the princes had drawn back in fear at the fury some claimed Luther had unleashed, then the Protestant Reformation might have been penned in at least as effectively as the Hussites in Bohemia a century before, or even brought to the brink of extinction, like the Lollards in England. But Luther's robust repudiation of rebellion consolidated his credentials as a pillar of the social order. The man who had complained in 1524 about the cruelty of imperial edicts against heretics was now genially inviting the German princes to wade in the blood of their rebellious serfs.

So anyone who can ought to strike, pierce, or slaughter them, secretly or openly, and reckon nothing more poisonous, more dangerous, or more devilish than a rebel.[43]

Their brutality would be a good work in God's eyes, and the way he put this seemed to contradict his own theological principles, as was pointed out by Cochlaeus (who thought that reprinting this pamphlet with a critical commentary would discredit its author):

> Times now are so strange that one prince can do more to merit heaven by bloodshed than others can do by their prayers.[44]

His rant against the rebels was vile stuff, but it did the trick. Luther was unshakable in his commitment to political authority and authoritarian politics. Over the next few years he elaborated still more fully his scriptural justification for princely rule, eventually coming to found it in a patriarchal interpretation of the fourth commandment ("Honor your father and mother"). "All power derives from paternal power," he maintained, "worldly power flows from fatherly authority." As he summed it up a few years later:

> It can be manifestly demonstrated that government is founded in the fourth commandment.[45]

In consequence, Lutheranism became one of the most congenial versions of Christianity ever set before the powers of this world.

As Luther himself saw it, his thoroughly patriarchal account of political order and authority, predicated at first on the familiar tag from Saint Paul ("Let every soul be subject unto the higher powers," which he cited throughout his pamphlet against the peasants), and in due course on the fourth commandment, was vastly superior to anything the papacy or the schools had to offer.[46] The notion of kingship "by the grace of God" was a commonplace in medieval Catholicism, but earlier medieval notions which might have turned consecrated kingship into a sacrament had been stymied by the formal enumeration of the seven sacraments in the thirteenth century, a moment when the revival of Aristotle in the nascent universities made a more naturalistic account of politics prevalent in scholasticism. Obedience to political authority remained a Christian duty. But political order itself was seen by most Christian theorists as grounded in nature, not grace; while those who did see it as grounded in grace tended to subordinate it directly to the ecclesiastical supremacy of the papacy. Luther's new theology of politics answered to both the Christian convictions and the political predilections of the princes with such success that Lutheranism soon came to seem, and perhaps to be, more compatible with their interests than Catholicism or the more populist or radical accounts of politics found among "Anabaptist" or "Sacramentarian" reformers.

The complex crisis which enveloped Luther in the early 1520s completed the process by which the man was made. By 1525, in his early forties, his creative days were past and he had fixed his positions both in terms of Catholicism and in terms of the theological and intellectual challenges emerging on his other flank. He still did not know how it would end. And it was in the midst of crisis and worldly turmoil and uncertainty that he made the sudden and unexpected decision to take a wife. Although one or two people had mooted the possibility of his marrying over the previous couple of years, Luther himself had balked at the idea, not least out of concern that, should he be made a martyr, he would leave behind a poor widow.[47] And martyrdom still seemed likely to be his fate. Early that year Luther had been taken in by a classic scapegoating rumor, that a Jewish physician had been suborned by his foes to poison him. Typically, the physician, and some other unfortunate Jews, were seized and questioned over this nonsense, though Luther generously hoped that they would not be tortured if they did not reveal who had sent them.[48]

As the crisis of the Peasants' War unfolded, the situation was if anything less favorable than ever to any prospect of Luther's marrying, yet, in June 1525, quite out of the blue, he announced his intention to wed. His explanation was curious and revealing: "While I was thinking about other things, the Lord suddenly and amazingly put me in mind to marry that nun, Catharina von Bora."[49] It was, then, a marriage made in heaven. Yet this at the very time when the German princes were butchering rebellious peasants in their thousands, from Franconia to Alsace. More broadly, Luther had spent that year writing against Carlstadt and Zwingli, and was contemplating the time when he would be able to turn his fire against Erasmus. His decision to marry, though, was no idle romantic fancy, but a gesture of evangelical defiance. It was precisely because the dangers had mounted up to such a height, and precisely because the papists, as he put it, had been so heartened by evangelical divisions, by Erasmus's démarche, and most of all by the Peasants' War, that the gesture was so outlandish and so effective. This marriage was a declaration of faith in the Gospel, one in the eye, as it were, for Satan.

Luther's wedding should have been a gift to his enemies. Thomas More endlessly harped upon it in his English polemics against William Tyndale and Robert Barnes, mocking as a central principle of the new religion that "a lewd friar may wed a nun" and exploiting as far as he could not only the shock value in the fact that two persons vowed to virginity should break their vows with those of marriage but also the essentially comedic value of a monk in bed with a nun, an idea as funny then as now.[50] With his more acidic wit, Erasmus simply observed that, while he had thought at first that what was happening to Christendom was a tragedy, he had now come to see that it was really a comedy:

In comedies, all the to-ings and fro-ings tend to end in marriage. It now looks as though the Lutheran tragedy will end the same way.[51]

In his first tellings of this story, he added that to show how blessed Luther's union was, the bride had given birth just days later. But by March 1526 he was explaining that this second claim had just been a rumor. Nevertheless, he went on, in another dig at Luther's teachings:

> If there is any truth in the vulgar fable that Antichrist will be born to a monk and a nun, how many thousand Antichrists the world must have already![52]

The jokes were not bad. But it is a tribute to what Luther had achieved that nobody was laughing.

10

THE MEANING
OF MARTIN LUTHER

Only towards the end of 1525 did Luther at last find the leisure
to turn to the first of the three threats of that year, the challenge
from Erasmus. The culmination of the slow-motion controversy
between them broke little new ground. Although Luther show-
ered Erasmus with ironic praise as the one who "alone before
all the others set about the real issue," not pestering him with
trivialities like the papacy and indulgences, the first of his opponents to get to the root of his teachings by focusing on free
will and grace, this was mere rhetorical posing.[1] His opponents
had been picking out this issue for six years. His position on free
will had been condemned by the papal bull *Exsurge Domine* in
1520, and Erasmus himself borrowed much of the theological
substance of his case from the works of earlier controversialists such as John Fisher. From the Catholic point of view, from
which Erasmus entered the fray, it was too little, too late. He
was no longer in much of a position to damage Luther, as he
might have been had he weighed in five years earlier. Luther was
too big now to have any need to fear, or brook, contradiction.
Yet their exchanges are nonetheless important for our understanding of Luther and his development, largely because Erasmus was such an acute observer and managed to expose more
clearly than previous controversialists some of the internal methodological difficulties within Luther's theological position.

Luther's considered response to Erasmus, *The Enslaved Will*,
was finally released in December 1525. There was little new

on show, nor did Luther's ideas develop further to any significant extent across the remainder of his life.[2] The flat denial of the moral freedom of the human will was a position Luther had adopted years before, but this was a position he took not out of any commitment to philosophical determinism, but for entirely theological reasons. The point of his uncompromising teaching was to highlight the priority of divine grace in human salvation, and to emphasize divine predestination as its ultimate cause. Previous theologians of predestination, such as Augustine and Thomas Aquinas, had for the most part insisted, notwithstanding the absolute and unconditional nature of divine predestination, that the human will remained in some real sense free. The logical coherence of this claim might well be questioned, and Reformation theologians from Luther onwards tended to simplify matters by simply dismissing the concept of free will in relation to human salvation, noting that it was nowhere to be found in scripture. On the contrary, the very notion of *liberum arbitrium*, free will, was smoke blown into the eyes of the church by Satan precisely in order to compromise the theology of grace. On predestination as such there was little if anything to choose between Luther and Thomas Aquinas. The difference was that Luther entirely repudiated the concept of free will.

Erasmus's treatise *On Free Will* made two important contributions to the debate. The first was to deconstruct Luther's carefully crafted self-image as a purely biblical theologian. The humanist critic saw in Luther, for all his genuine insights into Paul, not a scholar after his own heart, but yet another scholastic theologian with an axe to grind, overthinking and over-arguing his insights out of a misplaced pride in his own intellectual ingenuity. Secondly, he forced Luther to address one of the deepest scriptural and philosophical difficulties with the doctrine of predestination in the extreme form in which he advanced it, a difficulty further sharpened by his rejection of free will. This difficulty was that of reconciling a divine decision to save only a fraction of humanity (and, it was generally accepted, a small fraction at that) with the plentiful scriptural testimony to the at least potentially universal mercy and benevolence of God. "Nolo mortem peccatoris" (Ezek 33:11), Erasmus cited, "I desire not the death of the sinner."[3] Luther was by no means unaware of this text. He had cited it himself on occasion. But he had skirted round it since developing his new theology. The problem lay in reconciling the divine choice of the elect out of the "mass of perdition" with the apparent universality of the offer of mercy and salvation both in scripture and in Luther's preaching. Erasmus's challenge was, essentially, to ask whether that offer was genuine or not. For if God had chosen but a small minority for salvation, the divine offer announced in the scriptures would not be as straightforward as it seemed, but would, on the contrary, seem at best equivocal and at worst mendacious. *Deus solus verax*?

Luther's answer to this question should probably not be regarded as a central plank of his theological platform, with which it is not obviously consistent. That answer was to distinguish between the "revealed" will of God—the scriptures, including their apparently universal and conditional offer of salvation—and a further "hidden" will of God, the inscrutable and unrevealed will of the Trinity, by which the actual choice of the elect was unconditionally determined. Ezekiel was therefore speaking only of God's revealed offer of mercy, not of that "hidden and fearsome will" by which he determined who would partake of it.[4] This solved the immediate problem, giving a perfectly plausible explanation for the theological data: God chose some and not others, and the Bible simply did not account for this, and it was not for mere human beings to pry into the most intimate and awesome counsels of the divine majesty. But the logical price was high. The appeal to a hidden will of God was at least counterintuitive for a theology that rested on what was revealed *sola scriptura*, by the Bible alone, and by a Bible that was to be read as a transparent text in accordance with what Luther elsewhere in this very work calls the "simple, pure, and natural signification of the words."[5] In the light of this hidden will, the revealed text of scripture nonetheless remained therefore equivocal, for the offer of salvation was not being made upon the stated conditions, but was being determined by further considerations not even to be found in the small print. Luther had no answer to this beyond assertion and imprecation, and it is tempting to conclude that the extraordinary ferocity of his subsequent hatred for Erasmus may be traced to the mental discomfort occasioned him by his opponent's drilling into this fault line in his theology.

On this occasion, as on innumerable others, Luther expressed himself with an otherwise unaccountable bitterness towards a man who had been by far the mildest of his critics. This started in *The Enslaved Will* itself. Erasmus may have been a prejudiced critic, so we need not concur with his claim that, of all Luther's books thus far, none contained as much "malicious vituperation" as this.[6] As Luther's polemics go, it is relatively restrained. But he was justified in feeling that the tone and wording of his own essay had done nothing to merit what was still a ferocious response. And from this time on, Luther spoke of Erasmus with unmitigated contempt. One of his milder claims was that for Erasmus, as for the pope and all the cardinals, "Religion is nothing but a fairy story," dreamed up to maintain papal power.[7] Erasmus was a clown, a Judas, an Arian and an Epicurean, an equivocator, an amphibologist, indeed an atheist.[8] This last allegation Erasmus found especially hurtful. Luther's default sneers were that Erasmus was "as slippery as an eel" and that he "spouts ambiguities."[9] So much might be taken merely for the niceties of sixteenth-century debate, but there is a disturbing solemnity to other comments which takes them close to the absolute zero of cold and considered hatred:

Therefore I enjoin upon you, by divine authority, hatred for Erasmus (this he said to me). He looks on our whole theology as if he were Democritus: he just laughs at it. So I shall write against him, even if he is killed; for I have decided to kill him with my pen. . . . What if I do kill him? So too I killed Muntzer.[10]

The scribe's parenthesis testifies to his shock at the deliberate solemnity of this execration, and it was no mere "one-off." Luther frequently delighted in the divine providence that brought so many of his foes to a bitter end, and he regarded hatred for Erasmus as an integral component of his legacy:

This I bequeath you as my testament when I am gone, and I call you present as witnesses of this, that I hold Erasmus for the greatest enemy of Christ there has been this thousand years.

The reason I hate Erasmus with all my heart is that he brings into dispute the things that ought to be our joy.[11]

Luther loved his enemies. He rejoiced in his hatreds and savored them, rolling them around his mouth like some fine vintage. He was not inclined, however, to bless those who cursed him. On the contrary, "everyone curses when they pray, so, when I pray 'Hallowed be thy name,' I curse Erasmus and all those who hold opinions contrary to the Word." "I pray all of you who care about glory and the Gospel, be enemies of Erasmus, for he hates religion."[12]

He saw where the appeal of Erasmus's argument lay:

This idea of Erasmus's is the ultimate temptation and the most perilous, namely that he thinks God unjust in dealing evil to the good and good to the evil.[13]

Of course he does not accurately represent the case here. Erasmus was as aware as any Christian moralist that bad things happen to good people and that this process of trial and temptation was part of the dispensation of providence. But lurking below this account is his sensitivity to the Erasmian question about what divine "justice" means in Luther's account of faith, justification, and predestination. His pervasive critique of Erasmus as a doubter and an equivocator is a reductive and instinctive response to the sort of mental subtlety that not only shied away from Luther's assertive certainties but also succeeded in problematizing them.

Luther had piggybacked quite successfully on the humanist critique of scholasticism, which had been voiced *par excellence* by Erasmus. But from where Erasmus stood, Luther looked like just one more quarrelsome scholastic with a bee in his bonnet, leading Christians astray into endless agonizing about the finer points of dogma when the crucial task was to initiate them into faith and justice by presenting them with the teaching, example, and person of Jesus as depicted in the Gospels. Ultimately there were two very different understandings of religion at work here. Erasmus saw all the weaknesses and drawbacks of the established Church. After all, few had pointed them out more insistently than he. But when challenged by the Reformers as to why he did not therefore join their brave new church, he simply observed that, when he saw a better one, he might. He saw nothing in the convulsions and upheavals of the civic Reformations of Germany and Switzerland to persuade him that the new establishment had anything better to offer than the old. And the instant fissiparousness of what we now call "the Reformation" gave him no cause to prefer it to the still imposing unity of the Catholic Church, no matter how striated and pitted that ancient monolith now seemed. Luther was offering a highly cerebral account of Christianity powered by a surge of emotional commitment, and the rhetoric of "faith alone" and "faith not works," even when qualified by the insistence that the Christian life was meant to be fruitful in good works and personal sanctification, was perhaps unlikely in principle to drive any dramatic movement of moral and social reform. At any rate it did not evidently do so. The first Lutheran convert to Catholicism of any note, Georg Witzel, a young priest who, coming under the influence of Luther at Wittenberg, took a wife and served a while as Lutheran pastor of a parish near Eisenach, reverted to the faith of his fathers in the later 1520s largely out of a growing feeling that the new teaching was failing to bring forth the fruits of good works predicted for it.[14]

Luther had never intended to "start the Reformation." He had not even intended to launch a new theology, a new doctrine, on the world, let alone the new religion that actually transpired, the first in a rapidly expanding family. As a Christian, he could not actually conceive of himself as founding a new religion, so he dutifully credited the truth to scripture. His intention, like that of so many reformers before him, was to call Christians back to the original and central truths of the Gospel. Yet in the end, he had a shrewd sense of the originality of his own intellectual achievement. He saw clearly enough that he was the first to bring the truth to light, at least in his own times. In his showdown with Carlstadt at Wittenberg in spring 1522 he reminded his audience that it was he, Luther, who had opened the way to truth. Like Paul, he took a legitimate pride in his apostolic role, even though he did not claim to have been snatched up into heaven to meet Christ in person.[15]

Although it does not do to romanticize the perceptions and intuitions of "ordinary people," who are no less prone to flattery, self-deception, willful blindness, and obstinacy as whoever we imagine we exclude from that category, yet the evidence set before us by the linguistic record of our kind, by the everyday usage of ordinary vernacular speech, can help us understand the past. And ordinary people, as witnessed by everyday speech and usage, had a clear idea of what was going on. What they saw in Luther's movement, and in Zwingli's, and in due course in Calvin's, not to mention in the "Anabaptist" traditions denounced by the others, was novelty. Luther's movement was as much a novelty in sixteenth-century Germany as Islam in seventh-century Arabia or Mormonism in nineteenth-century America. From Cajetan onwards, the whiff of novelty hung about it, for two or three generations—until Lutheranism and Calvinism had become so much part of Europe that they were themselves established, traditional, comfortable, and every bit as complacent as the late medieval Catholic Church before the tidal wave of dissident print swept over it with Luther precariously surfing on top.

This common perception was somewhat bruising to the tender consciences of the new evangelists. They knew, after all, that all they were doing was summoning people back to the true, original Word of God, stripped of its human accretions, the barque of Peter scoured of the limpets which had accumulated on its hull through 1500 years on the seas of history. So the charge of innovation was especially hurtful and offensive. And innovation was a "charge." Sixteenth-century Europe was a traditional society, not a modern society. The "new" was not, as it is today, a challenge, or an opportunity, or at the very least a marketing ploy. The "new" was a disruption, a risk, a threat. The charge of reckless innovation (innovation was by definition reckless) was a surefire way, for the most part, to put a thinker or writer in the doghouse.

The evidence for this is most visibly preserved in a pamphlet produced by a Protestant controversialist to rebut the charge of innovation. Urbanus Rhegius, the leading Lutheran preacher in Augsburg in the 1520s, produced his pamphlet *New Learning* in 1526.[16] The burden of his argument was that people had got it all wrong. The "new doctrine," the "new learning," was in fact popery. It was the *evangelium*, the "Gospel," which, as its name showed, was really the "old" religion, because it was the religion of the New Testament itself, not the religion that had gradually overlaid that old religion through the intervening centuries, until eventually it had completely obscured the truth. The charge of innovation, of "new doctrine," he pointed out, had been levelled by the Pharisees against Jesus himself, so the prevalence of the charge in modern times itself became evidence that it was false. As Luther put it:

> The peasants are brutes who think we made up the religion we preach. When they are examined, they say "yeah, yeah," and don't believe a word of it.[17]

The charge of novelty stung, and was rebutted. Protestants insisted that it was the Catholics who were the real innovators. But the peasants never called Catholicism the "new religion," and it is revealing that the Catholic preachers and pamphleteers never felt they needed to defend the claim that their faith was the "old religion." Instead, they relentlessly appealed to an antiquity and a tradition that they felt able to take for granted, irrespective of the objections of their opponents.

Notwithstanding the novel character of his thought, Luther owed more than he realized to medieval theology. But it is his conscious repudiation of medieval theology, rather than his unconscious assimilation of many of its obsessions and presuppositions, that is the most important thing about his relationship with it: "Before our time, none of the universities had any idea about the real subject of theology."[18]

Luther is commonly praised by modern theologians, Catholic as well as Protestant, for putting Christ at the center of his theology. Yet in this, of all his thinking, he showed himself at his most medieval. As he himself noted in one of his *obiter dicta*, Bernard of Clairvaux (a Cistercian monk of the twelfth century) excelled all the ancient Fathers of the Church in his preaching "because he preached Christ so beautifully."[19] A focus on Christ, "Christocentrism," was very much the creation of medieval Christian sensibility: because the humanity of Christ, especially the suffering humanity of Christ, in solidarity with sinners and with the human race in general, loomed ever larger in the artistic and devotional imagination of the later Middle Ages. This intense devotion to Christ is all over late medieval spiritual literature: among the best-selling religious books in 1500 was the *Imitation of Christ*. The centrality of Christ is even more obvious in late medieval art. No one was depicted more commonly in painting, sculpture, or illumination than Jesus, usually on the cross or in his mother's arms. Luther's "theology of the cross" is stylistically (though not theologically) prefigured in the south German ivory carvings of the crucifixion and other passion scenes. It is no surprise that Dürer, a product and a master of this artistic movement, was drawn to Luther's teachings. Luther's focus on Christ was no radical departure from late medieval Christianity, it was its fruit: perhaps its culmination, perhaps its exaggeration, but most certainly its fruit.

This profound Christocentric legacy in Luther's thought may help explain what are from one perspective the two anomalous, if likewise medieval, features of his mature theology: his continued adherence to the doctrine of the "real presence" in the Eucharist and his continued acceptance of the place of visual imagery in the Christian life. Most traditions of early modern Protestantism other than his own abandoned both the Catholic and the Lutheran doctrines of eucharistic presence[20] and excluded visual imagery from public worship. More generally, the use of images in worship has been closely correlated in Christian history with more "realist" doctrines of eucharistic presence. Other evangelical theologians found it hard to see what role that kind of real presence could have in the world of "justification by faith alone." And it is easy to understand how, in the world of "scripture alone," the Old Testament's relentless polemic against idolatry could be turned against the elaborate apparatus of imagery at work in late medieval Catholic life and worship. Luther's position on these issues was somewhat anomalous, even if he was able to defend the real presence, to his own satisfaction, in terms of a straightforward reading of scripture, while justifying the place of images by excluding the worship of images but not their use for purposes of instruction and meditation. The theologians of the other Reformation traditions, who were mostly ready to acknowledge their debt to him (Zwingli alone, rather unconvincingly, denied any such debt), seem to have felt that his papist past simply clung too closely to allow him to jettison all its errors. Like Moses, he had led people towards the promised land but had not lived to enter it. If this view does get near to explaining the anomalies, the reason is that Luther's own personal engagement with Christ had been shaped so deeply by the artistic and imaginative resources of late medieval devotion. The cross of Christ, so central to the emergence of his theology, was inseparable for him from its artistic depictions. And his sense of Christ was inseparable from a realist understanding of the Eucharist, as is evident in his later reminiscences of his first mass and of the "horror" he experienced when Staupitz was carrying the consecrated host in a Corpus Christi procession.

If the role of Christ is part of the medieval inheritance in his thought, so too is the role of Antichrist, which is indeed one of the deepest marks of medieval Catholicism on his mind. The scriptural basis for the doctrine of the Antichrist was scanty at best, and far from clear, but this medieval legacy left its mark on the entire early modern Protestant tradition. The meaning Luther, Calvin, and so many others attached to those scattered texts had been forged through centuries of speculative interpretation. It was a thoroughly medieval myth which Luther took up and reforged as a weapon against the papacy.

The very bibliocentrism of Luther's theology, one of its most powerfully attractive features, was rooted in medieval Christianity. It was movable print, that last fruit of medieval Catholicism,[21] that brought the Bible within the reach first of all scholars and then of almost everyone. But veneration of the very words of the Bible was already a cultural reality. Luther's appeal to the Bible was thoroughly traditional, even though his growing disdain for tradition, "human tradition," was not. He did not have to give the Bible central place: it held that already. All he had to do was to disconnect it from the institutional structures that had hitherto controlled its interpretation, to emancipate the divine word from human bondage. The rhetorical device with which he achieved that was the key phrase "Word of God." This was already in limited use as a synonym for the Bible, albeit chiefly in a liturgical context or as part of a phrase, "preaching the Word of God," which was a late medieval periphrasis for "preaching." Luther took up the phrase "Word of God," in its narrow sense as a synonym for scripture, and popularized it. It thus became simultaneously a synonym not only for scripture but also for his particular message, for his particular interpretation of scripture. It was a powerful slogan with which to challenge the papal church.

At a deeper level, the problems that worried Luther were thoroughly medieval problems. The intensity of his engagement with sin and guilt is the legacy of centuries of monastic piety. Self-examination and confession lay at the root of his concept of justification by faith alone, and while these practices have deep roots in the Christian past, most notably in the reflections of Saint Augustine, they were developed in the Middle Ages with an intensity and profundity that shaped both Luther's spiritual growth and his theological journey. His conception of the "imputation" of divine justice to the Christian by virtue of their faith (itself elicited in the Christian by divine action) could hardly have been formulated until the medieval nominal-ists had forged their concept of divine "acceptation," by which God accepted human good deeds as good works despite their imperfections. Luther's doctrines of the intrinsic sinfulness of all human works (even good works) and the consequent impossibility of the commandments was an imaginative elaboration on such ideas, and led him ultimately towards the radically new, ultra-Augustinian thesis that baptism—notwithstanding a thousand years of tradition to the contrary—did not take away all sin. Even his powerful anti-Pelagian rhetoric and his successful characterization of Catholic theology as Pelagian (or semi-Pelagian) owed their impact to the fact that Augustine's condemnation of Pelagius had been so universally assimilated by Christian theologians (even when they inadvertently compromised it).[22] Everyone knew that Pelagius was wrong.

Luther's problems were medieval problems, but his solutions were new solutions. The big novelties in his thought were the invisible church, the ineradicable persistence of sin in this life, and the certainty of grace (through justification by faith alone). Each of these central ideas directly contradicted the presuppositions of a thousand years of Christian writing and preaching—and, ironically, contradicted Luther's favorite ancient Christian writer, Augustine of Hippo. For Augustine, the Catholic Church was emphatically visible. That was the whole point of his lengthy controversy against a North African Christian splinter group, the so-called Donatists. For Augustine, baptism took away all sin: whatever flaws remained, however difficult and problematic, were not, as such, sin, and he indignantly repudiated the suggestion that he thought otherwise. For Augustine, no one could be certain that they enjoyed the grace and favor of God. For a millennium, medieval Christian theologians echoed and embroidered his themes. Luther, starting each time with Augustinian insights, namely the persistent sinfulness of Christians, the flawed character of every human action, and the absolute priority of divine grace in justification, developed those insights in directions which fatally undermined other outworks of Augustine's theological structure. For Augustine the divine and the human cooperated in salvation, and salvation was therefore, from the human perspective, cooperative. For Luther, it was passive. Although Luther is commonly, and to some extent justifiably, classified as an "Augustinian" theologian, his theological achievement was to shatter, or at least to transcend, the Augustinian paradigm.

Luther had never intended to open a path to the individual and subjective interpretation of the scriptures. Truth was his object, and his notion of truth was as objective as everyone else's at that time. But the literalness of the literal sense of scripture was always going to be a debatable quality, and the potential depth of the problem became apparent with the endless and intricate disputations that arose over one of the simplest statements in the New Testament, "Hoc est enim corpus meum," "For this is my body." For a statement which might seem, grammatically, in the "cat sat on the mat" class, this proved prodigiously contentious in sixteenth-century Europe. "Lutheranism" could barely be said to have come into existence before other preachers, such as Zwingli in Zurich, began weaving their own threads into the new religious fabric by proposing that this apparently apodictic utterance should be taken not literally but figuratively, lest Christ be imagined to have said something so manifestly contrary to the evidence of the senses. For Luther, it was obvious that Christ called it his body, and that, as Christ (God) could not lie, it must be so. But it was equally obvious that it was still bread, obvious both to the senses and because the Apostle Paul, also incapable of lying in such a matter thanks to the inspiration and guidance of the Holy Spirit, often called it bread. So it had to be both: body and bread. For Zwingli, it was obviously bread, not only because Paul called it bread but also because this was evident to the senses; therefore, though Christ had called it his "body," it could not be two things at once. It had to be either his body or bread. He went for bread, resolving the question by the evidence of the senses. But for him it was obvious that, if Christ's words were to be taken literally, it had to be his body and therefore not bread, because it could not be two things at once. He preferred the Catholic solution to the Lutheran one, though he preferred his own to both. For the Catholics, it was obvious that Christ called it his body and that Christ could not lie; therefore, the evidence of the senses was not in this case to be relied upon, and it was Paul's description of the sacrament as "bread" that was figurative, rather than Christ's description of it as his body.

Luther did not like the idea of having anyone else decide whether he was right or wrong. He incessantly demanded the right to be heard, but denied that anyone had the right to preside or judge at the hearing. After failing to persuade Cajetan at Augsburg, he returned home and appealed to a future general council of the Church, affiliating himself for the moment to the late medieval "conciliarist" tradition, which held that in matters of dogmatic definition a general council was superior even to the pope. But at the Leipzig Disputation he went out of his way to show how church councils had contradicted each other, and retreated to his last redoubt, the principle, which he derived from the fifteenth-century canon lawyer Panormitanus, that a single individual, properly reliant on solid scripture, might conceivably maintain the truth against a pope or even a council. The Leipzig Disputation itself was only submitted to the judgment of Paris because Eck refused to go on stage unless it was agreed that some judge be appointed. As the judgments of Louvain, Cologne, and Paris all came down against him, Luther showed a sturdy disregard for their cavilling. A couple of years later, at Worms, when Johannes Cochlaeus offered to dispute against Luther, he asked who might adjudicate the outcome, and Luther suggested they ask a boy, or else a youth who happened to be in the room.[23] The only judge, for Luther, was scripture, and he already knew that scripture was in his favor. What more was there to be said?

The "Panormitanus Principle," which Panormitanus himself seems to have advanced as a sort of thought experiment rather than as a practical policy, was powerfully corrosive because it was profoundly individualistic. Ultimately, although nothing could have been further from his mind, Luther's theological synthesis was a triumph of individualism. This individualism was evident in both the substance and the method of his theology. The focus of his teaching was the personal certitude of divine favor which grew out of the doctrine of justification by faith. Allied with the idea of the invisibility of the church (while one could be certain of one's own standing with God, one could never have such certainty about anyone else, so the true church had to be invisible), this tended theologically to put the individual's "relationship with God" (as it came to be called much, much later), rather than the church, at the heart of the Christian religion (even if that individual relationship with God has often been manifested in practice by transferring from one church community to another). In terms of theological method, the exaltation of the Word of God above all human authority necessarily conferred upon each and every person the right and duty to work out for themselves what the Word of God might actually mean. Opponents of the Reformation were prompt to attack what they thought was the fatal flaw in the Protestant scripture principle, arguing that Luther and his followers were establishing the right of private or individual judgment, which they saw as an unconscionable subordination of eternal truth to personal whim. None of the early Reformers was prepared for a moment to entertain such a preposterous notion. The pure Word of God was above all human authority, especially that of the random and perhaps uneducated individual. Each of the Reformers knew what the pure Word of God was, and if anybody failed to agree with them on it, that was evidently the outcome of pride or folly or both. Yet the interpretative maelstrom which this principle unleashed was irresoluble, and Protestants came to accept that this was so. Two hundred years later, it was widely accepted among Protestants themselves that "private judgment" was, precisely, one of the great achievements of the Reformation. The fundamental tenet of Protestantism, for many in that tradition, was now to be identified as the right of the individual conscience against the oppressive structures of popery.

Luther would never have subscribed to such a position, yet it was discernibly related to the rhetoric of conscience with which, especially in the years around 1520, he had justified his own stand for truth. No more than Thomas More did he make a stand for "conscience." Each made a stand, in conscience, for truth. Thomas More aligned his conscience with the definitions of the Catholic Church. Martin Luther aligned his with the pure Word of God, the plain text of scripture. Each of them took their departure from a conception of conscience which was very much the creation of medieval European Catholicism. Generations of primarily monastic reflection on sin and guilt, virtue and vice, within the context of sacramental confession had raised self-examination to an art form which in extreme cases could be psychologically damaging. "Conscience" was the mental process by which individuals assessed and passed judgment on their own lives and actions, measuring thoughts, words, deeds done and undone, against criteria supplied by scripture, tradition, and the Church. By 1500, it was an established principle of moral theology that no one should ever act, nor be expected or required to act, against their conscience; and that to act knowingly and willfully against one's conscience was a mortal sin. It was to this principle that Luther appealed loudly and often in his brushes with ecclesiastical authorities around 1520. There was nothing new in the principle. What was novel was appealing to this principle against not simply the judicial but the dogmatic authority of the Church.

Luther's conscience was lively but unruly. This is evident from his later reminiscences, which record how during his time as a friar his tender conscience fostered anxiety over the observance of minutiae of the rule of his religious order. Life in religious orders was envisaged as a training in conscience and a denial of self. Obedience in indifferent matters was a training in humility. Self was subordinated to community—via the paternal authority of the prior and his hierarchical superiors up to the pope. Luther's conscience, however, did not respond to this training, which troubled him and his confessors, who, as he remarked, simply could not understand the anxieties of a man whose life seemed relatively blameless. Luther went instead in a radically different direction, as he developed a new theology of justification which at least bestowed upon him that "peace of conscience" which became for him the practical measure of theological integrity. His peace of conscience rested not on the rigorous examination of conscience and the exhaustive cataloguing of failure in confession, nor even on the "perfect contrition" of which medieval theology spoke, but on the promise or guarantee of forgiveness which he found first in the words of absolution uttered by the priest to the penitent (words which, medieval theologians held, were the words of Christ uttered by the priest as his representative and in his name), and then in the more general promise of forgiveness that he identified as the central message of the Gospel. This peace of conscience was the fruit of his doctrine of certitude of grace, by which, for Luther, the burden of salvation was taken off the self.

Yet at a deeper level, the deployment of peace of conscience as a practical yardstick of doctrinal truth amounted to an assertion of the self shrouded beneath a professed subjection to scripture. In practice, introspection, often a psychologically harmful introspection, remained a marked feature of the Protestant traditions. And, as the emerging notion of "private judgment" showed, the appeal to the plain meaning of scripture alone necessarily thrust onto the individual the onus of deciding just which of the competing plain meanings of scripture was the authoritative one. The inherent individualism of this approach to scripture was obscured partly by Luther's insistence on scriptural transparency and supremacy, and partly by the sheer force of his personality. The egotism of his rhetoric drowned out the intrinsic individualism of his logic. This egotism manifested itself unmistakably in his life. Successive repudiations of paternal authority—first that of his father, then of his spiritual father (Staupitz), of his princely father (the Elector Frederick), of the *pater patriae* Charles V, and ultimately of the Holy Father himself (the supreme figure of Christian fatherhood on earth was unveiled by Luther as Antichrist)—marked the stages by which Luther emancipated his conscience and his own individuality from any earthly subjection.[24] By 1530 nobody told Luther what to do. The certainty of divine favor that he had uncovered in the certainty of scripture had freed this particular Christian from any merely human authority.

Abbreviations

WA, followed by volume number and page number, refers to the volumes of the best available edition of Luther's works, and specifically to the first and largest section of that edition, the *Schriften* (writings): *D. Martin Luthers Werke: Kritische Gesamtausgabe* (Weimar: Böhlau, 1893–2009).

WA Tr, followed by volume number, item number, page number, and date, refers to the second section of that edition, the volumes of *Tischreden* ("table talk"), e.g., WA Tr 1.446, p. 195, early 1533.

WA Br, followed by volume number, item number, and page number, refers to the fourth section of that edition, the volumes of *Briefwechsel* (correspondence), e.g., Luther to the Archbishop of Mainz, 31 Oct. 1517, WA Br 1.48, pp. 110–12.

Notes

I. WITTENBERG 1517

1. *Vie du bienheureux martyr Jean Fisher*, ed. F. Van Ortroy, *Analecta Bollandiana* 10 (1891), pp. 121–365, at pp. 229–35. The account in this source is confused about the nature of the document that was defaced, but it was written by someone with good knowledge of the University of Cambridge and it is clear about where the document was posted.

2. E. Iserloh, *The Theses Were Not Posted* (London: Chapman, 1968). His original challenge, as controversial as the *Ninety-Five Theses* themselves, was made in "Luthers Thesenanschlag, Tatsache oder Legende?," *Trierer theologische Zeitschrift* 70 (1961), pp. 303–12.

3. Leszek Kolakowski, *Religion* (Oxford: OUP, 1982), p. 16. For the debate among German scholars, see the articles collected in *Geschichte in Wissenschaft und Unterricht* 16 (1965), pp. 661–99. See also, more recently, J. Ott and M. Treu (eds.), *Luthers Thesenanschlag: Faktum oder Fiktion* (Leipzig: Evangelische Verlagsanstalt, 2008).

4. WA Tr 3, no. 3722, p. 564, 2 Feb. 1538. WA Tr 2.2455a, p. 467, Jan.–March 1532. The dating of this to the Feast of All Saints is evidently approximate. See also WA Tr 5.5349, p. 77, and 6431, pp. 657–58, for other versions.

5. Luther to the Elector Frederick, 21 Nov. 1518, WA Br 1.110, p. 245.

6. WA 59.180.

7. Iserloh, *The Theses Were Not Posted*, pp. 77–82.

8. Martin Luther, *Tomus Secundus Operum Omnium* (Wittenberg: Seitz, 1551), sig. *4v. For the disputation on scholastic theology, see ch. 3 below.

9. Luther notes Melanchthon's arrival in his letter to Georg Spalatin, 31 Aug. 1518, WA Br 1.88, p. 192. For Luther's communications with the bishops, see Iserloh, *The Theses Were Not Posted*, pp. 53–60.

10. Martin Luther, *Tomus Secundus Operum Omnium* (Wittenberg: Seitz, 1551), sig. *4v.

11. This transcript is taken from Martin Treu, "Urkunde und Reflexion: Wiederentdeckung eines Belegs von Luthers Thesenanschlag," *Luthers Thesenanschlag* (2008), pp. 59–67, at p. 59. The underlinings represent expansions, for clarity, of abbreviations and contractions in the original manuscript note. One word is left incomplete, as damaged or hard to read in the original manuscript. The likeliest conjectures here would be "primum" (first), or perhaps even more probably "publice," echoing Melanchthon.

12. Such a dependence was suggested by Hans Volz in 1972. See Treu, "Urkunde und Reflexion," p. 61.

13. Iserloh, *The Theses Were Not Posted*, p. 80.

14. Andrew Pettegree, *Brand Luther* (London: Penguin, 2015), pp. 13, 51–52, and 71–72. This counters earlier views, followed by Iserloh (p. 86), that the theses were not printed beforehand. Much later, though, Luther wrote of these events in terms which would sit more naturally with his having sent out the theses originally in manuscript form, only printing them for general publication after he had come to feel that his initial protest was being ignored. See the preface to the *Opera Omnia* of 1545, and also WA Tr 4.4446, p. 316, 25 March 1539.

15. F. Myconius, *Historia Reformationis*, ed. Ernst Salomon Cyprian (Leipzig, 1718), p. 23.

16. See *Wider Hans Worst* [1541], WA 51.461–572, at p. 540.

17. Luther to Spalatin, no date, WA Br 1.50, pp. 117–19, at p. 118. The WA editors place this letter in Nov. 1517, but this is probably based on the myth of the first fortnight. There is no internal evidence as to its date. It could as easily be from Dec. 1517 or even Jan. 1518.

18. For these letters, see Christoph Scheurl, *Briefbuch*, ed. F. F. von Soden and J. K. F. Knaake (2 vols., Potsdam: Gropius, 1867–72), vol. 1, nos. 156–58, pp. 40–42, and no. 160, pp. 42–43 (8 Jan. 1518).

19. *Kilian Leibs Briefwechsel und Diarien*, ed. J. Schlecht (Aschendorff, Münster 1909. Reformationsgeschichtliche Studien und Texte; 7), p. 85.

20. Luther to the Archbishop of Mainz, 31 Oct. 1517, WA Br 1.48, pp. 110–12.

21. Luther to the Archbishop of Mainz, 31 Oct. 1517, WA Br 1.48, p. 111.

22. *Dokumente zur Causa Lutheri (1517–1521)*, ed. P. Fabisch and E. Iserloh (2 vols., Münster: Aschendorff, 1988, Corpus Catholicorum 41–42), 1, p. 310.

23. *Dokumente zur Causa Lutheri* 1, p. 315.

24. *Album Academiae Vitebergensis ab A. Ch. MDII usque ad A. MDLX*, ed. C. E. Foerstemann (Leipzig: Tauchnitz, 1841), p. 76.

25. *Resolutiones disputationum de indulgentiarum virtute* [1518], WA 1, pp. 522–628. The title Luther gave this book might seem to confirm that there was a disputation, by analogy with the work he wrote after the Leipzig Disputation in 1519, *Resolutiones Lutherianae super propositionibus suis Lipsiae disputatis*. But equally, he had written his *Resolutio Lutheriana super propositione decima tertia* (Leipzig: Lotter, 1519) before the event at which it was to be debated (see WA 2.180–240). So this is far from decisive.

26. WA Br 1.58, pp. 135–41, at p. 139. The letter is undated, but thought to have been written about the middle of February. Melanchthon to Johannes Oecolampadius, 21 July 1519, *Epistola de Lipsica Disputatione* ([Leipzig: Landsberg, 1519. USTC 651522), sig. A2r: "Superiore anno sententias, quas Martinus de indulgentiis proposuit disputandas Eckius obelis notavit."

27. *Wider Hans Worst*, WA 51.539.

28. This is the burden of Staupitz's comments about indulgences in a sermon on contrition preached in Advent 1516. Franz Posset, *The Front-Runner of the Catholic Reformation* (Aldershot: Ashgate, 2003), p. 180, misconstrues his critique as an anticipation of Luther's.

29. For a helpful analysis of this work, see Livia Cárdenas, *Friedrich der Weise und das Wittenberger Heiltumsbuch* (Berlin: Lukas, 2002), on which this paragraph is mainly based.

30. Luther to Spalatin, 14 Dec. 1516, WA Br 1.30, p. 78.

31. *Canon Pietro Casola's Pilgrimage to Jerusalem in the year 1494*, ed. M. Margaret Newett (Manchester: University Press, 1907).

32. See *Tomus Primus Omnium Operum Reverendi Domini Martini Lutheri* (Wittenberg: Luft, 1550), fol. 291v: "Deus . . . a quo uno verae indulgentiae fluunt."

2. FROM ERFURT TO WITTENBERG

1. WA Tr 4.4707, p. 440, 16 July 1539, for the vow to Saint Anne; and WA Tr 1.119, p. 46, Nov. 1531, for the accident with the sword.
2. Dietrich Emme, *Martin Luthers Weg ins Kloster* (Regensburg: D. Emme, 1991), esp. pp. 9–10, and ch. 2, pp. 15–22, "Weshalb wurde Martin Luther ein Mönch?," a reissue of an article originally published in 1978. See also his *Martin Luther: seine Jugend- und Studentenzeit, 1483–1505* (2nd ed., Bonn: D. Emme, 1982). Emme weaves his diaphanous web from scattered threads pulled out of Luther's letters, treatises, and tabletalk, and then traverses the cavernous gaps with an insouciant flight of fancy for which his chief authority is his own work.
3. WA Tr 1.326, p. 134, summer or autumn 1532. See Emme, *Martin Luthers Weg ins Kloster*, pp. 26, 33, 40, 60, 80, and 178. The arguments circle around endlessly and self-referentially, returning always to the same handful of citations from Luther's works, none of which mention a duel, a death, or a murder.
4. Posset, *Front-Runner of the Catholic Reformation*, pp. 91–92. Posset avows himself impressed by Emme's case because of the difficulty the scholarly consensus has in explaining Luther's obscure references to the risk of "capture." But this is nothing as to the difficulty of giving even one good reason why this obscure reference should be connected with an alleged homicide for which there was neither a *corpus delicti* nor any recorded judicial proceedings. One could of course imagine countless possible explanations of what Luther meant by "capture" without resorting to a murder rap. Posset believes that it was "peculiar" of Luther to have commented that he "was made a friar" (p. 92). The phrase "factus sum monachus" is not in the least peculiar. The passive form of *facio* is standard Latin usage for "becoming."

5. Johannes Cochlaeus, *Commentaria Ioannis Cochlaei, De Actis et Scriptis Martini Lutheri* (Mainz: Behem, 1549), pp. 1–2.

6. For Dr. Usingen's publications, see Wilbirgis Klaiber, *Katholische Kontroverstheologen und Reformer des 16. Jahrhunderts* (Münster: Aschendorff, 1978), pp. 290–92. For his life, see *Deutsche Biographie* (https://www.deutsche-biographie.de/), under "Arnoldi."

7. Emme, *Martin Luthers Weg ins Kloster*, p. 24.

8. Crotus Rubianus to Luther, 28 April 1520, WA Br 2, no. 281, p. 91.

9. Martin Brecht, *Martin Luther*, tr. James L. Schaaf (3 vols., Minneapolis: Fortress, 1985–93), vol. 1, p. 49.

10. WA 8.573–74, mentions that "beset by the terror and fear of sudden death, I vowed a forced and necessary vow" (*coactum et necessarium votum*). See Emme, *Martin Luthers Weg ins Kloster*, pp. 3, 33, 39, 57, and 84. The force Luther mentions here is almost certainly the force of circumstances.

11. Luther to Melanchthon, 9 Sept. 1521, WA Br 2.428, p. 385. Luther's Latin here is not very correct, but note the present tense of "videtur," "it seems," which shows that he is reinterpreting his recollection in the light of his circumstances at that time, not recalling some long agony occasioned by his father's words, an impression given by the rendering "it seemed" in the American translation found in *Luther's Works*, ed. J. Pelikan (55 vols., St. Louis, MO: Concordia, 1955–), vol. 48, p. 301.

12. WA Tr 3.3556A, p. 410, March 1537. See also 3556B, p. 411, and Tr. 1.881, p. 439.

13. The term "apostate" was used for those who fled the religious life without proper canonical dispensation. A "gyrovague" was a monk who, though not actually casting off his monastic clothing or "habit," nevertheless spent as much time as he could on the road—the "monk out of his cloister" of the type Chaucer noted was likened to a fish out of water.

14. WA Tr 1.354, p. 148, autumn 1532.

15. Brecht, *Martin Luther*, vol. 1, p. 156.

16. From his lectures on 1 Timothy in 1528. See WA 26.21.

17. Brecht, *Martin Luther*, vol. 1, p. 69.
18. WA Tr 1.495, p. 220, spring 1533.
19. WA Tr 3.3556a, p. 410, March 1537.
20. WA Tr 1.137, p. 59, Dec. 1531. Brecht, *Martin Luther*, vol. 1, p. 75. Luther's report of Staupitz's comment filters it through his later "Law and Gospel"–inspired dichotomy between seeing Christ as judge and seeing Christ as savior. Staupitz's words are more likely to have meant simply the rather obvious point that, for a Christian, the presence of Christ should not evoke horror.
21. Cochlaeus's report that on one occasion Luther had a sort of fit during mass, when the gospel of the exorcism of a boy was read, is associated by Brecht with the story of his response to the eucharistic presence in 1515 (*Martin Luther*, vol. 1, p. 75). But Cochlaeus's story has all the hallmarks of malicious rumor: it is simply too good to be true. And, of course, the gospel is read out in the mass quite some time before the performance of the consecration that brings about the presence of Christ.
22. WA Tr 1.141, p. 62, 14 Dec. 1531.
23. WA Tr 1.518, p. 240, spring 1533.
24. WA 9.12. WA Tr 5.6475, p. 683: "Wimpfeling was almost killed when he questioned whether Augustine had been a monk."
25. WA Tr 1.116, pp. 44–45, Nov. 1531.
26. WA Tr 2.1240, pp. 5–6, Dec. 1531.
27. WA Tr 3.3767, p. 598, 22 Feb. 1538.
28. Brecht, *Martin Luther*, vol. 1, p. 85: "Until then he had believed that the only texts in the Bible were those which also appeared in the postils. Whether at that time Luther already possessed a postil or knew it only from the lessons read in the bursa cannot be determined." This sort of elephantine exegesis mistakes the genre. A man is not on oath when talking at his table. The point of the story is that the liturgical readings were all that most people knew of the New Testament. To take another example, if Luther is making a factual statement in claiming that Staupitz restored the Bible to the Augustinian Order (Brecht, pp. 84–85), then he is unlikely also to be making a factual statement in claiming that he himself was the only friar in the Erfurt house who read the

Bible (Brecht, p. 86), though of course one can imagine conditions under which both statements might be true. It is essential to bear in mind that Luther's "table talk" consists of second-hand reports of throwaway remarks uttered long after the events they relate.

29. WA Tr 1.116, pp. 44–45, Nov. 1531.
30. WA Tr 3.3016, p. 141, March 1533.
31. WA Tr 3.3593, p. 439, May–June 1537.
32. Brecht, *Martin Luther*, vol. 1, p. 81.
33. WA Tr 4.4707, p. 440 (16 July 1539): "Doctor Staupitius me incitabat contra papam." Luther's comment might also be more plausible if it is taken as shorthand for a more complex process of unintentional causation.
34. Posset, *Front-Runner of the Catholic Reformation*, p. 328. See also pp. 294–95 and 373 ("anti-papal"). See pp. 254 for the joke and 281 for the "true pope."
35. Fisher's denunciation of corruption at the papal curia, a one-paragraph *cri de coeur*, was sometimes cited by Protestant controversialists seeking to condemn the Catholic Church out of the mouths of its own spokesmen. See John Fisher, *Convulsio Calumniarum Ulrichi Veleni* (Antwerp: Vorstermann, 1522, USTC 403701), sig. O1v.
36. Posset's *Front-Runner of the Catholic Reformation* is the most recent and extensive.
37. For the sermons on Job, see Johann von Staupitz, *Tübinger Predigten*, ed. R. Wetzel (Berlin: De Gruyter, 1987), part 1, vol. 1 of his *Sämtliche Schriften*, ed. L. Dohna and R. Wetzel.
38. Staupitz's reading of Augustine changed over time. By 1516 he was himself the author of a treatise on predestination. See *Libellus de exsecutione aeternae praedestinationis*, ed. L. Dohna (Berlin: De Gruyter, 1979), part 1, vol. 2 of the *Sämtliche Schriften*. In that text the anti-Pelagian writings of Augustine held an important place (see pp. 335–42). This may reflect the publication between 1505 and 1508 of the first reasonably complete and critical edition of Augustine's works, which gathered the anti-Pelagian writings in one volume.
39. Brecht, *Martin Luther*, vol. 1, p. 105.

40. Brecht, *Martin Luther*, vol. 1, pp. 99–100.
41. WA Tr 3, no. 3582a, pp. 431–32, March–May 1537.
42. WA Tr 4, no. 4785, p. 502, ca. 1540.
43. Thomas More, *A Dialogue concerning Heresies*, ed. T. M. C. Lawler et al. (New Haven: Yale UP, 1981; The Complete Works of St Thomas More, 6), vol. 1, pp. 87–88.
44. Brecht, *Martin Luther*, vol. 1, p. 104. WA Tr 4.4925, pp. 582–83, May 1540, where he says that when he asked her whether she was willing to die, she replied certainly not, because she knew what life was like here, but not what it would be like there. See also Tr 6.7005, p. 320.
45. WA Tr 1.221, p. 94, from April 1532.

3. THE CATHOLIC LUTHER

1. Brecht, *Martin Luther*, vol. 1, p. 96.
2. WA Tr 2.1552, p. 129, 20 May 1532. He added that Carlstadt had taken his doctorate in theology without owning one.
3. Martin Luther, *Dictata super Psalterium*, WA 3–4. For the origins and fate of these materials, see the introduction, WA 3.1–8.
4. The National Archives (UK), SP2/R, fols. 28–274, for John Fisher's voluminous and often badly damaged draft commentary, on roughly the first 50 psalms. There are passing comments against Jews in a handful of psalms. See, e.g., fols. 92r (where Jews are denounced together with tyrants and heretics) and 246v (where Jews are described as "worse than dogs").
5. See, e.g., WA 3.154 on Ps 27, and 176–77, on Ps 31.
6. WA 3.289.
7. Theological discussion is not aided by the tendency, common among theologians in the Lutheran and Reformed traditions, to label this doctrine simply "justification by faith." All medieval and early modern Catholic theologians who reflected on the subject were aware that Christians were justified by faith in Jesus Christ. The question that established the difference between Catholicism and Protestantism was whether they were justified by faith "alone" (or, still more exactly in some formula-

tions, by faith "only"). There are, as we shall see later, further issues about the connotations of both "justification" and "faith."

8. WA 4.61: "Cooperatores enim sumus dei."
9. WA 4.204–5.
10. WA 3.17 and 25.
11. WA 3.68 and 649.
12. WA 3.258.
13. WA 3.621 and 645.
14. WA 3.47, 65, 91, and 249.
15. WA 3.127.
16. WA 3.29, 288, and 370.
17. WA 3.172 and 283.
18. WA 3.174, 251, and 258.
19. WA 3.289.
20. WA 6.183 (Luther's response to the condemnations of his teaching issued by the universities of Louvain and Cologne); and WA Tr 2.2544a, p. 516, March 1532.
21. WA Tr 4.3944, p. 25, 5 Aug. 1538. This was part of a longer comment on how far it was from his original intention to attack the old ways, and on how divine providence had called him to the task. The *Encomium Moriae* (1511) and the *Julius Exclusus* (1514) are the likeliest of Erasmus's writings to have irked the young Luther. Later on, he had toyed with the idea of translating the *Julius Exclusus*, but found he could not quite manage it. WA Tr 4.4902, p. 574, May 1540.
22. WA 3.269.
23. See Colet's sermon to the convocation of the clergy of Canterbury Province, *Oratio habita a D. Ioanne Coleto Decano Sancti Pauli ad Clerum in Conuocatione, Anno. M.D.xj.* (London: R. Pynson, 1511 or 1512, STC 5545), sigs. B1v and B4v. For a similar sermon by Clichtove, to a diocesan synod at Paris, see Josse Clichtove, *Sermones Iudoci Clichtovei* (Paris: Kerver, 1534), fol. 372v, "Integritas presidentium / salus est subditorum."
24. WA 3.308 and 421.
25. WA 3.509.
26. WA 3.332 and 4.386.

27. WA 3.292 and 334; and WA 4.77 and 345.
28. WA 3.161, 280, 460, and 470.
29. WA 3.262.
30. WA 3.95, 419, and 453. See also WA 9.75–76, his notes on Lombard's *Sentences*, where, likewise, he proposes an entirely traditional understanding of concupiscence, seen primarily as "malum" rather than intrinsically as "peccatum." See also WA 9.90–91, on faith, where Luther's understanding is entirely within bounds of medieval tradition.
31. WA 3.223.
32. WA 3.416 and 424.
33. WA Tr 1.160, p. 76, autumn 1532. According to Luther, Carlstadt threatened to delate him to the pope as a heretic for this, though this claim does not seem very plausible.
34. WA 4.248.
35. WA 3.319 and 382.
36. WA 3.575.
37. WA 3.577–78.
38. WA 4.82.
39. WA 3.287 and 320.
40. WA 3.11–12.
41. WA 4.12.
42. WA 4.516–17.
43. WA 4.211.
44. It had been preceded in this by Lorenzo Valla's *Annotationes in Novum Testamentum*, which made substantial reference to the original Greek, and had been published by Erasmus as *In Latinam Novi Testamenti interpretationes ex collatione Graecorum exemplarium Adnotationes* (Paris: Bade, 1505, USTC 143044). But Lefèvre's commentary on Paul was more substantial and more theological than Valla's.
45. See, e.g., WA 56.154 and plate A for the notes on Romans.
46. WA Tr 1.335, first half of 1532, p. 136, reporting his move away from allegorical interpretation.
47. WA 56.502.
48. WA 3.171–78 for his earliest comment on Ps 31; WA 56.1–

154 for the notes on Romans; and WA 1.167 for the devotional reflections on Ps 31. One might add that there is no sign of Luther's new understanding of concupiscence after baptism in his sermons on the Ten Commandments, which, although published in 1518, are generally agreed to have been delivered earlier, probably in Lent 1517. It could be that Luther was not yet sure enough of his ground to publish his ideas on concupiscence after baptism in print. Or it may be that the text of the scholia which we have dates from after Easter 1517. The concern with indulgences which is manifested at various points in this text would suit such a dating. For the preaching of indulgences only seems to catch Luther's eye around that time, when the indulgence for contributing to the rebuilding of Saint Peter's was being preached in his vicinity.

49. Augustine exempted Jesus Christ from this law, and hence hesitated to include his mother, Mary, under it. See his *De natura et gratia* 36.42.

50. Augustine, trained in the schools of classical rhetoric, liked to define his figures of speech precisely. In this case, the figure of speech he detected was "metonymy," when the name of a cause or effect of a thing is used in place of the name of the thing itself. The concupiscence of the flesh was both a cause and an effect of sin, and could therefore be described metonymically as "sin" in the baptized. See *On Marriage and Concupiscence*, book 1, ch. 23.

51. WA 56.273–74. The words of Augustine are from his anti-Pelagian treatise *On Marriage and Concupiscence*, book 1, ch. 25. In this citation, Luther misplaced the word "peccatum." Augustine's words were: "concupiscentiam in baptismate remitti non ut non sit, sed ut non imputetur in peccatum," namely, "concupiscence is remitted in baptism not so that it does not exist but so that it is not reckoned as sin." See *Octaua pars librorum diui Aurelii Augustini* (Basel: Amerbach, 1506), sig. k4v, probably the text Luther used. Luther's formulation here—"peccatum concupiscentiam in baptismate remitti, non ut non sit, sed ut non imputetur"—was the nearest he ever got to citing the text accurately. In countless later references, doubtless working from

memory, he omitted the word "concupiscence" and spoke only of "sin." Thus, for Luther, "sin" (rather than "concupiscence") was what was said by Augustine to be forgiven but not entirely removed in baptism. This erroneous recollection was probably responsible for Luther's original adoption of this idiosyncratic position, though he later argued that his position was justified from the words of Paul alone. Augustine always insisted that the concupiscence of the flesh was not sin in the baptized, because baptism took away all sin.

52. WA 56.172. See Augustine, *De spiritu et litera*, 11.18, and Aristotle, *Nicomachean Ethics*, III.7, p. 1114a.

53. WA 1.224–28.

54. It is striking that Thomas Aquinas is not once specified as the target of any of these 97 theses, probably an indication that Luther was not familiar with his work. Within a few years, Thomas would become Luther's supreme bugbear among theologians, standing for the whole scholastic tradition. This is probably because several of Luther's early opponents were from the Order of Preachers (or Dominicans), to which Thomas himself had belonged.

4. THE QUEST FOR CERTAINTY

1. WA 47.682, emphasis added. For a typical interpretation of Ishmael and Isaac, see Augustinus von Alveldt, *Super apostolica sede* (Leipzig: Lotther, 1520), sig. D1v, where the Christian Church is compared to Sarah's son, and the Synagogue of the Jews to Hagar's.

2. Thomas Aquinas, *Summa Theologiae*, 1a 2ae q. 112, art. 5.

3. The standard proof text for this, Eccles 9:1, "no one knows whether they deserve love or hatred," was cited in Cambridge by the Observant Franciscan Stephen Baron, *Sermones declamati coram alma universitate Cantibrigiensi* (London: Wynkyn de Worde, n.d. [ca. 1510]), sermon 10, sig. D7v; in Cologne by the Dominican Cornelius de Snekis, *Sermones XXI super Confraternitate de Serto Rosaceo* (Paris: Bade, 1514), sermon 21, fols.

LXIr–v; and in Tübingen by Staupitz in his sermons on Job, in *Tübinger Predigten*, ed. R. Wetzel, p. 83.

4. WA 1.373: "Aut certus erit de gratia, quod omnes negant."

5. WA 57.215, emphasis added. The prepositional phrase *pro me* (or similar—*pro te, pro se, pro nobis*) itself became one of the features distinguishing Luther's new theology from that which he henceforth rejected. Mere belief that Christ was a savior, he insisted, was not faith, merely informed opinion. The devils in hell acknowledged as much, to no avail. Faith was when the individual believed that Christ was a savior *pro se*, for himself or herself, when people believed, with utter certainty, that the general principle of salvation had been specifically applied in their particular, individual case.

6. Thomas Aquinas, *Summa Theologiae*, 1a 2ae q. 112, art. 5. I have translated the technical term "gratia gratum faciens" as "justifying grace." The exposition of this conclusion makes it clear that the knowledge of which Thomas speaks entails certainty.

7. WA 56.252.

8. WA 57.216, emphasis added.

9. J. Wicks (ed. and tr.), *Cajetan Responds: a Reader in Reformation Controversy* (Eugene, OR: Wipf & Stock, 2011), p. 55. See also ch. 5 below.

10. Luther to the Archbishop of Mainz, 31 Oct. 1517, WA Br 1.48, p. 111.

11. *Instructio pro confessione peccatorum* [1518], WA 1.257–65, and *Sermo de digna praeparatione cordis pro suscipiendo sacramento eucharistiae* [1518], WA 1.325–34.

12. WA 1.264 (*Instructions*). Compare WA 57.170–71 (*Hebrews*).

13. WA 1.330.

14. WA 1.332.

15. WA Tr 3, no. 3232b, p. 228 (June or July 1532).

16. E. H. Erikson, *Young Man Luther: A study in psychoanalysis and history* (London: Faber, 1959). John Osborne, *Luther* (London: Faber, 1961).

17. Luther to Spalatin, 10 June 1521, from the Wartburg, mentions his bowel problems (WA Br 2.417, p. 354). Although his letter of 15 July reports that the laxative Spalatin sent him has done

its work (WA Br 2.420, p. 364), he continued to be troubled. He was in agonies in September (WA Br 2.429, 9 Sept., p. 388), but he declared that his anus and belly were "finally back in favor" a month later (WA Br 2.434, 7 Oct., p. 434).

18. WA Tr 1.141, p. 61, 14 Dec. 1531; and Tr. 1, no. 122, p. 47, 30 Nov. 1530.

19. WA Tr 1.495, p. 220, spring 1533; Tr 4.5094, p. 654, June 1540; and Tr 4.4422, pp. 305–6, March 1539.

20. WA Tr 2.2066, p. 309, June–Aug. 1531.

21. *Disputatio Heidelbergae habita* [1518], WA 1.350–74, at p. 354, no. 13.

22. See Staupitz's sermons on Job, *Tübinger Predigten*, ed. R. Wetzel, p. 95, where he cites Thomas Aquinas and Giles of Rome as authorities for this position. This is further strong evidence against Luther's statement that he "got all his stuff from Staupitz."

23. WA 1.373.

24. Luther to Spalatin, 18 May 1518, WA Br 1.75, pp. 173–74.

25. Lowell C. Green, *How Melanchthon Helped Luther Discover the Gospel* (Fallbrook, CA: Verdict, 1980) interprets the preface to support dating the crucial breakthrough as late as 1519. A. E. McGrath, *Luther's Theology of the Cross* (Oxford: Blackwell, 1985), p. 146, following the emphasis on *iustitia*, places it in 1515, while Luther was still working on the *Dictata super Psalterium*. He adds in *Reformation Thought* (3rd ed. Oxford: Blackwell, 1999), p. 110, that this is the "general consensus among Luther scholars." James Atkinson, *Martin Luther and the Birth of Protestantism* (Harmondsworth: Pelican, 1968), finds "the real evangelical Luther" (p. 94) from the start of the *Dictata*. I stand with what McGrath notes as the "significant minority opinion" (p. 311, note 8) in placing it in 1518. For this tradition see Daniel Oliver, *Luther's Faith* (St Louis, MO: Concordia, 1978).

26. *Vorrede zum ersten Bande der Gesamtausgaben seiner lateinischer Schriften* [1545], WA 54.176–87.

27. To this extent, the moment at which scholars date Luther's crucial breakthrough tends to reflect precisely what they take that crucial breakthrough to consist in, as Leif Grane observed in

Modus Loquendi Theologicus: Luthers Kampf um die Erneuerung der Theologie, 1515–1518 (Leiden: Brill, 1975), pp. 11–12.

28. Luther's unsympathetic assessment of Catholicism as a religion preaching justification by works is often taken as normative. See, e.g., Lyndal Roper, *Martin Luther: Renegade and Prophet* (London: Bodley Head, 2016), p. 337.

29. On the tradition of cooperative grace, see A. McGrath, *Iustitia Dei: a History of the Christian Doctrine of Justification* (2 vols., Cambridge: Cambridge University Press, 1986), vol. 1, pp. 31 and 105–9.

30. For the concept of historical faith (*fides historica*), see Philip Melanchthon, *Loci communes rerum theologicarum* (Wittenberg: [Lotter], 1521. USTC 673141), sig. K3r–v.

31. WA Tr 1.347, summer or autumn 1532, p. 140.

32. WA Tr 3.3131, p. 180, from spring 1533. See also WA Tr 2.1581, p. 140, May 1532.

33. Bucer to Beatus Rhenanus, 1 May 1518, in *Briefwechsel des Beatus Rhenanus*, ed. A, Horawitz & K. Hartfelder (Leipzig: Teubner, 1886), p. 107, "Martinus ille indulgentiarum . . . sugillator." This aspect of the Luther phenomenon has been lucidly expounded by Andrew Pettegree, *Brand Luther* (London: Penguin, 2015).

34. *Resolutiones disputationum de indulgentiarum virtute* [1518], WA 1.522–628, at p. 594.

35. WA 1.525–26.

36. WA 1.541. And see, in general, "Conclusio VII," WA 1.539–45.

37. WA 1.541–42.

38. WA 1.543.

39. WA 1.540.

40. WA 1.544.

41. WA 1.595.

42. WA 1.610.

43. WA 1.616.

44. For the biography of Prierias, I rely on Michael M. Tavuzzi, *Prierias: The Life and Works of Silvestro Mazzolini da Prierio, 1456–1527* (Durham, NC: Duke University Press, 1997).

45. S. Prierias, *In Presumptuosas Martini Luther Conclusiones de Potestate Pape Dialogus* ([Rome]: [Silber], 1518, USTC 841732). For a modern edition, see *Dokumente zur Causa Lutheri (1517–1521)*, ed. P. Fabisch and E. Iserloh (2 vols., Münster: Aschendorff, 1988), vol. 1, pp. 33–107.
46. *Dokumente zur Causa Lutheri* 1, p. 84.
47. *Dokumente zur Causa Lutheri* 1, p. 88.
48. *Dokumente zur Causa Lutheri* 1, pp. 89–93.
49. WA 1.589.
50. WA 1.525.
51. *Ad dialogum Silvestri Prieratis de potestate papae responsio* [1518], WA 1.644–86. Luther to Spalatin, 8 Aug. 1518, WA Br 1.85, p. 188.
52. Luther to Staupitz, 1 Sept. 1518, WA Br 1.89, p. 194.
53. Luther to Reuchlin, 14 Dec. 1518, WA Br 1.120, pp. 268–69.
54. WA 1.662.
55. WA 1.666.
56. WA 1.541.
57. WA Tr 1.423, p. 183, Dec. 1532.

5. INTIMATIONS OF ANTICHRIST

1. Luther to Spalatin, 28 Aug. 1518, WA Br 1.87, pp. 190–91.
2. Luther to Staupitz, 1 Sept. 1518, WA Br 1.89, p. 193. His letter to Melanchthon, 11 Oct. 1518, WA Br 1.98, pp. 212–13, is in a more heightened key. See WA Tr 1.509, p. 233, spring 1533, for his later admission, "valde metuebam."
3. Luther to Spalatin, 10 Oct. 1518, WA Br 1.97, p. 209 (Peutinger). Luther to Melanchthon, 11 Oct. 1518, WA Br 1.98, p. 213.
4. Luther to Spalatin, 31 Oct. and 13 Nov. 1518, WA Br 1.105 and 108, pp. 225 and 230.
5. Luther to Spalatin, 10 Oct 1518, WA Br 1.97, p. 210.
6. These briefing papers have been helpfully translated and published by Jared Wicks in *Cajetan Responds: A Reader in Reformation Controversy* (Washington, DC: Catholic University of America Press, 1978; repr. Eugene, OR: Wipf & Stock, 2011),

pp. 47–98. Wicks's introduction offers an account of the Augsburg meeting and its aftermath, pp. 21–28.

7. WA 2.13. Luther repeated this observation of Cajetan's about new doctrine (*nova dogmata*) in his letter to Elector Frederick, 25 Oct. 1518, WA Br 1.110, p. 234.

8. Cajetan, *In primam partem secundae partis Summe Theologie* ([Paris]: Chevallon, [1520]), sig. B4v–B5r (near the end of the book).

9. This account of their meetings is based on Luther's *Acta Augustana* (WA 2.6–26) and a letter from Cajetan to Elector Frederick, 25 Oct. 1518, WA Br 1.110, pp. 232–35.

10. For the full text of Luther's formal protestation, see WA 2.8–9.

11. WA 2.9–16.

12. Luther to Cajetan, 17 and 18 Oct. 1518, WA Br 1.103 and 104, pp. 220–23, esp. p. 220.

13. See Niccolò de' Tudeschi (aka Panormitanus), *Commentariorum Prima in Primum Lib. Decretalium* (Lyon: Gryphius, 1534), "De electione," ca. 4, "Significasti," fol. 122r. Luther had already cited this text in his *Response* to Prierias (WA 1.656), and did so again in his letter to the Franciscans of Jüterbog, 15 May 1519, WA Br 1.172, pp. 387–93, at p. 391.

14. See Brad S. Gregory, *The Unintended Reformation* (Cambridge, MA: Belknap, 2012), pp. 95 and 107–9 for an exploration of the long-term consequences of this.

15. Luther to Staupitz, 14 Jan. 1521, WA Br 2.366, pp. 245–46, at p. 245. He goes on to say that he takes these words as having come "through" rather than "from" Staupitz.

16. WA Tr 1.445, p. 194, early 1533: "Ich wolt gern wissen, wie der man wer selig worden!"

17. WA Tr 2.2250, p. 376, from late 1531. The tone of this recollection is a touch rueful.

18. Scheurl to Otto Beckmann on 21 October 1518, *Briefbuch*, no. 170, pp. 51–52. Link had got back to Nuremberg the day before.

19. WA Tr 1.225, p. 96, April 1532, on the threefold excommunication. The first "excommunication" was that Staupitz "absolved me from the observance and rule of the order," in case the pope

commanded Staupitz to imprison or silence him, so that he could reply that Luther was not under his obedience. WA Tr 2.2250, p. 376, late 1531, talks of a threefold "absolution" or release. Staupitz, he says on this occasion, left him alone at Augsburg. See also WA Tr 2.2455a, p. 467, early 1532: "Anno 17. in die omnium sanctorum incepit primum scribere contra papam et indulgentias. Anno 18. excommunicabar. Anno 19. Disputabam Lipsiae contra Eccium." The excommunication here must allude to the Staupitz event, as not even Luther's memory could have malfunctioned to the extent of putting his papal excommunication ahead of the Leipzig Debate.

20. See, e.g., D. C. Steinmetz, *Reformers in the Wings* (Philadelphia: Fortress, 1971), p. 26.
21. WA Tr 4.4414, p. 303, March 1539.
22. WA Tr 1.409, p. 177, Dec. 1532, "reliquit me Deo."
23. WA Tr 1.1203, pp. 597–98, 30 July 1535.
24. Luther to Staupitz, 20 Feb. 1519, WA Br 1.152, pp. 344–45, at p. 344.
25. Cajetan to the Elector Frederick, 25 Oct. 1518, WA Br 1.110, p. 233.
26. Cajetan to the Elector Frederick, 25 Oct. 1518, WA Br 1.110, pp. 234–35.
27. Luther to Staupitz, 12 Nov. and 25 Nov. 1518, WA Br 1.107 and 112, p. 228 and no. 112, p. 253 (in press). See also Luther to Wenzel Link, 18 Dec. 1518, WA Br 1.121, p. 270, sending a copy, and noting that the appeal had also been printed.
28. Christoph Scheurl to Staupitz, 10 Dec. 1518, in Scheurl, *Briefbuch*, no. 178, p. 63. He had probably heard about this from Melanchthon. His account might be taken to mean that Luther made his appeal at each place on both days, but the formal notarial dating of his appeal to the parish churchyard on 28 Nov. 1518 (3.00 pm) suggests the interpretation adopted here. For the appeal itself, see WA 2.34–40.
29. Luther to Wenzel Link, 18 Dec. 1518, WA Br 1.121, p. 270.
30. Luther to Spalatin, 13 March 1519, WA Vr. 1.161, p. 359.

31. WA 2.17.
32. WA 2.18.
33. *Acta Augustana* (1518), WA 2.17–18.
34. Luther to Christoph Langemantel, 25 Nov. 1518, WA Br 1.113, pp. 256–57.
35. Luther to the Elector Frederick, Nov. 1518, WA Br 1.110, p. 244.
36. Luther to Eck, 15 Nov. 1518, WA Br 1.109, p. 231.

6. LUTHER AND ECK

1. Petrus Mosellanus, *De ratione disputandi* (Leipzig: Lotter, 1519. USTC 631252), sigs. B4v–C1r.
2. *Dokumente zur Causa Lutheri* 1, p. 376.
3. For a brief biography of Eck, see E. Iserloh, *Johannes Eck (1486–1543): Scholastiker, Humanist, Kontroverstheologe* (Münster: Aschendorff, 1981).
4. J. P. Wurm, *Johannes Eck und der Oberdeutsche Zinsstreit, 1513–15* (Münster: Aschendorff, 1997, Reformationsgeschichtliche Studien und Texte 137), esp. pp. 1 and 82–89.
5. For a modern edition of the *Obelisks*, see *Dokumente zur Causa Lutheri* 1, pp. 376–447.
6. *Dokumente zur Causa Lutheri* 1, pp. 424, 431, 435, and 442.
7. Luther to Johannes Sylvius Egranus, 24 March 1518, WA Br 1.65, p. 158.
8. Brecht, *Martin Luther*, vol. 1, p. 211.
9. Like the inimitable Psmith, Luther was "a very fair purveyor of good, general invective." See P. G. Wodehouse, *Psmith, Journalist* (London: A. & C. Black, 1915), p. 58.
10. Luther to Eck, 19 May 1518, WA Br 1.77, p. 178. Is Luther looking in a mirror?
11. *Dokumente zur Causa Lutheri* 1, p. 402.
12. *Dokumente zur Causa Lutheri* 1, pp. 416–20, 422, 424, 430–31, and 435.
13. *Dokumente zur Causa Lutheri* 1, p. 397.

14. A. Carlstadt, *CCCLXX et Apologeticae Conclusiones* (Wittenberg: Grunenberg, 1518). The text numbers Carlstadt's original theses as far as 380, though there is no number 87. Is it a coincidence that 380 is four times 95? Carlstadt was always somewhat envious and emulous of Luther. Confusingly, though, the book adds a further 26 theses to those originally drafted for the disputation, making 406 (or perhaps 405) in all.

15. E. Iserloh, *Johannes Eck (1483–1543: Scholastiker, Humanist, Kontroverstheologe* (Aschendorff: Münster, 1981), p. 28.

16. See *Disputatio D. Iohannis Eccii et D. Martini Lutheri in studio Lipsiensi futura* [1519], WA 9.206–12, which reprints Eck's original 12 theses, his cover letter to Cardinal Matthäus Lang, 29 Dec. 1519 (207–8), and Luther's letter to Carlstadt (210–12). For Luther's realization that he was Eck's real target, see his letter to Johannes Sylvius Egranus, 2 Feb. 1519, WA Br 1.140, pp. 313–14, at p. 314.

17. WA 9.210–12. Luther had received a copy of Eck's theses in February. See Luther to Pirckheimer, 20 Feb. 1519, WA Br 1.154, p. 348.

18. Luther to Eck, 7 Jan. 1519, WA Br 1.132, pp. 295–97 at p. 295; Eck to Abbot Caspar, Ingolstadt, 14 March 1519, WA Br 1, p. 321.

19. Luther to Eck, 18 Feb. 1519, WA Br 1.149, p. 340. See his letters to Spalatin of 7 and 12 Feb. 1519, WA Br 1.144 and 145, pp. 325 and 326, for the general agreement to dispute with Eck at Leipzig some time after Easter.

20. *Dokumente zur Causa Lutheri* 2, p. 256.

21. Bernhard Adelmann to Pirckheimer, Augsburg, 10 April 1519, *Pirckheimers Briefwechsel* ed. E. Reicke, H. Scheible, et al. (7 vols.. Munich: Beck, 1940–2009), 4.599, pp. 44–45.

22. Luther to Spalatin, 13 March 1519, WA Br 1.161, p. 359.

23. *Resolutio Lutheriana super propositione sua decima tertia de potestate papae* [1519], WA 2.180–240.

24. WA 2.227.

25. Luther, *Auff des Bocks zu Leypczick Antwort*, WA 7.271–83, at p. 272.

26. *Ein Sermon gepredigt zu Leipzig auf dem Schloss am Tage Petri und Pauli* [1519], WA 2.241–49, at p. 249.

27. Eck to Jacob van Hoogstraten, Leipzig, 24 July 1519, *Dokumente zur Causa Lutheri* 2, pp. 258–65, at p. 265.

28. J. Wicks (ed. and tr.), *Cajetan Responds: a Reader in Reformation Controversy* (Eugene, OR: Wipf & Stock, 2011), p. 55.

29. WA 2.260. See also his letter to Hoogstraten, *Dokumente zur Causa Lutheri* 2, p. 264.

30. Eck might well have read the *Disputation on Scholastic Theology*. Luther had sent him a copy of those theses via Scheurl (*Dokumente zur Causa Lutheri* 1, p. 377), though we do not know for certain that Eck ever received them.

31. WA 2.255–57.

32. WA 2.605.

33. WA 2.256 (4 July).

34. WA 2.275 (5 July).

35. WA 2.275 and 279.

36. Johannes Eck, *Ad Eruditum Virum Gervasium Vaim* ([Ingolstadt], 1520), sig. E3r–v. Gervase Wain was a theologian then based at the Sorbonne.

37. WA 2.288 (6 July).

38. WA 2.279 and 287. Hus derived his view directly from the writings of Wycliffe.

39. WA 2.323 and 328–29. A year before, in the *Resolutions on Indulgences*, he had said that the existence of purgatory was "most certain" (*certissimum*) to him (WA 1.555).

40. WA 2.335. Eck cites the key term as "homousia."

41. WA 2. 346–49.

42. WA 2.352.

43. WA 2.346. That said, he did not always maintain this position. Arguing against Carlstadt in 1522, he opposed active iconoclasm while claiming that, although the veneration of the saints was not necessary to Christians, one could admit it to be lawful and good. See Luther to J. Lang, 29 May 1522, WA Br 2.501, p. 548: "ad Christum omnes voca, ut sciant non necessarium esse cultum Sanctorum, ut demus licitum, et bonum esse."

44. Lucien Febvre, *Martin Luther: a Destiny*, tr. R. Tapley (London: Dent, 1930), p. 45
45. WA 2.359–61.
46. WA 2.361 (12 July). (I cite; you snip; he, she, or it twists; . . .)
47. Luther to Spalatin, 20 July 1519, WA Br 1.187, pp. 420–24; Philip Melanchthon, *Epistola de Lipsica Disputatione* ([Wittenberg: Grunenberg], 1519. USTC 651523); J. Eck, *Excusatio Eckii ad ea que falso sibi Philippus Melanchton . . . adscripsit* ([Leipzig: Landsberg], 1519. USTC 636161).
48. WA Tr 2.1267, p. 17, Dec. 1531.
49. WA 2.391–403, dedication of the *Resolutiones Lutherianae super propositionibus suis Lipsiae disputatis*. This letter is discussed (but not printed) at WA Br 1.191, pp. 435–39, where it is dated ca. 10 Aug. 1519.
50. Luther to Spalatin, 18 Aug. 1519, WA Br 1.194, p. 503.
51. See Rhenanus to Zwingli, 19 March 1519, and Lefèvre to Rhenanus, 9 April 1519, nos. 97 and 105 in *Briefwechsel des Beatus Rhenanus*, ed. A. Horawitz & K. Hartfelder (Leipzig, 1886), pp. 143–45 (p. 145) and 151–52.
52. Ulrich von Hutten, *Expostulatio*, ed. M. Samuel-Scheyder (Turnhout: Brepols, 2012), pp. 50 and 57–61.
53. Hieronymus Dungersheim, *Confutatio* (Leipzig: Wolfgang Monacensis, 1514), fols. 130r (Emser) and 131r (Hessus).
54. Pellican to Luther, 16 March 1520, WA Br 1.266, pp. 64–68.
55. Luther, *In Epistolam Pauli ad Galatas* (Wittenberg: [Lotther], 1519), sig. A5r ("ab ERASMO, viro in Theologia summo") and fol. 1r. See WA 2.449 and 452 (the Weimar edition does not reproduce the capitalization of Erasmus's name seen in the original).
56. WA 2.458.
57. WA 2.493 (Aristotle); and 453, 459, & 464 (*omnis homo mendax*).
58. WA 2.523 (originality); and 584 (Augustine).
59. WA 2.534, 557, and 560.
60. See e.g. WA 2.541 and 567. Pellican to Luther, 16 March 1520, WA Br 1.266, p. 67.
61. WA 2.461. A point already made in *Resolutions on Indulgences* (WA 1.616).

62. *Canonici indocti Lutherani* (No place, no date; probably Augsburg, 1520), esp. sig. B2r–v.
63. Luther to Spalatin, 2 March 1520, WA Br 2.263, p. 59. The attribution to Pirckheimer has been widely agreed. See *Eccius Dedolatus: a Reformation Satire*, tr. T. W. Best (Lexington: Kentucky UP, 1971), pp. 22–23. Luther's judgment on such matters was far from infallible. See for example his mistaken insistence that Hieronymus Emser was the true author of an attack on Luther which had appeared over the name of Thomas Rhadinus. *Auff des Bocks zu Leypczick Antwort* [1519], WA 7.271–83, at p. 276. Rhadinus was an Italian Dominican.
64. Adelmann to Pirckheimer, Augsburg, 11 July 1520, *Pirckheimers Briefwechsel* 4.703, p. 271. No sign of such a pamphlet survives, so this may well simply have been a rumor. Adelmann claimed to have heard about it, not to have seen it.
65. Bucer to Rhenanus, 2 April 1520, WA Br 2.250, p. 34.
66. The young Ingolstadt humanist Martin Borrhaus (aka Cellarius) reproved Melanchthon for his attack on their "mutual friend" Eck, reminding him of the regard in which he had formerly held Eck at Tübingen. See his dedication to Melanchthon in the Ingolstadt edition of Eck's *Excusacio Eckii ad ea que falso sibi Philippus Melanchton . . . adscripsit* ([Ingolstadt: Lutz], 1519. USTC 655188), Sig. A1v. And Rhenanus regretted that his old friend Eck had entered the arena against Luther. See his letter to Jakob Spiegel, n.d. 1519, *Briefwechsel des Beatus Rhenanus*, no. 140, p. 194.

7. ROME AND WITTENBERG

1. He reported on 3 Dec. 1519, in an open letter addressed to Gervase Waim of Memmingen, who had just become Rector of the University of Paris, that he had been working on it for a month and a half, that is, since about mid-October. See Johannes Eck, *Ad Eruditum Virum Gervasium Vaim* ([Ingolstadt], 1520), sig. E4r. For information on Waim, see J. K. Farge, *Biographical Register of Paris Doctors of Theology, 1500–1536* (Toronto: PIMS, 1980), pp. 431–35.

2. Johannes Eck, *De primatu Petri adversus Ludderum libri tres* (Paris: Conrad Resch, 1521), lib. III, fol. LXIXv.

3. Eck, *De primatu Petri*, sig. A2r for the address, and lib. III, fol. LXIXv for the presentation. His work was accorded a papal privilege dated 11 Sept. 1520, reproduced in the Paris edition. His afterword, to Leo X and Charles V, enumerates the ills that would arise from Luther's teachings, and calls on pope and emperor together to defend the Christian religion and republic entrusted to them.

4. The number of condemned articles appears in some texts as 40, in others as 41, depending on how they were set up in print.

5. For the text of the bull, see *Magnum Bullarium Romanum* (Luxembourg: Chevalier, 1727), vol. 1, pp. 610–14. For the bull excommunicating Luther, *Decet Romanum Pontificem*, 3 Jan. 1521, see pp. 614–15.

6. Luther to Spalatin, 24 Feb. 1520, WA Br 2.257, pp. 48–49. A manuscript of Valla's polemic had been discovered by the German humanist Johannes Cochlaeus, then based at Bologna as tutor to the nephews of Willibald Pirckheimer, and Hutten had come to know it thanks to him. Cochlaeus and Hutten were at this point friends, but would end up on opposite sides of the Reformation divide.

7. See, e.g., Peter Matheson, *The Rhetoric of Reformation* (Edinburgh: T. & T. Clark, 1998), p. 162. Augustin von Alveldt, *Super apostolica sede* (Leipzig: Lotther, 1520).

8. *Von dem Bapstum zu Rome: widder den hochberumpten Romanisten zu Leiptzck* [1520], WA 6.285–324. For the writing and printing of this, see his letters to Spalatin of 31 May (WA Br 2.291, p. 111) and 25 June 1520 (WA Br 2.305, p. 130).

9. In conceding the laurel for personal invective to Alveldt, Luther is unduly modest. The *Luther's Works* edition observes that "Alveld's Latin tract abounds in such [i.e. offensive] language" (*Luther's Works*, vol. 39, p. 62, note 17). His pamphlet is strongly worded, especially in referring to condemned heretics such as Wycliffe and Hus. But abuse is anything but abundant, and the tone is less obnoxiously personal than Luther's. Alveldt does not, for example, suggest—as Luther does—that his opponent is not

worthy to look after pigs (WA 6.301). And Luther was not as well disposed towards that species as, say, Clarence, ninth Earl of Emsworth, on whose porcine predilections see P. G. Wodehouse, *Pigs Have Wings* (London: Herbert Jenkins, 1952), p. 8.

10. WA 6.307.
11. WA 6. 301.
12. WA 6.294.
13. WA 6.298.
14. WA 6.300–301.
15. WA 6.289 and 308.
16. Augustine, *Contra epistolam Manichaei quam vocant Fundamenti*, lib. 1, ca. 5, *Patrologia Latina* 42, p. 176.
17. WA Tr 4.4440, p. 312, March 1539. Luther's use of the invisibility of the church to evacuate Augustine's observation about scripture and the church is enough in itself to invalidate the widespread misconception that Luther's doctrine of the invisible church can be traced to Augustine. The idea that Luther derived this idea from Wycliffe or Hus is equally far from the mark. John Wycliffe's church was in principle invisible, but he did not explicitly draw (nor perhaps see) this inference from his understanding of the church as the body of the predestined. See Wycliffe, *Tractatus de Ecclesia*, ed. J. Loserth (London: Wyclif Society, 1886), p. 2, for the church as the body of the predestined. Loserth's marginal notes twice mention the "visible" church (pp. 89 and 100), but there is no basis for this in the text on either occasion, nor elsewhere. Nor is there any talk of a visible or invisible church from Jan Hus, whose ecclesiology (as Loserth notes, pp. xxvi–xxvii) is almost a carbon-copy of Wycliffe's. See Jan Hus, *Tractatus de Ecclesia*, ed. S. H. Thomson (Cambridge: University of Colorado Press & W. Heffer, 1956), p. 3, for the church as the body of the predestined. There is nothing in Luther's writings of this period to indicate that he was even aware of Wycliffe's teaching on the church. Luther had been sent a copy of Hus's treatise after the Leipzig Disputation in 1519, but his writings in 1520 betray no marked Hussite influence (although there are a number of warm references to him). The phrase and

the concept of the "invisible church" seem to have been coined by Luther and were certainly put into circulation by him.

18. See Per Frostin, *Luther's Two Kingdoms Doctrine: a Critical Study* (Lund: Lund University Press, 1994), for a fine and delicate analysis of the diverse and not unproblematic ways in which Luther developed this idea.

19. *An der christlichen Adel deutscher Nation . . .* [1520], WA 6.381–469, esp. pp. 445–53.

20. WA 6.407. See also *De captivitate Babylonica*, WA 6.566.

21. Luther to Johann Voigt, 3 Aug. 1520, WA Br 2.323, p. 162.

22. For examples of these conditional or veiled remarks, see WA 6.414 and 434.

23. WA 6.453 and 454 ("Doch davon ein ander mal mehr und besser"). Even in the formulation on p. 453, the use of indirect speech within a conditional construction ending in a subjunctive clause stops short of flat assertion.

24. See the notes of his sermons in WA 9, at, e.g., pp. 447, 453, 455, 460 (April and May).

25. Bishop of Merseburg and Archbishop of Mainz to Luther, 25 and 26 Feb. 1520, WA Br 2.258 and 259, pp. 52 and 54.

26. *Von den guten Werken* [1520], WA 6.196–276.

27. WA 6.230. The point is reiterated throughout the treatise.

28. WA 6.205 and 206.

29. WA 6.208–9.

30. *De captivitate Babylonica ecclesiae praeludium* [1520], WA 6.484–573. A little of this was in print, Luther wrote, right at the end of August, and the final text was ready at the start of October. Luther to Spalatin, 3 Oct. 1520, WA Br 2.340, p. 191.

31. WA 6.501.

32. The Christians of Eastern Europe had also signed up to the doctrine of the seven sacraments at the Council of Florence in the mid-fifteenth century. But that agreement had been almost immediately repudiated by the Eastern churches when their representatives returned home.

33. WA 6.572.

34. WA 6.520. See also *Von den guten Werken*, WA 6.230.

35. WA Tr 3.3354b, pp. 280–81, June–Sept. 1533.
36. WA 6.521.
37. WA 6.525. Luther acknowledges that these masses are generally called votive ("votivas quas vocant"). His use of "missa privata" here seems simply to emerge from the immediate exigencies of argument, but it was not long before he came to appreciate its rhetorical potential. See below, ch. 8, for further discussion of this.
38. WA 6.526.
39. WA 6.527.
40. WA 6.528–29.
41. WA 6.543–44.
42. E.g. John Fisher, *Assertionis Lutheranae Confutatio* (Antwerp: Hillenius, 1523), fol. 13v.
43. WA 6.509, "in simplicissima significatione." Luther's theory was known to the scholastics as "consubstantiation" (even as they argued against it). Luther had no more time for the "consubstantiation" than he had for that "transubstantiation" (a word found neither in the Bible nor in the ancient Fathers). Indeed, he never coined a name for his eucharistic doctrine at all, an omission which has caused problems for historians and theologians ever since.
44. R. Rex, *The Lollards* (Basingstoke: Palgrave, 2002), pp. 42–45.
45. WA 6.502–7.
46. WA 6.203.
47. WA 2.742.
48. *Ein Sermon von dem neuen Testament . . .* [1520], WA 6.373.
49. WA 6.505 and 507.
50. Luther to Spalatin, 1 Sept.1520, WA Br 2.335, p. 180, on the discussion that day with Staupitz and Link; and 11 Sept. 1520, WA Br 2.337, p. 184, on the point of the meeting and on Miltitz's role in bringing it about.
51. Luther to Spalatin, 3 and 11 Oct. 1520, WA Br 2.340 and 341, pp. 191 and 195.
52. *Epistola Lutheriana ad Leonem Decimum summum pontificem. Tractatus de libertate christiana* [1520], WA 7.39–73 (letter, 42–49; essay, 49–73).

53. WA 7.49.
54. WA 7.50–53. The phrase "priesthood of all believers" is a later formulation, rather than Luther's own, but the doctrine for which that phrase serves as a label is certainly present in Luther's writings from 1520 onwards.
55. Leopold von Ranke, *History of the Reformation in Germany*, (London: Routledge, 1905), p. 290.
56. WA 7.71.
57. Luther to Spalatin, 11 Oct. 1520, WA Br 2.341, p. 195.
58. Luther to Spalatin, 16 Jan. 1521, WA Br 2.368, p. 249. *Adversus execrabilem Antichristi bullam* [1520], WA 6.595–612. *Assertio omnium articulorum M. Lutheri per bullam Leonis X novissimam damnatorum* [1520] WA 7.91–151.
59. Philip Melanchthon, *Loci communes rerum theologicarum* (Wittenberg: [Lotter], 1521. USTC 673141).
60. WA 9.493, from Melanchthon's notes of Luther's sermons over the autumn and winter of 1520–21.
61. Luther to Spalatin, 10 Dec. 1520, WA Br 2.361, p. 234.
62. See *Bulla Leonis Decimi, contra errores Martini Lutheri*, ed. U. Hutten (Strasbourg: Schott, 1520). Hutten comments copiously on the preamble (sigs. a2r–b2r), but hardly at all on the condemned extracts from Luther's writings (b2v–b4v).
63. *Ad librum eximii Magistri Nostri Ambrosii Catharini . . . Responsio*, WA 7.698–778. For this extract, see p. 710 (emphasis added).
64. See e.g. Marc Lienhard, *L'Évangile et l'Église chez Luther* (Paris: Cerf, 1989), pp. 107–30.
65. WA 7.708.
66. I should like to thank Dr. David Pratt, of Downing College, Cambridge, for the conversation we had about this on 23 Feb. 2010, after a meeting of the Maitland Society, during which the full significance of Luther's identification of the papacy as Antichrist first became apparent to me.
67. See WA 7.722–36 for the exposition of three verses of Daniel over several thousand words. For the specific citation, see WA 7.729.

68. WA 7.722–23.

69. WA Tr 4.4487, p. 339, April 1539.

8. WORMS AND THE WARTBURG

1. WA Tr 4.3944, p. 25, 5 Aug. 1538.

2. Erwin Iserloh, *Johannes Eck, 1486–1543* (Münster: Aschendorff, 1981), p. 51. On 17 July 1520 Eck was appointed a papal protonotary and named alongside Aleander as papal nuncio.

3. WA Tr 2.2020, pp. 296–97 (summer 1531): "Doctor Lazarus Spengler Norinbergensis unus est, qui euangelium invexit in Norinbergam, et hactenus ut in ea maneret, unus effecit."

4. *Letters and Papers, Foreign and Domestic, of the Reign of Henry VIII*, ed. J. S. Brewer et al. (21 vols., London: HMSO, 1862–1932; henceforth cited as *LP*), vol. 3, part 1, no. 1043, Tunstall to Wolsey, Cologne, 6 Nov. 1520. See also Spinelly to Wolsey, 7 Nov. 1520, *LP* 3, part 1, no. 1044. Earlier in October he had made a splendid entry into Aachen, and had received his lesser coronation there. Spinelly comments on Elector Frederick's considerable reputation in the Empire, and that he is generally thought the best choice for viceroy in Charles V's absence—failing him, his cousin Duke George!

5. Erasmus to Reuchlin, 8 Nov. 1520, *Opus Epistolarum Des. Erasmi Roterodami*, ed. P. S. and H. M. Allen (12 vols., Oxford: Clarendon, 1906–58), vol. 4, no. 1155, pp. 370–72. Marcel Bataillon, *Érasme et l'Espagne: Recherches sur l'histoire spirituelle du 16ème siècle* (Paris: Droz, 1937), pp. 111–23.

6. Spinelly to Wolsey, Worms 2 Feb. 1520, *LP* 3, part 1, no. 1155.

7. Aleander to Giulio de Medici, n.d. [ca. 1 March 1521], *Monumenta Reformationis Lutheranae*, ed. P. Balan (Regensburg: Pustet, 1884), pp. 97–105, at p. 99.

8. Aleander to Giulio de Medici, 19 Jan. 1521 and 28 Feb. 1521, *Monumenta Reformationis Lutheranae*, pp. 38–41, at p. 40 (cultic images), and pp. 77–81, at p. 80 (the ark picture).

9. Aleander to Giulio de Medici, 16 April 1521 and May 1521, *Monumenta Reformationis Lutheranae*, pp. 170–71, at 170 (miracles), and pp. 205–13, at p. 207 (posters).

10. *LP* 3, part 1, no. 1106, notes of a dispatch from Tunstall to Wolsey, undated, but from Dec. 1520.
11. WA Br 2.383, pp. 280–81 for the summons; 387, p. 286, for Frederick's cover letter.
12. Luther to Spalatin, 19 March 1521, WA Br 2.389, p. 289. There is no reason to think that he dared write to the emperor in such terms.
13. Luther to an unnamed person, 24 March (Palm Sunday) 1521, WA Br 2. 391, p. 293.
14. Luther to Lang, 29 March 1521, WA BR 2.392, p. 293.
15. Aleander to Giulio de Medici, 16 April 1521, *Monumenta Reformationis Lutheranae*, pp. 170–71, at 170.
16. *Acta et res gestae D. Martini Lutheri Augustiniani in comitiis Principum Wormaciae*, WA 7.825–57, at p. 838. I have followed the version in *Acta et res gestae* ([Strasbourg: Schott], 1521. USTC 608616), sig. B3v, which lacks the famous addition, "I cannot do otherwise, here I stand," which figures in some accounts of this statement but not others.
17. *Acta et res gestae D . . . Wormaciae*, WA 7.825–57, the main source for the narrative offered here. See the Strasbourg 1521 edition, sig. B4v, for the marginal note, "Irridetur Dei vir." Compare the text, "All those who see me, deride me" (Ps 21:8), which all Christian commentators applied to Christ.
18. WA 8.842.
19. WA 7.851. For the lampoon and Cochlaeus's response, see his letter to Aleander, 5 May 1521, pp. 109–11 of W. Friedensburg, "Beiträge zum Briefwechsel der katholischen Gelehrten Deutschlands im Reformationszeitalter," *Zeitschrift für Kirchengeschichte* 18 (1898), pp. 106–31, pp. 109–11, at p. 110. See WA Tr 3.3709, p. 553, Jan. 1538, for Luther's recollection of early encouragement from Cochlaeus, after which "he turned viper"; and Tr. 3, no. 3357b, p. 286, 27 Sept. 1533, for the friend who dissuaded him.
20. See the excellent study by Johannes Schilling, *Passio Doctoris Martini Lutheri: Bibliographie, Texte und Untersuchungen* (Gütersloh: Mohn, 1989), on which these comments are based.
21. R. W. Scribner, "Incombustible Luther: the Image of the Re-

former in Early Modern Germany," *Past & Present* 110 (1986), pp. 38–68, and *For the Sake of Simple Folk* (Cambridge: CUP, 1981), esp. pp. 123–25.

22. *Passional Christi und Antichristi* [1521], WA 9.677–715 (the text, without the pictures, at pp. 701–15). For a prepublication reference to it, see Luther to Spalatin, 7 March 1521, WA Br 2.385, p. 283. For comment, see Scribner, *For the Sake of Simple Folk*, pp. 149–57.

23. Heiko A. Oberman, *Luther: Man between God and Devil* (New Haven: Yale UP, 1989).

24. WA 6.404–69. The only occurrences of "Satan" are on pp. 414 (citing 2 Thess 2:9) and 453. For comparison, in the final 50 pages of the *De servo arbitrio* in the WA edition, "Satan" occurs 23 times, and "diabolus" twice. See WA 18.748–87 (the sample analyzed).

25. WA Tr 3.2885, p. 50, Jan. 1533.

26. *Rationis Latomianae Confutatio* [1521], WA 8.36–128.

27. Jacobus Latomus, *Articulorum doctrinae fratris Martini Lutheri per theologos Louanienses damnatorum Ratio* (Antwerp: Hillenius, 1521. USTC 404722), esp. sigs. b4v for the sheer absurdity of good works as sins, c3v–d1r for Augustine (and thereafter some other fathers), and d4v–e2r for the interpretation of Eccles 7:21.

28. Latomus, *Ratio*, sigs. d2r–d3v.

29. WA 8.62.

30. WA 8.63.

31. WA Tr 3.3165, p. 206, June 1535, "quidquid ego scribebam, imitabatur."

32. A. Carlstadt, *Super coelibatu, monachatu et viduitate axiomata* (Wittenberg: Grunenberg, 1521. USTC 695190). The preface to the reader is dated SS. Peter and Paul (29 June) 1521.

33. *Themata de Votis* [1521], WA 8.323–35, and the cover letter, Luther to Melanchthon, 1 Aug. 1521, at WA Br 2.424, pp. 370–73.

34. Luther to Melanchthon, 9 Sept. 1521, WA Br 2.428, pp. 382–86, at p. 385 for his father's remark. See also *De votis monasticis Martini Lutheri iudicium* [1521], WA 8.564–669, pp. 573–76 for the dedication, with the remark in slightly different wording

at p. 574. For other versions, see WA Tr 1.623, p. 294 (autumn 1533), and 881, p. 439; and Tr. 3.3556a, p. 410, March 1537.
35. WA 8.593.
36. WA 8.593.
37. WA 8.594.
38. WA 8.640.
39. WA Tr 2.1313, pp. 37–38, early 1532.
40. WA Tr 2.1538, p. 126, May 1532, recalls abandoning the monastic cowl in 1524, after 19 years.
41. WA 2.519, commenting on Gal 3:15, a key text in this interpretation of the Eucharist.
42. WA 9.445. This is from a collection of notes taken down at Luther's sermons by listeners.
43. *De Abroganda Missa Privata* [1521], WA 8.398–476.
44. WA 8.412.
45. WA 8.441.
46. WA 8.441.

9. THE BEGINNING AND END OF REFORMATION

1. Luther to Amsdorf, Wartburg, [15 July?] 1521, WA Br 2.419, pp. 361 and 32.
2. Luther to Nikolaus Gerbel, Wartburg, 1 Nov. 1521, WA Br 2.435, p. 397. The plural "Satans" here appears to be a metonymical usage for what he describes elsewhere as the "spectres" (*spectris*: illusions or manifestations) occasioned by Satan. See WA Tr 3.2885, p. 50, early 1533: "Saepe me vexavit Sathan spectris suis, praesertim in arce illa."
3. This account of the "Wittenberg Stirs" is largely dependent on James S. Preus, *Carlstadt's Ordinances and Luther's Liberty: A Study of the Wittenberg Movement, 1521–1522* (Cambridge, MA: Harvard UP, 1974), pp. 28–29. Preus puzzles over the way that some sources place this event on Christmas Day while others place it on New Year's Day. But in Saxony the new year was counted as starting on Christmas Day.

4. Luther to the Elector Frederick, 5 and 7/8 March 1522, WA Br 2.455–56, pp. 455 and 460.
5. WA 10:3.8.
6. Luther to Kaspar Güttel, 30 March 1522, WA Br 2.471, p. 491.
7. This was happening at many other places. A group of Zwingli's followers marked Lent in Zurich in 1522 by sharing some sausage. See G. R. Potter, *Zwingli* (Cambridge: CUP, 1976), pp. 74–75.
8. Luther dismisses "these new prophets" in a letter to Spalatin, 12 April 1522, WA Br 2.472, p. 493. WA Tr 2.1796, p. 217, Sept. 1532. In his *Grund and Ursach aller Artikel* [1520], WA 7.299–457, at p. 313, he remarks, "I do not say that I am a prophet, but I say rather that they should worry in case I am one."
9. *Contra Henricum Regem Angliae*, WA 10:2.175–262, at p. 193.
10. WA Tr 4.4979, p. 598, May–June 1540.
11. See *Dass Jesus Christus ein geborner Jude sei* [1523], WA 11.307–336 and *Von den Juden and ihren Lügen* [1543], WA 53.417–552.
12. Brad S. Gregory, *Salvation at Stake* (Cambridge, MA: Harvard UP, 1999), pp. 139 and 144–50. See also M. Gielis, "Érasme, Latomus et le martyre de deux augustins luthériens à Bruxelles en 1523," in *Erasmus of Rotterdam: the Man and the Scholar*, ed. J. Sperna Weiland and W. T. M. Frijhoff (Leiden: Brill, 1988), pp. 61–68.
13. *Rationis Lutheranae Confutatio* [1521], WA 8.36–128, at p. 89.
14. WA Tr 3.3292a, p. 253, early 1533.
15. WA 10:2, pp. 160–62, lists the editions.
16. WA 10:2, pp. 164–68.
17. *Martini Lutheri Epistolarum Farrago*, tr. V. Obsopoeus (Hagenau: Secer, 1525. USTC 675228).
18. *Von weltlicher Uberkeitt* [1523], WA 11.229–281, at pp. 249–50.
19. WA 11.262.
20. WA 11.262.
21. WA 11.269.
22. Few Catholic responses to Luther enjoyed more than one print run. Henry's went through nine editions in Latin and another four in German in the 1520s. See Henry VIII, *Assertio septem sacramentorum adversus Martinum Lutherum*, ed. P. Fraenkel

(Münster: Aschendorff, 1992. Corpus Catholicorum 43), pp. 77–80 and 84.

23. WA 10:2.184 (ordure) and, e.g., 189 ("Thomistitate sua"—"His Thomisticity").

24. For the most penetrating account of this unwinding of the Protestant problematic, see Brad S. Gregory, *The Unintended Reformation* (Cambridge, MA: Belknap, 2012), pp. 86–112.

25. See Johannes Cochlaeus, *Adversus cucullatum Minotaurum Wittenbergensem*, ed. J. Schweizer (Münster: Aschendorff, 1920), p. 48. For Luther's interpretation of "faith" in Gal 5:22, see his 1519 commentary on Galatians, WA 2.595, where he says that he had for a long time followed Jerome in taking this simply as "faith," and then credits Melanchthon with helping him undo this knot by taking it for "truthfulness, fidelity, or candor."

26. WA 11.260.

27. WA 10:2.219.

28. *Enarrationes Martini Lutheri in Epistolas D. Petri duas* (Strasbourg: Hervagius, 1525), fol. 102r.

29. WA Tr 3.2891a and b, pp. 54–55, early 1533.

30. WA Tr 2.1391, p. 82, early 1532. Luther's implication is that Muntzer's somewhat indefinite expression of faith was nothing like adequate as a profession of truth.

31. See, e.g., Luther to the Council at Leisnig, 25 Jan. 1523, WA Br 3.576, p. 22; and his letters to the Christians of the Netherlands and of Riga, ca. Aug. 1523, WA 12.77–80 and 147–50. See also his *Epistolarum Farrago* (1525).

32. J. Lohmüller, City Secretary of Riga, to Luther, 20 Aug. 1522, WA Br 2.532, p. 592.

33. Luther to the Estates of Bohemia, 15 July 1522, WA 10, part 2, pp. 172–74. See *Epistolarum Farrago* for a contemporary collection of these pastoral epistles.

34. Luther to Hess, 29 March 1523, WA Br 3.596, p. 50.

35. Luther to Oecolampadius, 20 June 1523, WA Br 3.626, pp. 96–97.

36. Luther to Conrad Pellican, 1 Oct. 1523, WA Br 3.661, p. 160: "Si hoc est spongia abstergere, rogo, quid est maledicere et con-

viciari?" For comment on Erasmus's controversy with Hutten, see the excellent commentary in Ulrich von Hutten, *Expostulatio*, ed. and tr. Monique Samuel-Scheyder (Turnhout: Brepols, 2012), pp. 85–124. Samuel-Scheyder's assessment of the tone of *Spongia* (p. 117–18) does not bear out Luther's *tu quoque*.

37. Luther to Nikolas Gerbel, 6 May 1524, WA Br 3.739, p. 284.

38. Wimpfeling to Luther and Zwingli, 23 May 1524, WA Br 3.747, p. 297.

39. See Luther to Amsdorf, 2 Dec. 1524, WA Br 3.802, p. 397, blaming Carlstadt; and Capito et al. to Luther, 23 Nov. 1524, WA Br 3.797, pp. 381–87.

40. *Wider die himmlischen Propheten . . .* [1525], WA 18.37–125 (part 1) and 126–214 (part 2).

41. WA Tr 2.1883, p. 246, from Dec. 1534.

42. *Ermahnung zum Frieden . . .* [1525], WA 18.279–334; and *Wider die raübischen und mörderischen Rotten der Bauern* [1525], WA 18.344–361.

43. WA 18.358.

44. WA 18.361. See also J. Cochlaeus (ed.), *Adversus Latrocinantes et Raptorias Cohortes Rusticorum. Mar. Lutherus. Responsio Iohannis Cochlaei Wendelstini* (Cologne: [Kruffter], 1525), sig. B1v and C2r, for these citations and Cochlaeus's caustic comments on them.

45. See Luther's second series of sermons on the catechism, Sept. 1528, WA 30, part 1, p. 35. For the last comment, WA Tr 1, no. 415, p. 181, Dec. 1532.

46. See Luther's third series of sermons on the catechism, Dec. 1528, WA 30, part 1, p. 67. He was well aware of the relative novelty of his interpretation.

47. See Luther to Spalatin, 30 Nov. 1524, WA Br 3.801, p. 394, for Argula von Grumbach's speculations about his matrimonial prospects, and his own assurance that nothing could be further from his mind given the danger of imminent death.

48. Luther to Amsdorf, 23 Jan. 1525, WA Br 3.821, p. 428, and subsequent letters.

49. WA Br 3.896, to Wenzel Link, 20 June 1525, p. 537.
50. See R. Rex, "Thomas More and the Heretics: Statesman or Fanatic?," in George M. Logan (ed.), *The Cambridge Companion to Thomas More* (Cambridge: Cambridge University Press, 2011), pp. 93–115, at pp. 101–3.
51. Erasmus to Francis Craneveldt, 24 Dec. 1525, *Opus Epistolarum Des. Erasmi*, vol. 6, no. 1655, p. 242.
52. Erasmus to Francis Sylvius, 13 March 1526, *Opus Epistolarum Des. Erasmi*, vol. 6, no. 1677, p. 283. Luther returned the compliment years later, cheerfully announcing that Erasmus was the son of a monk and a nun. WA Tr 4.4902, p. 574, May 1540.

10. THE MEANING OF MARTIN LUTHER

1. *De servo arbitrio* [1525], WA 18.551–787, p. 786.
2. His eucharistic theology was deepened as he pursued his controversy against Zwingli, and his political theology underwent some minor modifications in order to justify the Lutheran princes of the Schmalkaldic League in their resistance to their emperor.
3. Erasmus, *De Libero Arbitrio Διατριβη, siue Collatio* (Basel: Froben, 1524. USTC 630368), sig. C1r.
4. WA 18.664.
5. WA 18.700.
6. Erasmus to Duke John of Saxony, 2 March 1526, 1525, *Opus Epistolarum Des. Erasmi*, vol. 6, no. 1670, p. 269. It would be invidious indeed to decide which was Luther's most intemperate tract.
7. WA Tr 1.37, p. 13, 1531 "Religio tota est fabula." The notion that Leo X dismissed Christianity as a "fable" has a certain currency, and this is the earliest trace of it that I have ever found. It is unlikely that Luther is doing anything other than repeat and embroider a story he heard from someone else, but I have no idea, if so, where he got it from.
8. WA Tr 1.811 (pp. 390–91); 797 (pp. 376–77); Tr. 2.3795, p. 620, March 1538; Tr. 2.3392b, p. 302, autumn 1533; Tr. 2.2205, p. 363, late 1531.

9. WA Tr 1.131, p. 55, Dec. 1531; and Tr 1.446, p. 195, early 1533.
10. WA Tr 1.446, p. 195, early 1533.
11. WA Tr 1.494, p. 219, 25 March 1533. He had made a similar point about the papacy in his *Contra Henricum Regem Angliae*, WA 10:2.187: "Verius autem sic de Papatu dico, Papatus est, Principis Satanae pestilentissima abominatio, quae sub coelo fuit aut futura est."
12. WA Tr 3.3028, p. 147, 1533 (curse); WA Tr 3.3144, p. 189, 26 May 1532.
13. WA Tr 1.1193, p. 592, first half of the 1530s.
14. Witzel henceforth ploughed an Erasmian furrow within the Catholic Church, seeking to combine defense of orthodoxy with policies of conciliation and unity.
15. Except perhaps once. In his sermon on Pentecost Sunday, 1523 (WA 11.117), he says: "et ego semel raptus fui in 3um celum" ("I was once snatched up to the third heaven"). This ends a sentence which starts "I have seen many monks and clergy who are uncertain." To me it sounds like a figurative rather than a literal claim, contrasting the Pauline certainty of his own faith with the Pelagian uncertainty of their works.
16. It appeared in Latin as *Nova doctrina* (Augsburg: Simprecht Ruff, 1526. USTC 678508), and in German as *Neue lere* (Wittenberg: Klug, 1526. USTC 677079). It was frequently reprinted, translated, or imitated.
17. WA Tr 3.3366, pp. 292–93, autumn 1533. See also Tr. 3.3594, p. 440, May–June 1537.
18. WA Tr 2.1868, p. 242, 16 Oct. 1532. His term "subiectum theologiae" refers not to the academic discipline in itself, but to that which it is really about.
19. WA Tr 3.3370b, p. 295, June–Sept. 1533.
20. They offered instead an account of "spiritual" presence, which they sometimes argued was as "real" as, if not more real than, what they called the "corporal" presence which they rejected. In common parlance, "real presence" tended, then as now, to denote the Catholic and Lutheran doctrines.

21. Historians have been so ready to see in printing the nemesis of medieval Catholicism that they have often overlooked the fact that the mother's milk of the industry in its infancy was meeting the massive demand for liturgical texts which was generated by the almost hyperventilated piety of late medieval Catholicism.

22. Luther's success in defining Catholicism as Pelagianism has left an abiding impression on Reformation historiography, evident to this day in the way that theologically unsophisticated historians (especially but by no means exclusively those in the Lutheran or other Protestant traditions) recycle and thus reinforce his view.

23. Cochlaeus to Aleander, 5 May 1521, W. Friedensburg, "Beiträge zum Briefwechsel der katholischen Gelehrten Deutschlands im Reformationszeitalter," *Zeitschrift für Kirchengeschichte* 18 (1898), pp. 106–31, pp. 109–11, at p. 110.

24. It is noteworthy that Luther's fullest affirmations of paternal and patriarchal authority came only after, in the mid-1520s, he had married and become a father himself.

Index